CONTENTS

INTRODUCTION

The Ninja brand skyrocketed in popularity after their amazing Ninja Foodi multi-cooker took the whole market by storm and became a prime challenger for the King of multi-cookers, the Instant Pot!

But that wasn't enough for them now was it? With culinary technologies advancing with each passing day, consumers demanded more and Ninja listened! And hence, Ninja Foodi Smart XL Grill was born.

The Ninja Foodi Smart XL Grill aims to completely revolutionize how people grill their meals. Long gone are the days when you had to carry a bulky outdoor grill and a bucket of charcoals to grill your food!

The Ninja Foodi Smart XL Grill makes the whole process extremely easy and convenient, even for newcomers!

For those of you who are completely new, the Ninja Foodi Smart XL Grill is essentially an extremely compact indoor Grill that utilizes the power of superheated air to perfectly grill and cooks your meals from all sides, without even needing to flip them!

But that's not all, apart from Grilling, the Ninja Foodi Smart XL Grill is also capable of Air Frying, Roasting and even Baking! And the best part? You can even directly put frozen items in your appliance without defrosting them!

This is not only an appliance that helps to prepare healthy meals, but it also helps to save a lot of time!

That being said, this particular book has been designed to help beginners get a grip of the appliance and keeping that in mind, the first chapter of the book covers all the basic information that you might need to know regarding the Ninja Foodi Grill.

After this, you will find a plethora of absolutely amazing recipes to choose from and experiment with!

So, what are you waiting for? Jump right in and start exploring!

Everything about the Ninja Foodi Smart XL Grill

What is the Ninja Foodi Smart XL Grill?

The Ninja Foodi Smart XL Grill is an exceptional cooking appliance that has the capacity to act as an indoor grill, roasting machine, air fryer, baking oven and more all under singlehood! Using its amazing Cyclonic Grill Technology, the Ninja Foodi Smart XL Grill can use superheated air to Grill proteins and vegetables to perfection, all without any of the hassles of an outdoor grill.

With a temperature that can reach up to 500 degrees F, the Ninja Foodi Smart XL Grill gives perfect sear to any food, while the awesome grill grate helps the food to get a beautiful char-grilled finish.

This is one of the most innovative and advanced cooking appliances out there in the market right now, and you just can't go wrong with it! If you were impressed by the Ninja Foodi, just wait till you start using this one! Outdoor Grills will slowly be a thing of the past thanks to this little nifty device.

Functions and Buttons of the Ninja Foodi Smart XL Grill

Now that you have a basic idea of what the Ninja Foodi Smart XL Grill is, let's have a look at the core functions and buttons that you should know about. Keep in mind that you have five different types of cooking that you can do using your Ninja Foodi Grill.

Grill

At its heart, the Ninja Foodi Smart XL Grill is an indoor grill, so to unlock its full potential, you must have a good understanding of how the grill function of the appliance works, so let me break it down to you.

Now you should understand that each set of the Grill is specifically designed for different types of food.

But regardless of which function you choose, the first step for you will always be

Place your cooking pot and grill grate in the Ninja Foodi

Let it pre-heat

Then add your food

The next thing would be to select the Grill function and choose the Grill Temperature, here you have 4 settings to choose from.

Low: This mode is perfect for bacon and sausages.

Medium: This is perfect for frozen meats or marinated meats.

High: This mode is perfect for steaks, chicken, and burgers.

Max: This is perfect for vegetables, fruits, fresh and frozen seafood, and pizza.

Air Crisp

The Air Crisp mode will help you to achieve a very crispy and crunchy golden brown finish to your food. Using the Air Crisp mode combined with the crisper basket is the perfect combination to cook your frozen foods such as French Fries, Onion rings, Chicken Nuggets, etc.

Air Crisp is also amazing for Brussels Sprouts and other fresh vegetables. Just always make sure to shake the crisper basket once or twice to ensure even cooking.

Bake

As mentioned earlier, the Ninja Foodi Smart XL Grill is essentially a mini convection oven. All you need to bake bread, cakes, pies, and other sweet treats is a Cooking Pot and this function. The Pre-heat time for the Bake mode is just 3 minutes.

Roast

The Roast function is used to make everything from slow-roasted pot roast to appetizers to casual sides. Large pieces of protein can be put directly in your Ninja Foodi Smart XL Grill and roasted using this function. You can further make this mode more effective by using a Roasting Rack accessory.

Dehydrate

Generally speaking, Dehydrators are pretty expensive and take a lot of space in your kitchen. Luckily, using the Dehydrate function, you can very easily dehydrate fruits, meats, vegetables, herbs, etc. using just your Ninja Foodi Grill!

What Technologies Make Ninja Foodi Smart XL Grill So Amazing?

There are certain elements build inside the Ninja Foodi Smart XL Grill that makes this appliance so awesome and unique. The core technologies that you should know about include:

Cyclonic Grill Technology

The Ninja Foodi Smart XL Grill is unlike any other indoor grill out there! And what makes it so unique is the "Cyclonic Grill Technology" that is installed under its hood. This technology combines high-density Grill Grate and super-heated Cyclonic Air that is circulated all around the meal to give you that perfect grill.

This means that in the end, you will be getting a well-cooked food that is perfectly seared and deliciously caramelized from all sides, creating a fine and crispy crust on the outside.

This not only helps to cook everything evenly but also helps to completely bring out the flavors inside with the added char-grilled goodness.

No-Flip Grilling

This is an extension of the previous technology. Since air is circulated all around the food, there is no need to flip the food to grill it properly. Thanks to the heated air going all around, the food gets evenly cooked and grilled regardless.

Imagine having a perfectly grilled fish that won't fall apart because it is perfectly cooked on all sides! Thanks to No-Flip Grilling, you will even get Char Marks and beautiful sear on all sides as well!

Frozen To Char-Grilled

Unlike most grills out there, the Ninja Foodi Smart XL Grill is capable of grilling foods right out of your freezer without the need of thawing it first. So, whether you bought flash-frozen meat or fish from the market, you are always just minutes away from having your amazing meal cooked and ready to eat!

How To Clean And Maintain Your Ninja Foodi Smart XL Grill?

Just like any other appliance, the Ninja Foodi Smart XL Grill also needs to be maintained and cleaned to keep it in tip-top shape and prolong its longevity. Over time, dirt and debris might accumulate, which might prevent the appliance from working properly.

Therefore, you must keep it clean. However, some things that you should keep in mind while cleaning:

For the accessories, you may clean them by hand or use a cleaning brush. What you need to keep in mind though is that most of the accessories are ceramic coated, so you should refrain yourself from using abrasive cleaners. Always remember to be gentle. However, if you see that there is food debris that is stuck, then you may simply add the accessories to the cooking pot and submerge them under soapy warm soapy water, and let it stay overnight. Then clean them using a soft brush.

If you are planning on cooking your Ninja Foodi after cooking, then you should keep in mind that the appliance will be extremely hot. So, what you have to do is unplug it and keep the hood open after removing your food and let it cool.

Once done, take the cooking pot and grill grate and dip them under soapy warm water and let them stay overnight or a couple of hours. Then clean them using a soft brush.

For the body of the appliance, never use a brush or anything harsh. Just take a damp soft cloth and wipe the body gently.

Common mistakes that you might make

As a new user of the Ninja Foodi Grill, there are certain mistakes that you might make. You must know some of the most common ones so that you can avoid making them during your early days.

Always make sure to give enough time to your Ninja Foodi Smart XL Grill to let it pre-heat. Pre-heating the appliance will bring the internal temperature to an optimum level and you will get the best results possible.

Some people might think that it is not possible to grill or cook vegetables in the Ninja Foodi Grill, don't make that mistake! Make sure to cook your veggies as well!

The Ninja Foodi Smart XL Grill is best for when you are making recipes from scratch, don't try to add ingredients that are already cooked or fried.

If you overcrowd the cooking basket, the ingredients won't get enough space and as a result, the appliance won't be able to circulate heated air all around it properly, resulting in uneven cooking. So cook in batches if needed, but always make sure to keep spaces in between.

When you own a grilling appliance, baking doesn't come first to mind! But it is very much possible to bake goods in your Ninja Foodi Grill, so give it a try!

While using the Ninja Foodi Grill, some people often try to cook meals without using any oil at all! That is not ideal. You should keep in mind that a minimum of 1 to 2 teaspoons of oil is needed to cook meals properly, while 1-2 tablespoons are needed for breaded items.

You must learn how to properly cook the Ninja Foodi Grill, otherwise, you might end up damaging the appliance. Make sure to go through the section titled "How To Clean And Ninja Foodi Grill?" to properly learn how to.

FAQ's

If this is your first time using the Ninja Foodi Grill, then naturally you might have some questions. Below are some of the most common ones that you might want to know about:

Q1. Why is my food burned?

You should understand the no two proteins are ever the same and for that very reason, the time taken to cook them will be different as well. Always make sure to pay very close attention to the size of the meat as well as the shape, as they play a huge role in the time taken for them to cook. Some sizes may require you to lower time while others may need you to increase the time. For the best result, always make sure to check the meat for doneness while it is cooking (use a meat thermometer if needed).

Q2. Can I Cook Frozen Food In Ninja Foodi Grill?

Yes, one of the best features of the Ninja Foodi Smart XL Grill is that you can cook frozen food straight out of the fridge without waiting for them defrost!

Q3. Can I Crisp Air battered ingredients?

Yes, it is possible to do that, however, you should use the proper breading technique. It is very much important to keep in mind that you coat your food first with flour ad then with egg and lastly with breadcrumbs. Finally, always make sure to press the bread crumbs onto the protein to ensure that they stick well. And lastly, make sure to spray some oil in order.

Q4. How long should I pre-heated the Ninja Foodi Grill?

The Ninja Foodi Smart XL Grill has a temperature-sensitive Grill Grate so that it can monitor the temperature while cooking. It is essential that you always let the appliance pre-heat before adding your ingredients, generally speaking, the Grill function takes about 8 minutes to preheat. Once the appliance is heated, it will let you know with a "Beep" sound. You can easily track the progress by waiting for the beep or looking at the indicator on the control panel. Once the Ninja Foodi Smart XL Grill is heated, it will also show "Add Food" denoting that it is not alright to add food.

General Tips

Below are some tips that might help you to further enhance your grilling experience and ensure that you come up with the best possible grilled result possible!

Always make sure to give your appliance enough time to pre-heat before starting to cook your meals.

You must use a bit of oil while cooking. Brushing your vegetables and meats with a bit of oil helps to promote charring and crisping. If you want less smoke, then try to go for oil with high smoke point such as canola oil, avocado oil, etc.

Once you are ready to put food into your appliance, make sure to evenly arrange them well keeping a good amount of space between them to ensure even charring.

If you are worried about burning your food, you can always lift the hood to check the condition of your food. The Ninja Foodi Smart XL Grill automatically pauses the cooking process when you lift it and start again once you close it.

Always make sure to season your protein generously and let them sit at room temperature for at least 30 minutes. It will not only infuse flavors but will promote faster cooking as well.

Always try to keep a meat thermometer handy so that you can check your meat for doneness.

APPETIZERS AND SIDE DISHES

1. Cauliflower Mash

Servings: 4
Cooking Time: 6 Minutes
Ingredients:
- 1½ cups water
- ½ teaspoon turmeric
- 1 tablespoon butter
- 1 cauliflower, separated into florets
- Salt and ground black pepper, to taste
- 3 chives, diced

Directions:
1. Put water in the pot immediately, place the cabbage - flower in the basket for cooking, immediately cover the pot and cook 6 minutes to steam.
2. Release the pressure naturally for 2 minutes and quickly release the rest.
3. Transfer the cauliflower to a bowl and mash with a potato masher. Add salt, pepper, butter and saffron, mix, transfer to a blender and mix well. Serve with chives sprinkled on top.
- **Nutrition Info:** Calories: 70, Fat: 5, Fiber: 2, Carbohydrate: 5, Proteins: 2

2. Chili Corn On The Cob

Servings:4
Cooking Time: 15 Minutes
Ingredients:
- 2 tablespoon olive oil, divided
- 2 tablespoons grated Parmesan cheese
- 1 teaspoon garlic powder
- 1 teaspoon chili powder
- 1 teaspoon ground cumin
- 1 teaspoon paprika
- 1 teaspoon salt
- ¼ teaspoon cayenne pepper (optional)
- 4 ears fresh corn, shucked

Directions:
1. Grease the air fryer basket with 1 tablespoon of olive oil. Set aside.
2. Combine the Parmesan cheese, garlic powder, chili powder, cumin, paprika, salt, and cayenne pepper (if desired) in a small bowl and stir to mix well.
3. Lightly coat the ears of corn with the remaining 1 tablespoon of olive oil. Rub the cheese mixture all over the ears of corn until completely coated.
4. Arrange the ears of corn in the greased basket in a single layer.
5. Put the air fryer basket on the baking pan and slide into Rack Position 2, select Air Fry, set temperature to 400ºF (205ºC), and set time to 15 minutes.
6. Flip the ears of corn halfway through the cooking time.

7. When cooking is complete, they should be lightly browned. Remove from the oven and let them cool for 5 minutes before serving.

3. Rosemary Red Potatoes

Servings: 4
Cooking Time: 20 Minutes
Ingredients:
- 1½ pounds (680 g) small red potatoes, cut into 1-inch cubes
- 2 tablespoons olive oil
- 2 tablespoons minced fresh rosemary
- 1 tablespoon minced garlic
- 1 teaspoon salt, plus additional as needed
- ½ teaspoon freshly ground black pepper, plus additional as needed

Directions:
1. Toss the potato cubes with the olive oil, rosemary, garlic, salt, and pepper in a large bowl until thoroughly coated.
2. Arrange the potato cubes in the baking pan in a single layer.
3. Slide the baking pan into Rack Position 1, select Convection Bake, set temperature to 350ºF (180ºC), and set time to 20 minutes.
4. Stir the potatoes a few times during cooking for even cooking.
5. When cooking is complete, the potatoes should be tender. Remove from the oven to a plate. Taste and add additional salt and pepper as needed.

4. Red Beans And Rice

Servings: 6
Cooking Time: 25 Minutes
Ingredients:
- 1 teaspoon vegetable oil
- 1 pound red kidney beans, soaked overnight and drained
- Salt, to taste
- 1 pound smoked sausage, cut into wedges
- 1 yellow onion, peeled and chopped
- 4 garlic cloves, peeled and chopped
- 1 celery stalk, chopped
- 1 green bell pepper, seeded and chopped
- 1 teaspoon dried thyme
- 5 cups water
- 2 bay leaves
- Long grain rice already cooked
- 2 tablespoons parsley, minced, for serving
- Hot sauce, for serving
- 2 green onions, minced, for serving

Directions:
1. Put the Instant Pot in the sauté mode, add the oil and heat. Add sausage, onion, pepper, celery, garlic, thyme and salt, mix and cook for 8 minutes.

2. Add beans, bay leaves and water, stir, cover the Instant Pot and cook for 15 minutes.
3. Release the pressure naturally for 20 minutes, discard the bay leaves and put 2 cups of beans and a little liquid in the mixer. Clean them well and return to the plate.
4. Divide the rice between the dishes, add the beans, sausage and vegetables on top, sprinkle with chives and parsley and serve with a hot sauce.
- **Nutrition Info:** Calories: 160, Fat: 3.8, Fiber: 3.4, Carbohydrate: 24, Proteins: 4.6

5.   Ranch Potatoes

Servings: 6
Cooking Time: 20 Minutes
Ingredients:
- 1 1/2 lbs baby potatoes, cut in half
- 1/2 tsp paprika
- 1/2 tsp onion powder
- 1/2 tsp dill
- 1/2 tsp chives
- 1/2 tsp parsley
- 1/2 tsp garlic powder
- 2 tbsp olive oil
- 1/2 tsp salt

Directions:
1. Fit the oven with the rack in position 2.
2. Add baby potatoes and remaining ingredients into the mixing bowl and toss until well coated.
3. Transfer baby potatoes in air fryer basket then place air fryer basket in baking pan.
4. Place a baking pan on the oven rack. Set to air fry at 400 F for 20 minutes.
5. Serve and enjoy.
- **Nutrition Info:** Calories 108 Fat 4.8 g Carbohydrates 14.6 g Sugar 0.2 g Protein 3 g Cholesterol 0 mg

6.   Crunchy Cheese Twists

Servings: 8
Cooking Time: 45 Minutes
Ingredients:
- 2 cups cauliflower florets, steamed
- 1 egg
- 3 ½ oz oats
- 1 red onion, diced
- 1 tsp mustard
- 5 oz cheddar cheese, shredded
- Salt and black pepper to taste

Directions:
1. Preheat on Air Fry function to 350 F. Place the oats in a food processor and pulse until they are the consistency of breadcrumbs.
2. Place the cauliflower florets in a large bowl. Add in the rest of the ingredients and mix to combine. Take a little bit of the mixture and twist it into a straw.

3. Place onto a lined baking tray and repeat the process with the rest of the mixture. Cook for 10 minutes, turn over, and cook for an additional 10 minutes. Serve.

7.   Savory Chicken Nuggets With Parmesan Cheese

Servings: 4
Cooking Time: 25 Minutes
Ingredients:
- 1 lb chicken breasts, cubed
- Salt and black pepper to taste
- 2 tbsp olive oil
- 5 tbsp plain breadcrumbs
- 2 tbsp panko breadcrumbs
- 2 tbsp grated Parmesan cheese

Directions:
1. Preheat on Air Fry function to 380 F. Season the chicken with salt and pepper; set aside. In a bowl, mix the breadcrumbs with the Parmesan cheese.
2. Brush the chicken pieces with the olive oil, then dip into breadcrumb mixture, and transfer to the Air Fryer basket. Fit in the baking tray and lightly spray chicken with cooking spray. Cook for 10 minutes, flipping once halfway through until golden brown on the outside and no more pink on the inside. Serve warm.

8.   Air-fried Herb Mushrooms

Servings: 2
Cooking Time: 25 Minutes
Ingredients:
- 1 lbs mushrooms, wash, dry, and cut into quarter
- 1 tbsp white vermouth
- 1 tsp herb de Provence
- 1/4 tsp garlic powder
- 1/2 tbsp olive oil

Directions:
1. Fit the oven with the rack in position 2.
2. Add all ingredients to the bowl and toss well.
3. Transfer mushrooms in the air fryer basket then place the air fryer basket in the baking pan.
4. Place a baking pan on the oven rack. Set to air fry at 350 F for 25 minutes.
5. Serve and enjoy.
- **Nutrition Info:** Calories 99 Fat 4.5 g Carbohydrates 8.1 g Sugar 4 g Protein 7.9 g Cholesterol 0 mg

9.   Rosemary Potato Chips

Servings:4
Cooking Time: 30 Minutes
Ingredients:

- 1 pound potatoes, cut into thin slices
- ¼ cup olive oil
- 1 tbsp garlic puree
- ½ cup heavy cream
- 2 tbsp fresh rosemary, chopped

Directions:
1. Preheat on AirFry function to 390 F. In a bowl, mix oil, garlic puree, and salt. Add in the potato slices and toss to coat. Lay the potato slices onto the frying basket and place in the oven. Press Start and cook for 20-25 minutes. Sprinkle with rosemary and serve.

10. Chicken Wings In Alfredo Sauce

Servings:4
Cooking Time: 30 Minutes
Ingredients:
- 1 ½ pounds chicken wings
- Salt to taste
- ½ cup Alfredo sauce

Directions:
1. Preheat on AirFry function to 390 F. Season the wings with salt. Arrange them on the frying basket without touching. Press Start and cook for 20-22 minutes until no longer pink in the center. Remove to a large bowl and coat well with the sauce. Serve.

11. Baked Cauliflower & Tomatoes

Servings: 4
Cooking Time: 20 Minutes
Ingredients:
- 4 cups cauliflower florets
- 1 tbsp capers, drained
- 3 tbsp olive oil
- 1/2 cup cherry tomatoes, halved
- 2 tbsp fresh parsley, chopped
- 2 garlic cloves, sliced
- Pepper
- Salt

Directions:
1. Fit the oven with the rack in position
2. In a bowl, toss together cherry tomatoes, cauliflower, oil, garlic, capers, pepper, and salt and spread in baking pan.
3. Set to bake at 450 F for 25 minutes. After 5 minutes place the baking pan in the preheated oven.
4. Garnish with parsley and serve.
- **Nutrition Info:** Calories 123 Fat 10.7 g Carbohydrates 6.9 g Sugar 3 g Protein 2.4 g Cholesterol 0 mg

12. Zucchini Spaghetti

Servings: 4
Cooking Time: 20 Minutes
Ingredients:
- 1 lb. zucchinis, cut with a spiralizer

- 1 cup parmesan; grated
- ¼ cup parsley; chopped.
- ¼ cup olive oil
- 6 garlic cloves; minced
- ½ tsp. red pepper flakes
- Salt and black pepper to taste.

Directions:
1. In a pan that fits your air fryer, mix all the ingredients, toss, introduce in the fryer and cook at 370°F for 15 minutes
2. Divide between plates and serve as a side dish.
- **Nutrition Info:** Calories: 200; Fat: 6g; Fiber: 3g; Carbs: 4g; Protein: 5g

13. Cheesy Sticks With Thai Sauce

Servings: 4
Cooking Time: 20 Minutes + Freezing Time
Ingredients:
- 12 mozzarella string cheese
- 2 cups breadcrumbs
- 3 eggs
- 1 cup sweet Thai sauce
- 4 tbsp skimmed milk

Directions:
1. Pour the crumbs in a bowl. Crack the eggs into another bowl and beat with the milk. One after the other, dip each cheese sticks in the egg mixture, in the crumbs, then egg mixture again and then in the crumbs back. Place the cheese sticks in a cookie sheet and freeze for 2 hours.
2. Preheat on Air Fry function to 380 F. Arrange the sticks in the frying basket without overcrowding. Fit in the baking tray and cook for 8 minutes, flipping them halfway through cooking until browned. Serve with the Thai sauce.

14. Cheddar Broccoli Fritters

Servings: 4
Cooking Time: 30 Minutes
Ingredients:
- 3 cups broccoli florets, steam & chopped
- 2 cups cheddar cheese, shredded
- 1/4 cup breadcrumbs
- 2 eggs, lightly beaten
- 2 garlic cloves, minced
- Pepper
- Salt

Directions:
1. Fit the oven with the rack in position
2. Add all ingredients into the large bowl and mix until well combined.
3. Make patties from broccoli mixture and place in baking pan.
4. Set to bake at 375 F for 35 minutes. After 5 minutes place the baking pan in the preheated oven.

5. Serve and enjoy.
- **Nutrition Info:** Calories 311 Fat 21.5 g Carbohydrates 10.8 g Sugar 2.1 g Protein 19.8 g Cholesterol 141 mg

15. Pineapple And Cauliflower Rice

Servings: 6
Cooking Time: 20 Minutes
Ingredients:
- 2 cups rice
- 1 cauliflower, separated into florets and chopped
- 4 cups water
- ½ pineapple, peeled and chopped
- Salt and ground black pepper, to taste
- 2 teaspoons extra virgin olive oil

Directions:
1. In the Instant Pot, mix the rice with the pineapple, cauliflower, water, oil, salt and pepper, mix, cover and cook 2 minutes in manual mode.
2. Release the pressure naturally for 10 minutes, uncover the Instant Pot, mix with a fork, add more salt and pepper, divide between the plates and serve.
- **Nutrition Info:** Calories: 100, Fat: 2.7, Fiber: 2.9, Carbohydrate: 12, Proteins: 4.9

16. Amul Cheesy Cabbage Canapes

Servings: 2
Cooking Time: 15 Minutes
Ingredients:
- 1 whole cabbage, washed and cut in rounds
- 1 cube Amul cheese
- ½ carrot, cubed
- ¼ onion, cubed
- ¼ red bell pepper, cubed
- 1 tsp fresh basil, chopped

Directions:
1. Preheat on Air Fry function to 360 F. Using a bowl, mix onion, carrot, bell pepper, and cheese. Toss to coat everything evenly. Add cabbage rounds to the Air fryer baking pan.
2. Top with the veggie mixture and cook for 8 minutes. Garnish with basil and serve.

17. Roasted Garlic Fries

Servings: 1
Cooking Time: 30 Minutes
Ingredients:
- Roasted Garlic:
- 1 small head of garlic
- 2 teaspoons olive oil
- Baked Fries:
- 2 medium potatoes
- 2 teaspoons olive oil
- Salt
- Pepper

- Garlic Fries Topping:
- 1/4 cup minced parsley
- 1 teaspoon olive oil
- 1/8 teaspoon salt
- 2 cloves roasted garlic

Directions:
1. Start by preheating toaster oven to 425°F and lining a baking sheet with parchment paper.
2. Remove outer layer from garlic and chop off the top.
3. Drizzle oil over the garlic, filling the top.
4. Cut your potatoes into fries and toss with oil, salt, and pepper.
5. Place potatoes in a single layer on a greased baking sheet along with garlic head, and bake for 30 minutes, turning fries halfway through.
6. Remove two cloves of the garlic head, mince, and add parsley.
7. Stir the garlic mixture with olive oil and salt.
8. Drizzle over fries and serve.
- **Nutrition Info:** Calories: 513, Sodium: 326 mg, Dietary Fiber: 10.9 g, Total Fat: 23.9 g, Total Carbs: 70.8 g, Protein: 8.2 g.

18. Sweet Pickle Chips With Buttermilk

Servings: 3
Cooking Time: 20 Minutes
Ingredients:
- 36 sweet pickle chips
- 1 cup buttermilk
- 3 tbsp smoked paprika
- 2 cups flour
- ¼ cup cornmeal
- Salt and black pepper to taste

Directions:
1. Preheat on Air Fryer function to 400 F. In a bowl, mix flour, paprika, pepper, salt, cornmeal, and powder. Place pickles in buttermilk and set aside for 5 minutes. Dip the pickles in the spice mixture and place them in the greased air fryer basket. Fit in the baking tray and cook for 10 minutes. Serve warm.

19. Parsley Mushroom Pilaf

Servings: 4
Cooking Time: 35 Minutes
Ingredients:
- 2 tbsp olive oil
- 2 cups heated vegetable stock
- 1 cups long-grain rice
- 1 onion, chopped
- 2 garlic cloves, minced
- 2 cups cremini mushrooms, chopped
- Salt and black pepper to taste

- 1 tbsp fresh parsley, chopped

Directions:
1. Preheat on AirFry function to 400 F. Heat olive oil in a frying pan over medium heat. and sauté mushrooms, onion, and garlic for 5 minutes until tender. Stir in rice for 1-2 minutes.
2. Pour in the vegetable stock. Season with salt and pepper. Transfer to a baking dish and place in your oven. Press Start and cook for 20 minutes. Serve sprinkled with chopped parsley.

20. Parmesan Chicken Nuggets

Servings:4
Cooking Time: 25 Minutes
Ingredients:
- 1 lb chicken breast, cubed
- Salt and black pepper to taste
- 2 tbsp olive oil
- 5 tbsp plain breadcrumbs
- 2 tbsp panko breadcrumbs
- 2 tbsp grated Parmesan cheese

Directions:
1. Preheat on AirFry function to 380 F. Season the chicken with salt and pepper and drizzle with the olive oil. In a bowl, mix the crumbs with Parmesan cheese.
2. Coat the chicken pieces with the breadcrumb mixture and transfer them to the frying basket. Lightly grease chicken with cooking spray. Press Start. Cook the chicken for 10 minutes until golden brown on the outside and cooked on the inside. Serve warm.

21. Creamy Fennel(1)

Servings: 4
Cooking Time: 20 Minutes
Ingredients:
- 2 big fennel bulbs; sliced
- ½ cup coconut cream
- 2 tbsp. butter; melted
- Salt and black pepper to taste.

Directions:
1. In a pan that fits the air fryer, combine all the ingredients, toss, introduce in the machine and cook at 370°F for 12 minutes
2. Divide between plates and serve as a side dish.
- **Nutrition Info:** Calories: 151; Fat: 3g; Fiber: 2g; Carbs: 4g; Protein: 6g

22. Homemade Cheddar Biscuits

Servings: 8
Cooking Time: 35 Minutes
Ingredients:
- ½ cup + 1 tbsp butter
- 2 tbsp sugar

- 3 cups flour
- 1 ⅓ cups buttermilk
- ½ cup cheddar cheese, grated

Directions:
1. Preheat on Bake function to 380 F. Lay a parchment paper on a baking plate. In a bowl, mix sugar, flour, ½ cup of butter, half of the cheddar cheese, and buttermilk to form a batter. Make 8 balls from the batter and roll in flour.
2. Place the balls in your Air Fryer baking tray and flatten into biscuit shapes. Sprinkle the remaining cheddar cheese and remaining butter on top. Cook for 30 minutes, tossing every 10 minutes. Serve.

23. Japanese Tempura Bowl

Servings: 3
Cooking Time: 20 Minutes
Ingredients:
- 7 tablespoons whey protein isolate
- 1 teaspoon baking powder
- Kosher salt and ground black pepper, to taste
- 1/2 teaspoon paprika
- 1 teaspoon dashi granules
- 2 eggs
- 1 tablespoon mirin
- 3 tablespoons soda water
- 1 cup parmesan cheese, grated
- 1 onion, cut into rings
- 1 bell pepper
- 1 zucchini, cut into slices
- 3 asparagus spears
- 2 tablespoons olive oil

Directions:
1. In a shallow bowl, mix the whey protein isolate, baking powder, salt, black pepper, paprika, dashi granules, eggs, mirin, and soda water.
2. In another shallow bowl, place grated parmesan cheese.
3. Dip the vegetables in tempura batter; lastly, roll over parmesan cheese to coat evenly. Drizzle each piece with olive oil.
4. Cook in the preheated Air Fryer at 400 degrees F for 10 minutes, shaking the basket halfway through the cooking time. Work in batches until the vegetables are crispy and golden brown.
- **Nutrition Info:** 324 Calories; 12g Fat; 5g Carbs; 26g Protein; 9g Sugars; 2g Fiber

24. Traditional Greek Spanakopita

Servings: 6
Cooking Time: 40 Minutes
Ingredients:
- 3 tablespoons olive oil
- 2-1/2 pounds spinach

- 1 large onion
- 1 bunch green onions
- 2 cloves garlic
- 1/2 cup chopped fresh parsley
- 1/4 cup fresh dill
- 1/4 teaspoon ground nutmeg
- 2 eggs
- 1/2 cup ricotta cheese
- 1 cup crumbled feta cheese
- 3/4 teaspoon salt
- 1/2 teaspoon pepper
- 16 sheets of phyllo dough, thawed
- 1/4 cup olive oil

Directions:
1. Start by chopping all the vegetables into fine pieces.
2. Preheat the toaster oven to 350°F.
3. Heat olive oil in a large skillet over medium heat.
4. Sauté onions and garlic until garlic starts to brown.
5. Add spinach, parsley, dill, and nutmeg and stir until spinach begins to wilt.
6. Break eggs in medium bowl and mix in ricotta, feta, salt, and pepper.
7. Add spinach mixture to egg mixture and stir until combined.
8. Lay a sheet of phyllo dough on a baking sheet (it should overlap the edges) and brush with oil; repeat process 7 more times.
9. Spread the spinach mixture over dough and fold overlapping edges in.
10. Brush edges with olive oil. Add remaining dough one sheet at a time, brushing with oil as you go.
11. Tuck overlapping edges down to seal filling in dough.
12. Bake for 40 minutes or until lightly browned.
- **Nutrition Info:** Calories: 458, Sodium: 991 mg, Dietary Fiber: 5.8 g, Total Fat: 27.7 g, Total Carbs: 39.8 g, Protein: 16.9 g.

25. Mozzarella Cheese Sticks

Servings: 6
Cooking Time: 10 Minutes
Ingredients:
- Nonstick cooking spray
- 12 Mozzarella cheese sticks, halved
- 2 eggs
- ½ cup flour
- 1 ½ cups Italian panko bread crumbs
- ½ cup marinara sauce

Directions:
1. Blot cheese sticks with paper towels to soak up excess moisture.
2. In a shallow dish, beat eggs.
3. Place flour in a separate shallow dish.
4. Place bread crumbs in a third shallow dish.

5. Line a baking sheet with parchment paper.
6. One at a time, dip cheese sticks in egg, then flour, back in egg and finally in bread crumbs. Place on prepared pan. Freeze 1-2 hours until completely frozen.
7. Place baking pan in position 2 of the oven. Lightly spray fryer basket with cooking spray.
8. Place cheese sticks in a single layer in the basket and place in oven. Set to air fry on 375°F for 8 minutes. Cook until nicely browned and crispy, turning over halfway through cooking time. Serve with marinara sauce for dipping.
- **Nutrition Info:** Calories 199, Total Fat 3g, Saturated Fat 1g, Total Carbs 30g, Net Carbs 28g, Protein 13g, Sugar 3g, Fiber 2g, Sodium 368mg, Potassium 175mg, Phosphorus 220mg

26. Savory Stuffing

Servings: 4
Cooking Time: 20 Minutes
Ingredients:
- ½ cup butter
- 1½ cups water
- 1¼ cup turkey stock
- 1 yellow onion, peeled and chopped
- Salt and ground black pepper, to taste
- 1 teaspoon sage
- 1 bread loaf, cubed and toasted
- 1 cup celery, chopped
- 1 teaspoon poultry seasoning

Directions:
1. Put the Instant Pot in Saute mode, add the butter and melt. Add the stock, onion, celery, salt, pepper, sage and sauce and mix well. Add the bread cubes, mix and cook for 1 minute.
2. Transfer to a Bundt pan and cover with aluminum foil. Clean the Instant Pot, add the water and place the pan in the steamer basket, cover the Instant Pot and cook in the manual setting for 15 minutes.
3. Relieve the pressure, uncover the pan, bake at 100ºC and cook for 5 minutes. Serve hot.
- **Nutrition Info:** Calories: 230, Fat: 3.4, Fiber: 3.2, Carbohydrate: 23, Proteins: 11

27. Salty Baked Almonds

Servings: 4
Cooking Time: 25 Minutes
Ingredients:
- 1 cup raw almonds
- 1 egg white, beaten
- ½ teaspoon coarse sea salt

Directions:
1. Spread the almonds in the baking pan in an even layer.

2. Slide the baking pan into Rack Position 1, select Convection Bake, set temperature to 350ºF (180ºC) and set time to 20 minutes.
3. When cooking is complete, the almonds should be lightly browned and fragrant. Remove from the oven.
4. Coat the almonds with the egg white and sprinkle with the salt. Return the pan to the oven.
5. Slide the baking pan into Rack Position 1, select Convection Bake, set temperature to 350ºF (180ºC) and set time to 5 minutes.
6. When cooking is complete, the almonds should be dried. Cool completely before serving.

28. Grandma's Chicken Thighs

Servings: 2
Cooking Time: 30 Minutes
Ingredients:
- 1 pound chicken thighs
- ½ tsp salt
- ¼ tsp black pepper
- ¼ tsp garlic powder

Directions:
1. Season the thighs with salt, pepper, and garlic powder. Arrange thighs, skin side down, on the Air Fryer basket and fit in the baking tray. Cook until golden brown, about 20 minutes at 350 F on Bake function. Serve immediately.

29. Charred Green Beans With Sesame Seeds

Servings:4
Cooking Time: 8 Minutes
Ingredients:
- 1 tablespoon reduced-sodium soy sauce or tamari
- ½ tablespoon Sriracha sauce
- 4 teaspoons toasted sesame oil, divided
- 12 ounces (340 g) trimmed green beans
- ½ tablespoon toasted sesame seeds

Directions:
1. Whisk together the soy sauce, Sriracha sauce, and 1 teaspoon of sesame oil in a small bowl until smooth. Set aside.
2. Toss the green beans with the remaining sesame oil in a large bowl until evenly coated.
3. Place the green beans in the air fryer basket in a single layer.
4. Put the air fryer basket on the baking pan and slide into Rack Position 2, select Air Fry, set temperature to 375ºF (190ºC), and set time to 8 minutes.
5. Stir the green beans halfway through the cooking time.

6. When cooking is complete, the green beans should be lightly charred and tender. Remove from the oven to a platter. Pour the prepared sauce over the top of green beans and toss well. Serve sprinkled with the toasted sesame seeds.

30. Spicy Broccoli With Hot Sauce

Servings:6
Cooking Time: 14 Minutes
Ingredients:
- Broccoli:
- 1 medium-sized head broccoli, cut into florets
- 1½ tablespoons olive oil
- 1 teaspoon shallot powder
- 1 teaspoon porcini powder
- ½ teaspoon freshly grated lemon zest
- ½ teaspoon hot paprika
- ½ teaspoon granulated garlic
- $^1/_3$ teaspoon fine sea salt
- $^1/_3$ teaspoon celery seeds
- Hot Sauce:
- ½ cup tomato sauce
- 1 tablespoon balsamic vinegar
- ½ teaspoon ground allspice

Directions:
1. In a mixing bowl, combine all the ingredients for the broccoli and toss to coat. Transfer the broccoli to the air fryer basket.
2. Put the air fryer basket on the baking pan and slide into Rack Position 2, select Air Fry, set temperature to 360ºF (182ºC), and set time to 14 minutes.
3. Meanwhile, make the hot sauce by whisking together the tomato sauce, balsamic vinegar, and allspice in a small bowl.
4. When cooking is complete, remove the broccoli from the oven and serve with the hot sauce.

31. Baked Root Vegetables

Servings: 6
Cooking Time: 30 Minutes
Ingredients:
- 1 lb beetroot, cubed
- 3 tsp paprika
- 1/2 lb carrots, cut into chunks
- 1 lb sweet potato, cubed
- 2 tsp olive oil

Directions:
1. Fit the oven with the rack in position
2. Add all ingredients in a large mixing bowl and toss well.
3. Transfer root mixture onto a baking pan.
4. Set to bake at 350 F for 35 minutes. After 5 minutes place the baking pan in the preheated oven.
5. Serve and enjoy.

- **Nutrition Info:** Calories 133 Fat 2 g Carbohydrates 27.5 g Sugar 12.9 g Protein 3.3 g Cholesterol 0 mg

32. Garlic Herb Tomatoes

Servings: 4
Cooking Time: 45 Minutes
Ingredients:
- 10 medium-sized tomatoes
- 10 garlic cloves
- Bread crumbs
- Thyme
- Sage
- Oregano

Directions:
1. Start by finely chopping garlic and herbs.
2. Cut tomatoes in half and place cut-side up on a baking sheet lined with parchment paper.
3. Pour garlic and herb mixture over tomatoes.
4. Roast at 350°F for 30 minutes in toaster oven.
5. Top with bread crumbs and roast another 15 minutes.
- **Nutrition Info:** Calories: 103, Sodium: 68 mg, Dietary Fiber: 5.4 g, Total Fat: 1.3 g, Total Carbs: 21.4 g, Protein: 4.4 g.

33. Cheesy Chicken Breasts With Marinara Sauce

Servings:2
Cooking Time: 25 Minutes
Ingredients:
- 2 chicken breasts, beaten into ½ inch thick
- 1 egg, beaten
- ½ cup breadcrumbs
- Salt and black pepper to taste
- 2 tbsp marinara sauce
- 2 tbsp Grana Padano cheese, grated
- 2 mozzarella cheese slices

Directions:
1. Dip the breasts into the egg, then into the crumbs and arrange on the fryer basket. Select AirFry function, adjust the temperature to 400 F, and press Start. Cook for 5 minutes, turn over, and drizzle with marinara sauce, Grana Padano and mozzarella cheeses. Cook for 5 more minutes.

34. Hearty Eggplant Fries

Servings:2
Cooking Time: 20 Minutes
Ingredients:
- 1 eggplant, sliced
- 1 tsp olive oil
- 1 tsp soy sauce
- Salt to taste

Directions:
1. Preheat on AirFry function to 400 F. Make a marinade of olive oil, soy sauce, and salt and mix well in a bowl. Add in the eggplant and toss to coat.
2. Transfer them to the frying basket and place in the oven. Press Start and cook for 8 minutes. Serve drizzled with maple syrup.

35. Baked Artichoke Hearts

Servings: 6
Cooking Time: 25 Minutes
Ingredients:
- 15 oz frozen artichoke hearts, defrosted
- 1 tbsp olive oil
- Pepper
- Salt

Directions:
1. Fit the oven with the rack in position
2. Arrange artichoke hearts in baking pan and drizzle with olive oil. Season with pepper and salt.
3. Set to bake at 400 F for 30 minutes. After 5 minutes place the baking pan in the preheated oven.
4. Serve and enjoy.
- **Nutrition Info:** Calories 53 Fat 2.4 g Carbohydrates 7.5 g Sugar 0.7 g Protein 2.3 g Cholesterol 0 mg

36. Creamy Corn Casserole

Servings:4
Cooking Time: 15 Minutes
Ingredients:
- 2 cups frozen yellow corn
- 1 egg, beaten
- 3 tablespoons flour
- ½ cup grated Swiss or Havarti cheese
- ½ cup light cream
- ¼ cup milk
- Pinch salt
- Freshly ground black pepper, to taste
- 2 tablespoons butter, cut into cubes
- Nonstick cooking spray

Directions:
1. Spritz the baking pan with nonstick cooking spray.
2. Stir together the remaining ingredients except the butter in a medium bowl until well incorporated. Transfer the mixture to the prepared baking pan and scatter with the butter cubes.
3. Slide the baking pan into Rack Position 1, select Convection Bake, set temperature to 320ºF (160ºC), and set time to 15 minutes.
4. When cooking is complete, the top should be golden brown and a toothpick inserted in the center should come out clean. Remove from the oven. Let the casserole cool for 5

minutes before slicing into wedges and serving.

37. Delicious Chicken Wings With Alfredo Sauce

Servings: 4
Cooking Time: 60 Minutes
Ingredients:
- 1 ½ pounds chicken wings
- Salt and black pepper to taste
- ½ cup Alfredo sauce

Directions:
1. Preheat on Air Fry function to 370 F. Season the wings with salt and pepper. Arrange them on the greased basket without touching. Fit in the baking tray and cook for 20 minutes until no longer pink in the center. Work in batches if needed. Increase the heat to 390 F and cook for 5 minutes more. Remove to a large bowl and drizzle with the Alfredo sauce. Serve.

38. Air Fryer Corn

Servings: 2
Cooking Time: 10 Minutes
Ingredients:
- 2 fresh ears of corn, remove husks, wash, and pat dry
- 1 tbsp fresh lemon juice
- 2 tsp oil
- Pepper
- Salt

Directions:
1. Fit the oven with the rack in position 2.
2. Cut the corn to fit in the air fryer basket.
3. Drizzle oil over the corn. Season with pepper and salt.
4. Place corn in the air fryer basket then places an air fryer basket in the baking pan.
5. Place a baking pan on the oven rack. Set to air fry at 400 F for 10 minutes.
6. Serve and enjoy.
7. Drizzle lemon juice over corn and serve.
- **Nutrition Info:** Calories 122 Fat 5.6 g Carbohydrates 18.2 g Sugar 4.2 g Protein 3.1 g Cholesterol 0 mg

39. Party Pull Apart

Servings: 10
Cooking Time: 20 Minutes
Ingredients:
- 5 cloves garlic
- 1/3 cup fresh parsley
- 2 tbsp. olive oil
- 4 oz. mozzarella cheese, sliced
- 3 tbsp. butter
- 1/8 tsp salt
- 1 loaf sour dough bread

Directions:
1. Place the rack in position 1 of the oven.
2. In a food processor, add garlic, parsley, and oil and pulse until garlic is chopped fine.
3. Stack the mozzarella cheese and cut into 1-inch squares.
4. Heat the butter in a small saucepan over medium heat. Add the garlic mixture and salt and cook 2 minutes, stirring occasionally. Remove from heat.
5. Use a sharp, serrated knife to make 1-inch diagonal cuts across the bread being careful not to cut all the way through.
6. With a spoon, drizzle garlic butter into the cuts in the bread. Stack 3-4 cheese squares and place in each of the cuts.
7. Place the bread on a sheet of foil and fold up the sides. Cut a second piece of foil just big enough to cover the top.
8. Set oven to convection bake on 350°F for 25 minutes. After 5 minutes, place the bread in the oven and bake 10 minutes.
9. Remove the top piece of foil and bake 10 minutes more until the cheese has completely melted. Serve immediately.
- **Nutrition Info:** Calories 173, Total Fat 7g, Saturated Fat 3g, Total Carbs 18g, Net Carbs 17g, Protein 7g, Sugar 2g, Fiber 1g, Sodium 337mg, Potassium 68mg, Phosphorus 112mg

40. Mashed Squash

Servings: 4
Cooking Time: 20 Minutes
Ingredients:
- 2 acorn squashes, cut into halves and seeded
- ½ cup water
- ¼ teaspoon baking soda
- 2 tablespoons butter
- Salt and ground black pepper, to taste
- ½ teaspoon fresh nutmeg, grated
- 2 tablespoons brown sugar

Directions:
1. Sprinkle the pumpkin halves with salt, pepper and baking soda and place them in the steam basket of the Instant Pot.
2. Add water to the Instant Pot, cover and cook for 20 minutes in manual configuration. Relieve the pressure, take the pumpkin and set it on a plate to cool. Scrape the flesh of the pumpkin and place it in a bowl.
3. Add salt, pepper, butter, sugar and nutmeg and mash with a potato masher. Mix well and serve.
- **Nutrition Info:** Calories: 140, Fat: 1, Fiber: 0.5, Carbohydrate: 10.5, Proteins: 1.7

41. Bread Cheese Sticks

Servings:6
Cooking Time: 5 Minutes
Ingredients:
- 6 (6 oz) bread cheese
- 2 tbsp butter, melted
- 2 cups panko crumbs

Directions:
1. With a knife, cut the cheese into equal-sized sticks. Brush each stick with butter and dip into the panko crumbs. Arrange the sticks in a single layer on the basket tray. Select AirFry function, adjust the temperature to 390 F, and press Start. Cook for 10-12 minutes. Serve warm.

42. Asparagus Wrapped In Bacon

Servings:4
Cooking Time: 25 Minutes
Ingredients:
- 20 spears asparagus
- 4 bacon slices
- 1 tbsp olive oil
- 1 tbsp sesame oil
- 1 garlic clove, minced

Directions:
1. Preheat on AirFry function to 380 F. In a bowl, mix the oils, sugar, and garlic. Separate the asparagus into 4 bunches (5 spears in 1 bunch) and wrap each bunch with a bacon slice.
2. Drizzle the bunches with oil mix. Put them in the frying basket and place in the oven. Press Start and cook for 8 minutes. Serve warm.

43. Crispy Cauliflower Poppers

Servings: 4
Cooking Time: 20 Minutes
Ingredients:
- 1 egg white
- 1½ tablespoons ketchup
- 1 tablespoon hot sauce
- 1/3 cup panko breadcrumbs
- 2 cups cauliflower florets

Directions:
1. In a shallow bowl, mix together the egg white, ketchup and hot sauce.
2. In another bowl, place the breadcrumbs.
3. Dip the cauliflower florets in ketchup mixture and then coat with the breadcrumbs.
4. Press "Power Button" of Air Fry Oven and turn the dial to select the "Air Fry" mode.
5. Press the Time button and again turn the dial to set the cooking time to 20 minutes.
6. Now push the Temp button and rotate the dial to set the temperature at 320 degrees F.

7. Press "Start/Pause" button to start.
8. When the unit beeps to show that it is preheated, open the lid.
9. Arrange the cauliflower florets in "Air Fry Basket" and insert in the oven.
10. Toss the cauliflower florets once halfway through.
11. Serve warm.
- **Nutrition Info:** Calories 55 Total Fat 0.7 g Saturated Fat 0.3g Cholesterol 0 mg Sodium 181 mg Total Carbs 5.6 g Fiber 1.3 g Sugar 2.6 g Protein 2.3 g

44. Savory Parsley Crab Cakes

Servings: 6
Cooking Time: 20 Minutes
Ingredients:
- 1 lb crab meat, shredded
- 2 eggs, beaten
- ½ cup breadcrumbs
- ⅓ cup finely chopped green onion
- ¼ cup parsley, chopped
- 1 tbsp mayonnaise
- 1 tsp sweet chili sauce
- ½ tsp paprika
- Salt and black pepper to taste

Directions:
1. In a bowl, add crab meat, eggs, crumbs, green onion, parsley, mayo, chili sauce, paprika, salt and black pepper; mix well with your hands.
2. Shape into 6 cakes and grease them lightly with oil. Arrange them in the fryer basket without overcrowding. Fit in the baking tray and cook for 8 minutes at 400 F on Air Fry function, turning once halfway through.

45. Three Bean Medley

Servings: 4
Cooking Time: 15 Minutes
Ingredients:
- 4 cups water
- 1 cup garbanzo beans, soaked overnight and drained
- 1 cup cranberry beans, soaked overnight and drained
- 1½ cups green beans
- 1 garlic clove, peeled and crushed
- 1 bay leaf
- 1 small red onion, peeled and chopped
- 1 tablespoon sugar
- 2 celery stalks, chopped
- 1 bunch parsley, chopped
- Salt and ground black pepper, to taste
- 5 tablespoons apple cider vinegar
- 4 tablespoons extra virgin olive oil

Directions:

1. Place the water in the Instant Pot. Add the bay leaf, garlic and chickpeas. Also place the basket in the pan and add the cranberries.
2. Wrap the green beans in aluminum foil and place them in the steam basket. Cover the Instant Pot and cook in the Bean / Chili setting for 15 minutes.
3. Release the pressure naturally for 10 minutes, uncover the Instant Pot, drain the beans, discard them and place them all in a bowl. In another bowl, mix the onion with the vinegar and sugar, mix well and set aside for a few minutes.
4. Add the onion to the beans and mix well. Also add celery, olive oil, salt, pepper to taste and parsley, mix well, divide between plates and serve.
- **Nutrition Info:** Calories: 200, Fat: 1, Fiber: 6, Carbohydrate: 45, Proteins: 4

46. **Butterbeans With Feta & Bacon**

Servings:2
Cooking Time: 20 Minutes
Ingredients:
- 1 (14 oz) can butter beans
- 1 tbsp fresh chives, chopped
- ½ cup feta cheese, crumbled
- Black pepper to taste
- 1 tsp olive oil
- 2 oz bacon, sliced

Directions:
1. Preheat on AirFry function to 340 F. Blitz beans, oil, and pepper in a small blender. Arrange bacon slices on the frying basket.
2. Top with chives and place in the oven. Press Start and cook for 12 minutes. Add feta to the bean mixture and stir. Serve bacon with the dip.

47. **Crunchy Mozzarella Sticks With Sweet Thai Sauce**

Servings:4
Cooking Time: 20 Minutes
Ingredients:
- 12 mozzarella string cheese
- 2 cups breadcrumbs
- 3 eggs
- 1 cup sweet Thai sauce
- 4 tbsp skimmed milk

Directions:
1. Pour the crumbs in a bowl. Crack the eggs into another bowl and beat with the milk. One after the other, dip cheese sticks in the egg mixture, in the crumbs, then egg mixture again and then in the crumbs again. Place the coated cheese sticks on a cookie sheet and freeze for 1 hour.
2. Preheat on AirFry function to 380 F. Arrange the sticks in the frying basket

without overcrowding. Press Start and cook for 8 minutes until brown. Serve with sweet Thai sauce.

48. **Garlic & Parmesan Bread Bites**

Servings: 12
Cooking Time: 7 Minutes
Ingredients:
- 2 ciabatta loaves
- 1 stick butter at room temperature
- 4-6 crushed garlic cloves
- Chopped parsley
- 2 tablespoons finely grated parmesan

Directions:
1. Start by cutting bread in half and toasting it crust-side down for 2 minutes.
2. Mix the butter, garlic, and parsley together and spread over the bread.
3. Sprinkle parmesan over bread and toast in oven another 5 minutes.
- **Nutrition Info:** Calories: 191, Sodium: 382 mg, Dietary Fiber: 1.0 g, Total Fat: 9.4 g, Total Carbs: 21.7 g, Protein: 4.9 g.

49. **Jicama Fries(3)**

Servings: 4
Cooking Time: 20 Minutes
Ingredients:
- 1 small jicama; peeled.
- ¼ tsp. onion powder.
- ¾tsp. chili powder
- ¼ tsp. ground black pepper
- ¼ tsp. garlic powder.

Directions:
1. Cut jicama into matchstick-sized pieces.
2. Place pieces into a small bowl and sprinkle with remaining ingredients. Place the fries into the air fryer basket
3. Adjust the temperature to 350 Degrees F and set the timer for 20 minutes. Toss the basket two or three times during cooking. Serve warm.
- **Nutrition Info:** Calories: 37; Protein: 8g; Fiber: 7g; Fat: 1g; Carbs: 7g

50. **Shrimp With Spices**

Servings: 3
Cooking Time: 15 Minutes
Ingredients:
- ½ pound shrimp, deveined
- ½ tsp Cajun seasoning
- Salt and black pepper to taste
- 1 tbsp olive oil
- ¼ tsp paprika

Directions:
1. Preheat on Air Fry function to 390 F. In a bowl, mix paprika, salt, pepper, olive oil, and Cajun seasoning. Add in the shrimp and toss to coat. Transfer the prepared shrimp

to the AirFryer basket and fit in the baking tray. Cook for 10-12 minutes, flipping halfway through.

51. Simple Chicken Breasts

Servings: 4
Cooking Time: 30 Minutes
Ingredients:
- 4 boneless, skinless chicken breasts
- 1 tsp salt and black pepper
- 1 tsp garlic powder

Directions:
1. Spray the breasts and the Air Fryer basket with cooking spray. Rub chicken with salt, garlic powder, and black pepper. Arrange the breasts on the basket. Fit in the baking pan and cook for 20 minutes at 360 F on Bake function until nice and crispy. Serve warm.

52. Spicy Tortilla Chips

Servings: 4
Cooking Time: 5 Minutes
Ingredients:
- ½ teaspoon ground cumin
- ½ teaspoon paprika
- ½ teaspoon chili powder
- ½ teaspoon salt
- Pinch cayenne pepper
- 8 (6-inch) corn tortillas, each cut into 6 wedges
- Cooking spray

Directions:
1. Lightly spritz the air fryer basket with cooking spray.
2. Stir together the cumin, paprika, chili powder, salt, and pepper in a small bowl.
3. Place the tortilla wedges in the basket in a single layer. Lightly mist them with cooking spray. Sprinkle the seasoning mixture on top of the tortilla wedges.
4. Put the air fryer basket on the baking pan and slide into Rack Position 2, select Air Fry, set temperature to 375ºF (190ºC), and set time to 5 minutes.
5. Stir the tortilla wedges halfway through the cooking time.
6. When cooking is complete, the chips should be lightly browned and crunchy. Remove from the oven. Let the tortilla chips cool for 5 minutes and serve.

53. Garlicky Roasted Chicken With Lemon

Servings:4
Cooking Time: 60 Minutes
Ingredients:
- 1 whole chicken (around 3.5 lb)
- 1 tbsp olive oil
- Salt and black pepper to taste
- 1 lemon, cut into quarters
- 5 garlic cloves

Directions:
1. Rub the chicken with olive oil and season with salt and pepper. Stuff the cavity with lemon and garlic. Place chicken, breast-side down on a baking tray. Tuck the legs and wings tips under.
2. Select Bake function, adjust the temperature to 360 F, and press Start. Bake for 30 minutes, turn breast-side up, and bake it for another 15 minutes. Let rest for 5-6 minutes then carve.

54. Cheesy Garlic Biscuits

Servings: 4
Cooking Time: 20 Minutes
Ingredients:
- 1 large egg.
- 1 scallion, sliced
- ¼ cup unsalted butter; melted and divided
- ½ cup shredded sharp Cheddar cheese.
- ⅓ cup coconut flour
- ½ tsp. baking powder.
- ½ tsp. garlic powder.

Directions:
1. Take a large bowl, mix coconut flour, baking powder and garlic powder.
2. Stir in egg, half of the melted butter, Cheddar cheese and scallions. Pour the mixture into a 6-inch round baking pan. Place into the air fryer basket
3. Adjust the temperature to 320 Degrees F and set the timer for 12 minutes
4. To serve, remove from pan and allow to fully cool. Slice into four pieces and pour remaining melted butter over each.
- **Nutrition Info:** Calories: 218; Protein: 7.2g; Fiber: 3.4g; Fat: 16.9g; Carbs: 6.8g

55. Balsamic Cabbage(2)

Servings: 4
Cooking Time: 20 Minutes
Ingredients:
- 6 cups red cabbage; shredded
- 4 garlic cloves; minced
- 1 tbsp. olive oil
- 1 tbsp. balsamic vinegar
- Salt and black pepper to taste.

Directions:
1. In a pan that fits the air fryer, combine all the ingredients, toss, introduce the pan in the air fryer and cook at 380°F for 15 minutes
2. Divide between plates and serve as a side dish.
- **Nutrition Info:** Calories: 151; Fat: 2g; Fiber: 3g; Carbs: 5g; Protein: 5g

56. Cheese Herb Zucchini

Servings: 4
Cooking Time: 15 Minutes
Ingredients:
- 4 zucchini, quartered
- 1/2 tsp dried oregano
- 2 tbsp fresh parsley, chopped
- 2 tbsp olive oil
- 1/2 tsp dried thyme
- 1/2 cup parmesan cheese, grated
- 1/4 tsp garlic powder
- 1/2 tsp dried basil
- Pepper
- Salt

Directions:
1. Fit the oven with the rack in position
2. In a small bowl, mix parmesan cheese, garlic powder, basil, oregano, thyme, pepper, and salt.
3. Arrange zucchini in baking pan and drizzle with oil and sprinkle with parmesan cheese mixture.
4. Set to bake at 350 F for 20 minutes. After 5 minutes place the baking pan in the preheated oven.
5. Garnish with parsley and serve.
- **Nutrition Info:** Calories 130 Fat 9.8 g Carbohydrates 7.4 g Sugar 3.5 g Protein 6.1 g Cholesterol 8 mg

57. Lemon-thyme Bruschetta

Servings: 10
Cooking Time: 7 Minutes
Ingredients:
- 1 baguette
- 8 ounces ricotta cheese
- 1 lemon
- Salt
- Freshly cracked black pepper
- Honey
- 8 sprigs fresh thyme

Directions:
1. Start by preheating toaster oven to 425°F.
2. Thinly slice baguette, and zest lemon.
3. Mix ricotta and lemon zest together and season with salt and pepper.
4. Toast the baguette slices for 7 minutes or until they start to brown.
5. Spread ricotta mix over slices.
6. Drizzle with honey and top with thyme, then serve.
- **Nutrition Info:** Calories: 60, Sodium: 71 mg, Dietary Fiber: 0.6 g, Total Fat: 2.0 g, Total Carbs: 7.6 g, Protein: 3.5 g.

58. Winter Vegetables With Herbs

Servings: 2
Cooking Time: 20 Minutes

Ingredients:
- 1/2-pound broccoli florets
- 1 celery root, peeled and cut into 1-inch pieces
- 1 onion, cut into wedges
- 2 tablespoons unsalted butter, melted
- 1/2 cup chicken broth
- 1/4 cup tomato sauce
- 1 teaspoon parsley
- 1 teaspoon rosemary
- 1 teaspoon thyme

Directions:
1. Start by preheating your Air Fryer to 380 degrees F. Place all ingredients in a lightly greased casserole dish. Stir to combine well.
2. Bake in the preheated Air Fryer for 10 minutes. Gently stir the vegetables with a large spoon and cook for 5 minutes more.
3. Serve in individual bowls with a few drizzles of lemon juice.
- **Nutrition Info:** 141 Calories; 13g Fat; 1g Carbs; 5g Protein; 9g Sugars; 6g Fiber

59. Baked Sweet Potatoes

Servings: 6
Cooking Time: 35 Minutes
Ingredients:
- 4 large sweet potatoes, peel and cut into cubes
- 8 sage leaves
- 1 tsp honey
- 2 tsp vinegar
- 1/2 tsp paprika
- 2 tbsp olive oil
- 1/2 tsp sea salt

Directions:
1. Fit the oven with the rack in position
2. Add sweet potato, oil, sage, and salt in a baking dish and mix well.
3. Set to bake at 375 F for 40 minutes. After 5 minutes place the baking dish in the preheated oven.
4. Transfer roasted sweet potatoes into the large bowl and toss with honey, vinegar, and paprika.
5. Serve and enjoy.
- **Nutrition Info:** Calories 92 Fat 5.1 g Carbohydrates 12 g Sugar 1.2 g Protein 0.8 g Cholesterol 0 mg

60. Buffalo Quesadillas

Servings: 8
Cooking Time: 5 Minutes
Ingredients:
- Nonstick cooking spray
- 2 cups chicken, cooked & chopped fine
- ½ cup Buffalo wing sauce
- 2 cups Monterey Jack cheese, grated

- ½ cup green onions, sliced thin
- 8 flour tortillas, 8-inch diameter
- ¼ cup blue cheese dressing

Directions:
1. Lightly spray the baking pan with cooking spray.
2. In a medium bowl, add chicken and wing sauce and toss to coat.
3. Place tortillas, one at a time on work surface. Spread ¼ of the chicken mixture over tortilla and sprinkle with cheese and onion. Top with a second tortilla and place on the baking pan.
4. Set oven to broil on 400°F for 8 minutes. After 5 minutes place baking pan in position 2. Cook quesadillas 2-3 minutes per side until toasted and cheese has melted. Repeat with remaining ingredients.
5. Cut quesadillas in wedges and serve with blue cheese dressing or other dipping sauce.
- **Nutrition Info:** Calories 376, Total Fat 20g, Saturated Fat 8g, Total Carbs 27g, Net Carbs 26g, Protein 22g, Sugar 2g, Fiber 2g, Sodium 685mg, Potassium 201mg, Phosphorus 301mg

61. Creamy Fennel(3)

Servings: 4
Cooking Time: 20 Minutes
Ingredients:
- 2 big fennel bulbs; sliced
- ½ cup coconut cream
- 2 tbsp. butter; melted
- Salt and black pepper to taste.

Directions:
1. In a pan that fits the air fryer, combine all the ingredients, toss, introduce in the machine and cook at 370°F for 12 minutes

2. Divide between plates and serve as a side dish.
- **Nutrition Info:** Calories: 151; Fat: 3g; Fiber: 2g; Carbs: 4g; Protein: 6g

62. Flavored Mashed Sweet Potatoes

Servings: 8
Cooking Time: 9 Minutes
Ingredients:
- 3 pounds sweet potatoes, peeled and chopped
- Salt and ground black pepper, to taste
- 2 garlic cloves
- ½ teaspoon dried parsley
- ½ teaspoon dried rosemary
- ¼ teaspoon dried sage
- ½ teaspoon dried thyme
- 1½ cups water
- ½ cup Parmesan cheese, grated
- 2 tablespoon butter
- ¼ cup milk

Directions:
1. Place the potatoes and garlic in the Instant Pot, add 1 ½ cups of water to the Instant Pot, cover and cook for 10 minutes in the manual setting.
2. Relieve the pressure, drain the water, transfer the potatoes and garlic to a bowl and mix them using a hand mixer.
3. Add butter, cheese, milk, salt, pepper, parsley, sage, rosemary and thyme and mix well. Divide between plates and serve.
- **Nutrition Info:** Calories: 240, Fat: 1, Fiber: 8.2, Carbohydrate: 34, Proteins: 4.5

BREAKFAST RECIPES

63. Lamb And Feta Hamburgers

Servings: 4 Burgers
Cooking Time: 16 Minutes
Ingredients:
- 1½ pounds (680 g) ground lamb
- ¼ cup crumbled feta
- 1½ teaspoons tomato paste
- 1½ teaspoons minced garlic
- 1 teaspoon ground dried ginger
- 1 teaspoon ground coriander
- ¼ teaspoon salt
- ¼ teaspoon cayenne pepper
- 4 kaiser rolls or hamburger buns, split open lengthwise, warmed
- Cooking spray

Directions:
1. Spritz the air fryer basket with cooking spray.
2. Combine all the ingredients, except for the buns, in a large bowl. Coarsely stir to mix well.
3. Shape the mixture into four balls, then pound the balls into four 5-inch diameter patties.
4. Arrange the patties in the pan and spritz with cooking spray.
5. Put the air fryer basket on the baking pan and slide into Rack Position 2, select Air Fry, set temperature to 375ºF (190ºC) and set time to 16 minutes.
6. Flip the patties halfway through the cooking time.
7. When cooking is complete, the patties should be well browned.
8. Assemble the buns with patties to make the burgers and serve immediately.

64. Hearty Sweet Potato Baked Oatmeal

Servings: 6
Cooking Time: 30 Minutes
Ingredients:
- 1 egg, lightly beaten
- 1 tsp vanilla
- 1 1/2 cups milk
- 1 tsp baking powder
- 2 tbsp ground flax seed
- 1 cup sweet potato puree
- 1/4 tsp nutmeg
- 2 tsp cinnamon
- 1/3 cup maple syrup
- 2 cups old fashioned oats
- 1/4 tsp salt

Directions:
1. Fit the oven with the rack in position

2. Spray an 8-inch square baking pan with cooking spray and set aside.
3. Add all ingredients except oats into the mixing bowl and mix until well combined.
4. Add oats and stir until just combined.
5. Pour mixture into the prepared baking pan.
6. Set to bake at 350 F for 35 minutes. After 5 minutes place the baking pan in the preheated oven.
7. Serve and enjoy.
- **Nutrition Info:** Calories 355 Fat 6.3 g Carbohydrates 62.3 g Sugar 17.1 g Protein 10.9 g Cholesterol 32 mg

65. Spiced Squash Mix

Servings: 4
Cooking Time: 15 Minutes
Ingredients:
- 1 cup almond milk
- 1 butternut squash, peeled and roughly cubed
- ½ teaspoon cinnamon powder
- ¼ teaspoon nutmeg, ground
- ¼ teaspoon allspice, ground
- ¼ teaspoon cardamom, ground
- 2 tablespoons brown sugar
- Cooking spray

Directions:
1. Spray your air fryer with cooking spray, add the squash, milk and the other ingredients, toss, cover and cook at 360 degrees F for 15 minutes.
2. Divide into bowls and serve for breakfast.
- **Nutrition Info:** calories 212, fat 5, fiber 7, carbs 14, protein 5

66. Creamy Mushroom And Spinach Omelet

Servings: 2
Cooking Time: 10 Minutes
Ingredients:
- 4 eggs, lightly beaten
- 2 tbsp heavy cream
- 2 cups spinach, chopped
- 1 cup mushrooms, chopped
- 3 oz feta cheese, crumbled
- 1 tbsp fresh parsley, chopped
- Salt and black pepper to taste

Directions:
1. Spray a baking pan with cooking spray. In a bowl, whisk eggs and heavy cream until combined. Stir in spinach, mushrooms, feta, salt, and pepper.
2. Pour into the basket tray and cook in your for 6-10 minutes at 350 F on Bake function until golden and set. Sprinkle with parsley, cut into wedges, and serve.

67. Healthy Oatmeal Bars

Servings: 18
Cooking Time: 20 Minutes
Ingredients:
- 2 cups oatmeal
- 1/2 tsp allspice
- 1 tsp baking soda
- 1 tbsp maple syrup
- 1 cup butter
- 1 cup of sugar
- 1 cup flour

Directions:
1. Fit the oven with the rack in position
2. Add butter and maple syrup into a bowl and microwave until butter is melted. Stir well.
3. In a mixing bowl, mix oatmeal, sugar, flour, allspice, and baking soda.
4. Add melted butter and maple syrup mixture and mix until well combined.
5. Pour mixture into the parchment-lined 9*12-inch baking dish. Spread well.
6. Set to bake at 350 F for 25 minutes, after 5 minutes, place the baking dish in the oven.
7. Slice and serve.
- **Nutrition Info:** Calories 195 Fat 10.9 g Carbohydrates 23.4 g Sugar 11.9 g Protein 2 g Cholesterol 27 mg

68. Buttery Chocolate Toast

Servings: 1
Cooking Time: 5 Minutes
Ingredients:
- Whole wheat bread slices
- Coconut oil
- Pure maple syrup
- Cacao powder

Directions:
1. Toast the bread in toaster oven.
2. Spread coconut oil over the toast.
3. Drizzle maple syrup in lines over the toast.
4. Sprinkle cacao powder and serve.
- **Nutrition Info:** Calories: 101, Sodium: 133 mg, Dietary Fiber: 2.4 g, Total Fat: 3.5 g, Total Carbs: 14.8 g, Protein: 4.0 g.

69. Walnuts And Mango Oatmeal

Servings: 4
Cooking Time: 20 Minutes
Ingredients:
- 2 cups almond milk
- ½ cup walnuts, chopped
- 1 teaspoon vanilla extract
- 1 cup mango, peeled and cubed
- 3 tablespoons sugar
- ½ cup steel cut oats

Directions:

1. In your air fryer, combine the almond milk with the oats and the other ingredients, toss and cook at 360 degrees F for 20 minutes.
2. Divide the mix into bowls and serve for breakfast.
- **Nutrition Info:** calories 141, fat 4, fiber 7, carbs 8, protein 5

70. Cinnamon-orange Toast

Servings: 6
Cooking Time: 15 Minutes
Ingredients:
- 12 slices bread
- ½ cup sugar
- 1 stick butter
- 1½ tbsp vanilla extract
- 1½ tbsp cinnamon
- 2 oranges, zested

Directions:
1. Mix butter, sugar, and vanilla extract and microwave for 30 seconds until everything melts. Add in orange zest. Pour the mixture over bread slices. Lay the bread slices in your Air Fryer pan and cook for 5 minutes at 400 F on Toast function. Serve with berry sauce.

71. Delicious Baked Omelet

Servings: 6
Cooking Time: 25 Minutes
Ingredients:
- 8 eggs
- 1/2 cup green bell pepper
- 1/2 cup onion, diced
- 1 cup ham, chopped & cooked
- 1 cup cheddar cheese, shredded
- 1/2 cup half and half
- Pepper
- Salt

Directions:
1. Fit the oven with the rack in position
2. Spray 9*9-inch baking pan with cooking spray and set aside.
3. In a bowl, whisk eggs with half and half, pepper, and salt.
4. Add green bell pepper, onion, ham, and cheddar cheese and stir well.
5. Pour egg mixture into the prepared baking pan.
6. Set to bake at 400 F for 30 minutes. After 5 minutes place the baking pan in the preheated oven.
7. Serve and enjoy.
- **Nutrition Info:** Calories 230 Fat 16.4 g Carbohydrates 4.1 g Sugar 1.5 g Protein 16.6 g Cholesterol 258 mg

72. Blackberry French Toast

Servings: 6

Cooking Time: 20 Minutes
Ingredients:
- 1 cup blackberry jam, warm
- 12 ounces bread loaf, cubed
- 8 ounces cream cheese, cubed
- 4 eggs
- 1 tsp. cinnamon powder
- 2 cups half and half
- 1/2 cup brown sugar
- 1 tsp. vanilla extract
- Cooking spray

Directions:
1. Grease your air fryer with cooking spray and heat it up at 300 °F.
2. Add blueberry jam on the bottom, layer half of the bread cubes, then add cream cheese and top with the rest of the bread.
3. In a bowl, mix eggs with half and half, cinnamon, sugar and vanilla, whisk well and add over bread mix.
4. Cook for 20 minutes, divide among plates and serve for breakfast.
- **Nutrition Info:** Calories 113 Fat 8.2 g Carbohydrates 0.3 g Sugar 0.2 g Protein 5.4 g Cholesterol 18 mg

73. Bell Pepper Eggs

Servings: 4
Cooking Time: 30 Minutes
Ingredients:
- 4 medium green bell peppers
- ¼ medium onion; peeled and chopped
- 3 oz. cooked ham; chopped
- 8 large eggs.
- 1 cup mild Cheddar cheese

Directions:
1. Cut the tops off each bell pepper. Remove the seeds and the white membranes with a small knife. Place ham and onion into each pepper
2. Crack 2 eggs into each pepper. Top with ¼ cup cheese per pepper. Place into the air fryer basket
3. Adjust the temperature to 390 Degrees F and set the timer for 15 minutes. When fully cooked, peppers will be tender, and eggs will be firm. Serve immediately.
- **Nutrition Info:** Calories: 314; Protein: 24.9g; Fiber: 1.7g; Fat: 18.6g; Carbs: 6.3g

74. Oats, Chocolate Chip, Pecan Cookies

Servings:x
Cooking Time:x
Ingredients:
- ½ cup (115g) butter, softened
- ½ cup (100g) sugar
- 1 cup (170g) chocolate chips
- ½ cup (60g) pecan halves, chopped
- ½ cup (100g) firmly packed brown sugar
- 1 teaspoon vanilla extract
- 1 large egg
- 1L cup (160g) all-purpose flour
- 2 teaspoons baking powder
- ½ teaspoon kosher salt
- ¼ cup (20g) rolled oats

Directions:
1. Line 2 baking pans with parchment paper.
2. Assemble bench mixer with beater attachment. Place butter, sugar, brown sugar and vanilla in the mixing bowl. Mix on medium speed for 2 minutes until pale and creamy.
3. Add egg and beat until just combined. Sift flour, baking powder and salt, then add to egg mixture on low speed, mixing until just combined.
4. Add chocolate chips, pecans and oats and mix on low speed until just combined.
5. Roll heaping tablespoons of dough into balls and place 6 balls, 2 inches (4cm) apart, on each prepared pan.
6. Insert wire racks in rack positions 3 and Select COOKIES/315°F (155°C)/SUPER CONVECTION/12 minutes. Press START to preheat oven.
7. Bake cookies for 12 minutes, rotating halfway through baking (change top to bottom and front to back).
8. Let cool on baking pans for 5 minutes then transfer to a wire rack to cool completely. 9. Repeat with remaining dough.

75. French Toast Delight

Servings: 2
Cooking Time: 10 Minutes
Ingredients:
- 4 bread slices
- 2 tablespoons margarine
- 1/2 tsp. cinnamon
- 2 Eggs
- Pinch salt
- Pinch ground cloves
- Pinch Nutmeg
- Icing sugar and maple syrup, to serve

Directions:
1. Preheat Air fryer to350°F.Whisk together eggs, cloves, cinnamon, nutmeg, cloves and salt in a bowl. Margarine sides of each bread slice and cut into strips.
2. Soak the margarineed bread strips in the egg mixture one after the other and arrange in the tray. (Cook in two batches, if necessary).
3. Cook 2 minutes and then remove the strips. Lightly coat bread strips with cooking spray on both sides. Place back the tray into the

air fryer and cook another 4 minutes, checking to ensure they are cooking evenly.

4. Remove bread from Air fryer once it's golden brown. Sprinkle with icing sugar and drizzle with maple syrup.
- **Nutrition Info:** Calories 118 Fat 9.4 g Carbohydrates 0.2 g Sugar 0.3 g Protein 6 g

76. Ham And Egg Toast Cups

Servings: 2
Cooking Time: 5 Minutes
Ingredients:
- 2 eggs
- 2 slices of ham
- 2 tablespoons butter
- Cheddar cheese, for topping
- Salt, to taste
- Black pepper, to taste

Directions:
1. Preheat the Air fryer to 400-degree F and grease both ramekins with melted butter.
2. Place each ham slice in the greased ramekins and crack each egg over ham slices.
3. Sprinkle with salt, black pepper and cheddar cheese and transfer into the Air fryer basket.
4. Cook for about 5 minutes and remove the ramekins from the basket.
5. Serve warm.
- **Nutrition Info:** Calories: 202, Fat: 13.7g, Carbs: 7.4g, Sugar: 3.3g, Protein: 10.2g, Sodium: 203mg

77. Basil Dill Egg Muffins

Servings: 6
Cooking Time: 20 Minutes
Ingredients:
- 6 eggs
- 1 tbsp chives, chopped
- 1 tbsp fresh basil, chopped
- 1 tbsp fresh cilantro, chopped
- 1/4 cup mozzarella cheese, grated
- 1 tbsp fresh dill, chopped
- 1 tbsp fresh parsley, chopped
- Pepper
- Salt

Directions:
1. Fit the oven with the rack in position
2. Spray 6-cups muffin tin with cooking spray and set aside.
3. In a bowl, whisk eggs with pepper and salt.
4. Add remaining ingredients and stir well.
5. Pour egg mixture into the prepared muffin tin.
6. Set to bake at 350 F for 25 minutes. After 5 minutes place muffin tin in the preheated oven.
7. Serve and enjoy.

- **Nutrition Info:** Calories 68 Fat 4.6 g Carbohydrates 0.8 g Sugar 0.4 g Protein 6 g Cholesterol 164 mg

78. Avocado And Tomato Egg Rolls

Servings:5
Cooking Time: 5 Minutes
Ingredients:
- 10 egg roll wrappers
- 3 avocados, peeled and pitted
- 1 tomato, diced
- Salt and ground black pepper, to taste
- Cooking spray

Directions:
1. Spritz the air fryer basket with cooking spray.
2. Put the tomato and avocados in a food processor. Sprinkle with salt and ground black pepper. Pulse to mix and coarsely mash until smooth.
3. Unfold the wrappers on a clean work surface, then divide the mixture in the center of each wrapper. Roll the wrapper up and press to seal.
4. Transfer the rolls to the pan and spritz with cooking spray.
5. Put the air fryer basket on the baking pan and slide into Rack Position 2, select Air Fry, set temperature to 350ºF (180ºC) and set time to 5 minutes.
6. Flip the rolls halfway through the cooking time.
7. When cooked, the rolls should be golden brown.
8. Serve immediately.

79. Crispy Crab And Cream Cheese Wontons

Servings:6 To 8
Cooking Time: 10 Minutes
Ingredients:
- 24 wonton wrappers, thawed if frozen
- Cooking spray
- Filling:
- 5 ounces (142 g) lump crabmeat, drained and patted dry
- 4 ounces (113 g) cream cheese, at room temperature
- 2 scallions, sliced
- 1½ teaspoons toasted sesame oil
- 1 teaspoon Worcestershire sauce
- Kosher salt and ground black pepper, to taste

Directions:
1. Spritz the air fryer basket with cooking spray.
2. In a medium-size bowl, place all the ingredients for the filling and stir until well

mixed. Prepare a small bowl of water alongside.

3. On a clean work surface, lay the wonton wrappers. Scoop 1 teaspoon of the filling in the center of each wrapper. Wet the edges with a touch of water. Fold each wonton wrapper diagonally in half over the filling to form a triangle.
4. Arrange the wontons in the pan. Spritz the wontons with cooking spray.
5. Put the air fryer basket on the baking pan and slide into Rack Position 2, select Air Fry, set temperature to 350ºF (180ºC) and set time to 10 minutes.
6. Flip the wontons halfway through the cooking time.
7. When cooking is complete, the wontons will be crispy and golden brown.
8. Serve immediately.

80. Air Fryer Breakfast Frittata

Servings: 2
Cooking Time: 20 Minutes
Ingredients:
- ¼ pound breakfast sausage, fully cooked and crumbled
- 4 eggs, lightly beaten
- ½ cup Monterey Jack cheese, shredded
- 2 tablespoons red bell pepper, diced
- 1 green onion, chopped
- 1 pinch cayenne pepper

Directions:
1. Preheat the Air fryer to 365 ºF and grease a nonstick 6x2-inch cake pan.
2. Whisk together eggs with sausage, green onion, bell pepper, cheese and cayenne in a bowl.
3. Transfer the egg mixture in the prepared cake pan and place in the Air fryer.
4. Cook for about 20 minutes and serve warm.
- **Nutrition Info:** Calories: 464, Fat: 33.7g, Carbohydrates: 10.4g, Sugar: 7g, Protein: 30.4g, Sodium: 704mg

81. Avocado Oil Gluten Free Banana Bread Recipe

Servings:x
Cooking Time:x
Ingredients:
- 1/2 cup Granulated Sugar
- 1 cup Mashed Banana
- 1/2 cup Light Brown Sugar
- 1/3 cup Avocado Oil, (or canola oil)
- 2 cups All-Purpose Gluten Free Flour, (see notes)
- 3/4 teaspoon Xanthan Gum, (omit if your flour blend contains it)
- 1 teaspoon Baking Powder
- 1/2 teaspoon Baking Soda

- 1/2 teaspoon Fine Sea Salt
- 2 large Eggs, room temperature
- 2/3 cup Milk, (dairy free or regular milk), room temperature
- 1 teaspoon Pure Vanilla Extract

Directions:
1. Preheat oven to 350°F and spray a 9x9 inch square pan with non-stick spray and line with parchment paper.
2. In a large bowl, whisk together the flour, xanthan gum, baking powder, baking soda, salt, and granulated sugar.
3. In a separate bowl, whisk together the mashed banana, brown sugar, oil, eggs, milk, and vanilla extract. Pour the wet ingredients into the dry ingredients and stir to combine.
4. Pour the batter into the prepared pan and bake at 350°F for 25-30 minutes or until a toothpick or cake tester comes out clean or with a few moist crumbs attached. Cooking time will vary depending on your oven - mine took 29 minutes.
5. Cool the bread in the pan on a cooling rack. Cut into 16 pieces and serve slightly warm or room temperature.
6. To store, wrap tightly in foil or store slices in an air-tight container. It will stay fresh up to 3 days. This bread also freezes well. To freeze, slice into individual pieces and freeze in a freezer bag.

82. Chicken Breakfast Muffins

Servings: 12
Cooking Time: 15 Minutes
Ingredients:
- 10 eggs
- 1/3 cup green onions, chopped
- 1 cup chicken, cooked and chopped
- 1/4 tsp pepper
- 1 tsp sea salt

Directions:
1. Fit the oven with the rack in position
2. Spray 12-cups muffin tin with cooking spray and set aside.
3. In a large bowl, whisk eggs with pepper and salt.
4. Add remaining ingredients and stir well.
5. Pour egg mixture into the greased muffin tin.
6. Set to bake at 400 F for 20 minutes, after 5 minutes, place the muffin tin in the oven.
7. Serve and enjoy.
- **Nutrition Info:** Calories 71 Fat 4 g Carbohydrates 0.5 g Sugar 0.3 g Protein 8 g Cholesterol 145 mg

83. Protein Packed Breakfast Casserole

Servings: 8
Cooking Time: 40 Minutes
Ingredients:
- 12 eggs
- 2 cups cooked chicken, diced
- 1/2 cup cheddar cheese, shredded
- 1 tsp garlic powder
- 1 cup milk
- 1/4 cup onion, diced
- 1 green bell pepper, cubed
- 1 red bell pepper, cubed
- 2 medium potatoes, cubed
- 1/4 tsp pepper
- 1 tsp salt

Directions:
1. Fit the oven with the rack in position
2. Spray 9*13-inch baking pan with cooking spray and set aside.
3. Add bell peppers, potatoes, and cooked chicken into the prepared baking pan and spread evenly.
4. In a large bowl, whisk eggs with milk, garlic powder, pepper, and salt.
5. Pour egg mixture over vegetables and sprinkle with cheese and onion.
6. Set to bake at 350 F for 45 minutes. After 5 minutes place the baking pan in the preheated oven.
7. Serve and enjoy.
- **Nutrition Info:** Calories 240 Fat 10.7 g Carbohydrates 13.4 g Sugar 4.3 g Protein 22.5 g Cholesterol 282 mg

84. Thyme Cheddar Hash Browns

Servings:4
Cooking Time: 35 Minutes
Ingredients:
- 4 russet potatoes, peeled and grated
- 1 brown onion, chopped
- 3 garlic cloves, minced
- ½ cup cheddar cheese, grated
- 1 egg, lightly beaten
- Salt and black pepper to taste
- 1 tbsp fresh thyme, chopped

Directions:
1. In a bowl, mix potatoes, onion, garlic, cheese, egg, salt, black pepper, and thyme. Press the hash brown mixture into a greased baking dish and cook in the oven for 20-25 minutes at 400 F on Bake function until golden and crispy.

85. Beans And Pork Mix

Servings: 4
Cooking Time: 20 Minutes
Ingredients:

- 1-pound pork stew meat, ground
- 1 red onion, chopped
- 1 tablespoon olive oil
- 1 cup canned kidney beans, drained and rinsed
- 1 teaspoon chili powder
- Salt and black pepper to the taste
- ¼ teaspoon cumin, ground

Directions:
1. Heat up your air fryer at 360 degrees F, add the meat and the onion and cook for 5 minutes.
2. Add the beans and the rest of the ingredients, toss and cook for 15 minutes more.
3. Divide everything into bowls and serve for breakfast.
- **Nutrition Info:** calories 203, fat 4, fiber 6, carbs 12, protein 4

86. Spinach, Leek And Cheese Frittata

Servings:2
Cooking Time: 22 Minutes
Ingredients:
- 4 large eggs
- 4 ounces (113 g) baby bella mushrooms, chopped
- 1 cup (1 ounce / 28-g) baby spinach, chopped
- ½ cup (2 ounces / 57-g) shredded Cheddar cheese
- $^1/_3$ cup (from 1 large) chopped leek, white part only
- ¼ cup halved grape tomatoes
- 1 tablespoon 2% milk
- ¼ teaspoon dried oregano
- ¼ teaspoon garlic powder
- ½ teaspoon kosher salt
- Freshly ground black pepper, to taste
- Cooking spray

Directions:
1. Lightly spritz the baking pan with cooking spray.
2. Whisk the eggs in a large bowl until frothy. Add the mushrooms, baby spinach, cheese, leek, tomatoes, milk, oregano, garlic powder, salt, and pepper and stir until well blended. Pour the mixture into the prepared baking pan.
3. Slide the baking pan into Rack Position 1, select Convection Bake, set temperature to 300ºF (150ºC) and set time to 22 minutes.
4. When cooked, the center will be puffed up and the top will be golden brown.
5. Let the frittata cool for 5 minutes before slicing to serve.

87. Almond & Berry Oat Bars

Servings:6
Cooking Time: 35 Minutes + Cooling Time
Ingredients:
- 3 cups rolled oats
- ½ cup ground almonds
- ½ cup flour
- 1 tsp baking powder
- 1 tsp ground cinnamon
- 3 eggs, lightly beaten
- ½ cup canola oil
- ⅓ cup milk
- 2 tsp vanilla extract
- 2 cups mixed berries

Directions:
1. Spray a baking pan with cooking spray. In a bowl, add oats, almonds, flour, baking powder, and cinnamon in a bowl and stir well. In another bowl, whisk eggs, oil, milk, and vanilla.
2. Stir wet ingredients into oat mixture. Fold in the berries. Pour the mixture in the pan and place in the . Cook for 25 minutes at 330 F on Bake function. Let cool before slicing into bars.

88. Caprese Sandwich With Sourdough Bread

Servings: 2
Cooking Time: 15 Minutes
Ingredients:
- 4 slices sourdough bread
- 2 tbsp mayonnaise
- 2 slices ham
- 2 lettuce leaves
- 1 tomato, sliced
- 2 slices mozzarella cheese
- Salt and black pepper to taste

Directions:
1. On a clean board, lay the sourdough slices and spread with mayonnaise. Top 2 of the slices with ham, lettuce, tomato, and mozzarella cheese. Season with salt and pepper.
2. Top with the remaining two slices to form two sandwiches. Spray with oil and transfer to the Air Fryer basket. Fit in the baking tray and cook for 10 minutes at 350 F on Bake function, flipping once halfway through cooking. Serve hot.

89. Creamy Quesadillas With Blueberries

Servings:2
Cooking Time: 4 Minutes
Ingredients:
- ¼ cup nonfat Ricotta cheese
- ¼ cup plain nonfat Greek yogurt
- 2 tablespoons finely ground flaxseeds
- 1 tablespoon granulated stevia
- ½ teaspoon cinnamon
- ¼ teaspoon vanilla extract
- 2 (8-inch) low-carb whole-wheat tortillas
- ½ cup fresh blueberries, divided

Directions:
1. Line the baking pan with aluminum foil.
2. In a small bowl, whisk together the Ricotta cheese, yogurt, flaxseeds, stevia, cinnamon and vanilla.
3. Place the tortillas on the prepared pan. Spread half of the yogurt mixture on each tortilla, almost to the edges. Top each tortilla with ¼ cup of blueberries. Fold the tortillas in half.
4. Slide the baking pan into Rack Position 1, select Convection Bake, set temperature to 400ºF (205ºC) and set time to 4 minutes.
5. When cooking is complete, remove the pan from the oven. Serve immediately.

90. Smart Oven Baked Oatmeal Recipe

Servings:x
Cooking Time:x
Ingredients:
- 1 small Ripe Banana, (6 inches long, abut 1/4 cup mashed)
- 1 tablespoon Flax Meal
- 1/2 cup Non-Dairy Milk, plus 2 tablespoons (like Almond Milk or Soy Milk)
- 1 cup Old Fashioned Rolled Oats
- 2 teaspoons Pure Maple Syrup
- 2 teaspoons Olive Oil
- 1/2 teaspoon Ground Cinnamon
- 1/2 teaspoon Pure Vanilla Extract
- 1/4 teaspoon Baking Powder
- 1/8 teaspoon Fine Sea Salt
- 1/4 cup Pecan Pieces, (1 ounce)

Directions:
1. Adjust the cooking rack to the bottom position and preheat toaster oven to 350°F on the BAKE setting. Grease a 7 x 5-inch toaster oven-safe baking dish.
2. In a large bowl, add the banana and mash well. Stir in the flaxseed meal, maple syrup, olive oil, cinnamon, vanilla, baking powder, salt, milk, oats, and pecan pieces. Pour mixture into prepared baking dish.
3. Bake oatmeal until the middle is set and browned on the edges, about 25 to 35 minutes. (For softer scoop able oatmeal bake 25 to 30 minutes, for firm oatmeal bake 30 to 35 minutes.)
4. Let sit at least 10 minutes before slicing and serving.

91. Egg Florentine With Spinach

Servings:4
Cooking Time: 15 Minutes
Ingredients:
- 3 cups frozen spinach, thawed and drained
- 2 tablespoons heavy cream
- ¼ teaspoon kosher salt
- ⅛ teaspoon freshly ground black pepper
- 4 ounces (113 g) Ricotta cheese
- 2 garlic cloves, minced
- ½ cup panko bread crumbs
- 3 tablespoons grated Parmesan cheese
- 2 teaspoons unsalted butter, melted
- 4 large eggs

Directions:
1. In a medium bowl, whisk together the spinach, heavy cream, salt, pepper, Ricotta cheese and garlic.
2. In a small bowl, whisk together the bread crumbs, Parmesan cheese and butter. Set aside.
3. Spoon the spinach mixture into the baking pan and form four even circles.
4. Slide the baking pan into Rack Position 2, select Roast, set temperature to 375ºF (190ºC) and set time to 15 minutes.
5. After 8 minutes, remove the pan. The spinach should be bubbling. With the back of a large spoon, make indentations in the spinach for the eggs. Crack the eggs into the indentations and sprinkle the panko mixture over the surface of the eggs.
6. Return the pan to the oven and continue cooking.
7. When cooking is complete, remove the pan from the oven. Serve hot.

92. Peppered Maple Bacon Knots

Servings:6
Cooking Time: 7 To 8 Minutes
Ingredients:
- 1 pound (454 g) maple smoked center-cut bacon
- ¼ cup maple syrup
- ¼ cup brown sugar
- Coarsely cracked black peppercorns, to taste

Directions:
1. On a clean work surface, tie each bacon strip in a loose knot.
2. Stir together the maple syrup and brown sugar in a bowl. Generously brush this mixture over the bacon knots.
3. Place the bacon knots in the air fryer basket and sprinkle with the coarsely cracked black peppercorns.
4. Put the air fryer basket on the baking pan and slide into Rack Position 2, select Air Fry, set temperature to 390ºF (199ºC), and set time to 8 minutes.
5. After 5 minutes, remove the pan from the oven and flip the bacon knots. Return to the oven and continue cooking for 2 to 3 minutes more.
6. When cooking is complete, the bacon should be crisp. Remove from the oven to a paper towel-lined plate. Let the bacon knots cool for a few minutes and serve warm.

93. Blackberries Bowls

Servings: 4
Cooking Time: 30 Minutes
Ingredients:
- 1 ½ cups coconut milk
- ½ cup coconut; shredded
- ½ cup blackberries
- 2 tsp. stevia

Directions:
1. In your air fryer's pan, mix all the ingredients, stir, cover and cook at 360°F for 15 minutes.
2. Divide into bowls and serve
- **Nutrition Info:** Calories: 171; Fat: 4g; Fiber: 2g; Carbs: 3g; Protein: 5g

94. Crispy Ham Egg Cups

Servings: 2
Cooking Time: 30 Minutes
Ingredients:
- 4 large eggs.
- 4: 1-oz. slices deli ham
- ½ cup shredded medium Cheddar cheese.
- ¼ cup diced green bell pepper.
- 2 tbsp. diced red bell pepper.
- 2 tbsp. diced white onion.
- 2 tbsp. full-fat sour cream.

Directions:
1. Place one slice of ham on the bottom of four baking cups.
2. Take a large bowl, whisk eggs with sour cream. Stir in green pepper, red pepper and onion
3. Pour the egg mixture into ham-lined baking cups. Top with Cheddar. Place cups into the air fryer basket. Adjust the temperature to 320 Degrees F and set the timer for 12 minutes or until the tops are browned. Serve warm.
- **Nutrition Info:** Calories: 382; Protein: 29.4g; Fiber: 1.4g; Fat: 23.6g; Carbs: 6.0g

95. Cheddar Eggs With Potatoes

Servings:3
Cooking Time: 24 Minutes
Ingredients:
- 3 potatoes, thinly sliced
- 2 eggs, beaten

- 2 oz cheddar cheese, shredded
- 1 tbsp all-purpose flour
- ½ cup coconut cream

Directions:
1. Preheat on AirFry function to 390 F. Place the potatoes the basket and press Start. Cook for 12 minutes. Mix the eggs, coconut cream, and flour until the cream mixture thickens.
2. Remove the potatoes from the oven, line them in the ramekin and top with the cream mixture. Top with the cheddar cheese. Cook for 12 more minutes.

96. Crustless Broccoli Quiche

Servings:4
Cooking Time: 10 Minutes
Ingredients:
- 1 cup broccoli florets
- ¾ cup chopped roasted red peppers
- 1¼ cups grated Fontina cheese
- 6 eggs
- ¾ cup heavy cream
- ½ teaspoon salt
- Freshly ground black pepper, to taste
- Cooking spray

Directions:
1. Spritz the baking pan with cooking spray
2. Add the broccoli florets and roasted red peppers to the pan and scatter the grated Fontina cheese on top.
3. In a bowl, beat together the eggs and heavy cream. Sprinkle with salt and pepper. Pour the egg mixture over the top of the cheese. Wrap the pan in foil.
4. Put the air fryer basket on the baking pan and slide into Rack Position 2, select Air Fry, set temperature to 325ºF (163ºC) and set time to 10 minutes.
5. After 8 minutes, remove the pan from the oven. Remove the foil. Return to the oven and continue to cook for another 2 minutes.
6. When cooked, the quiche should be golden brown.
7. Rest for 5 minutes before cutting into wedges and serve warm.

97. Ultimate Breakfast Burrito

Servings: 8
Cooking Time:: 20 Minute
Ingredients:
- 16 ounces cooked bacon ends and pieces
- 16 eggs
- 1 tablespoon butter
- 8 hash brown squares
- 8 large soft flour tortillas
- 2 diced jalapeños
- 2 cups shredded sharp cheddar

Directions:

1. Place bacon on a baking sheet in toaster oven. Bake at 450°F until it reaches desired level of crispiness and set aside.
2. Whisk together eggs in a bowl and set aside.
3. Melt butter into a sauce pan and mix in eggs until they are starting to cook but not fully hardened.
4. While eggs are cooking, microwave and cool hash brown squares.
5. Roll out tortillas and top them with hash browns, bacon, jalapeños, and cheese.
6. Wrap up the burritos and place them seam-down on a baking sheet.
7. Bake at 375°F for 15–20 minutes.
- **Nutrition Info:** Calories: 698, Sodium: 1821 mg, Dietary Fiber: 3.4 g, Total Fat: 43.7 g, Total Carbs: 32.9 g, Protein: 42.1 g.

98. Vanilla Raspberry Pancakes With Maple Syrup

Servings:4
Cooking Time: 15 Minutes
Ingredients:
- 2 cups all-purpose flour
- 1 cup milk
- 3 eggs, beaten
- 1 tsp baking powder
- 1 cup brown sugar
- 1 ½ tsp vanilla extract
- ½ cup frozen raspberries, thawed
- 2 tbsp maple syrup
- A pinch of salt

Directions:
1. Preheat on Bake function to 390 F. In a bowl, mix flour, baking powder, salt, milk, eggs, vanilla extract, sugar, and maple syrup until smooth. Stir in the raspberries.
2. Drop the batter onto a greased baking dish. Just make sure to leave some space between the pancakes. Press Start and cook for 10 minutes. Serve.

99. Cheesy Eggs With Fried Potatoes

Servings: 4
Cooking Time: 30 Minutes
Ingredients:
- 2 lb potatoes, thinly sliced
- 1 tbsp olive oil
- 2 eggs, beaten
- 2 oz cheddar cheese, grated
- 1 tbsp all-purpose flour
- ½ cup coconut cream
- Salt and black pepper to taste

Directions:
1. Season the potatoes with salt and pepper and place them in the Air Fryer basket; drizzle with olive oil. Fit in the baking tray

and cook for 12 minutes at 350 F on Air Fry function.

2. Mix the eggs, coconut cream, and flour in a bowl until the cream mixture thickens. Remove the potatoes from the fryer oven, line them in a baking pan and top with the cream mixture. Sprinkle with cheddar cheese. Cook for 12 more minutes. Serve warm.

100. Cheesy Spring Chicken Wraps

Servings:12
Cooking Time: 5 Minutes
Ingredients:
- 2 large-sized chicken breasts, cooked and shredded
- 2 spring onions, chopped
- 10 ounces (284 g) Ricotta cheese
- 1 tablespoon rice vinegar
- 1 tablespoon molasses
- 1 teaspoon grated fresh ginger
- ¼ cup soy sauce
- $1/3$ teaspoon sea salt
- ¼ teaspoon ground black pepper, or more to taste
- 48 wonton wrappers
- Cooking spray

Directions:
1. Spritz the air fryer basket with cooking spray.
2. Combine all the ingredients, except for the wrappers in a large bowl. Toss to mix well.
3. Unfold the wrappers on a clean work surface, then divide and spoon the mixture in the middle of the wrappers.
4. Dab a little water on the edges of the wrappers, then fold the edge close to you over the filling. Tuck the edge under the filling and roll up to seal.
5. Arrange the wraps in the pan.
6. Put the air fryer basket on the baking pan and slide into Rack Position 2, select Air Fry, set temperature to 375ºF (190ºC) and set time to 5 minutes.
7. Flip the wraps halfway through the cooking time.
8. When cooking is complete, the wraps should be lightly browned.
9. Serve immediately.

101. Easy Grilled Pork Chops With Sweet & Tangy Mustard Glaze

Servings: 4
Cooking Time: 45 Minutes
Ingredients:
- For the glace 1 ½ tsp cider
- 1 tsp Dijon mustard
- 2 tsp brown sugar
- for the brine

- 3 cups light brown
- 2 bay leaves
- 2 tsp of salt
- 2 cloves smashed
- 1 ½ cups of ice cubes
- 4 boneless pork chops

Directions:
1. Make the glaze by placing all the ingredients in a small bowl and set them aside.
2. Brine your pork by placing it inside water with bay leaves, brown sugar, and garlic and heat it on medium heat. Cover and bring the mixture to boil. Uncover and stir it until the sugar is completely dissolved in the mixture. Add ice cubes to cool into it is slightly warm to the touch.
3. Once it is cooled submerge the pork chops and set aside for 15 minutes. Prepare your grill. Put the instant vortex fryer on GRILL mode and wait for it to attain the desired temperature. once it has attained 400 degree Celsius then it is time to add your pork chops. Usually the appliance will be indicated 'add food'.
4. Remove the pork chops from the salt mixture and pat them with paper towels. Place them on the grill and cover. Do not remove until they are well cooked. Once the instant fryer indicates TURN FOOD. flip your food and glaze it twice before allowing it to cook some more.
5. Transfer the pork to a clean cutting board once the appliance has indicated end. Serve while hot.
- **Nutrition Info:** Calories 355.9 Fat 20.7g, Carbs 21.2g, Fiber 0.3%, Protein 21.2g, Sodium:1086.5mg

102. Cherry Cinnamon Almond Breakfast Scones

Servings:x
Cooking Time:x
Ingredients:
- 2 cups all-purpose flour
- ½ cup chopped almonds
- ¾ cup milk
- ½ tsp cinnamon
- 2 tsp baking powder
- 3 Tbsp brown sugar
- Pinch of salt
- ½ cup cold butter
- 1½ cups dried cherries
- Zest of one lemon
- 2 Tbsp turbinado sugar

Directions:
1. Preheat oven to 375°F.
2. Combine flour, baking powder, brown sugar and salt.

3. Add cold butter, cut into small pieces, and pinch until dough becomes crumbly.
4. Add dried cherries, zest and chopped almonds to combine.
5. Add the milk and mix dough gently. Do not overwork.
6. Grease oven and spread dough uniformly.
7. Combine cinnamon and turbinado sugar and sprinkle on top.
8. Bake for about 25 minutes or until scone is cooked through.

103. Prosciutto & Mozzarella Crostini

Servings: 1
Cooking Time: 7 Minutes
Ingredients:
- ½ cup finely chopped tomatoes
- 3 oz chopped mozzarella
- 3 prosciutto slices, chopped
- 1 tbsp olive oil
- 1 tsp dried basil
- 6 small slices of French bread

Directions:
1. Preheat on Toast function to 350 F. Place the bread slices in the toaster oven and toast for 5 minutes. Top the bread with tomatoes, prosciutto and mozzarella. Sprinkle the basil over the mozzarella. Drizzle with olive oil. Return to oven and cook for 1 more minute, enough to become melty and warm.

104. Salty Parsnip Patties

Servings: 2
Cooking Time: 20 Minutes
Ingredients:
- 1 large parsnip, grated
- 3 eggs, beaten
- ½ tsp garlic powder
- ¼ tsp nutmeg
- 1 tbsp olive oil
- 1 cup flour
- Salt and black pepper to taste

Directions:
1. In a bowl, combine flour, eggs, parsnip, nutmeg, and garlic powder. Season with salt and pepper. Form patties out of the mixture. Drizzle the AirFryer basket with olive oil and arrange the patties inside. Fit in the baking tray and cook for 15 minutes on Air Fry function at 360 F. Serve with garlic mayo.

105. Spinach & Kale Balsamic Chicken

Servings: 1
Cooking Time: 20 Minutes
Ingredients:
- ½ cup baby spinach leaves
- ½ cup shredded romaine
- 3 large kale leaves, chopped
- 4 oz chicken breasts, cut into cubes
- 3 tbsp olive oil, divided
- 1 tsp balsamic vinegar
- 1 garlic clove, minced
- Salt and black pepper to taste

Directions:
1. Place the chicken, 1 tbsp of olive oil, and garlic in a bowl. Season with salt and pepper and toss to combine. Put on a lined Air Fryer pan and cook for 14 minutes at 390 F on Bake function.
2. Place the greens in a large bowl. Add the remaining olive oil and balsamic vinegar. Season with salt and pepper and toss to combine. Top with the chicken and serve.

106. Vanilla & Cinnamon Toast Toppet

Servings: 6
Cooking Time: 10 Minutes
Ingredients:
- 12 slices bread
- ½ cup sugar
- 1 ½ tsp cinnamon
- 1 stick of butter, softened
- 1 tsp vanilla extract

Directions:
1. Preheat on Toast function to 360 F. Combine all ingredients, except the bread, in a bowl. Spread the buttery cinnamon mixture onto the bread slices. Place the bread slices in the toaster oven. Cook for 8 minutes. Serve.

107. Olive & Tomato Tart With Feta Cheese

Servings: 2
Cooking Time: 25 Minutes
Ingredients:
- 4 eggs
- ½ cup tomatoes, chopped
- 1 cup feta cheese, crumbled
- 1 tbsp fresh basil, chopped
- 1 tbsp fresh oregano, chopped
- ¼ cup Kalamata olives, chopped
- ¼ cup onion, chopped
- 2 tbsp olive oil
- ½ cup milk
- Salt and black pepper to taste

Directions:
1. Preheat on Bake function to 360 F. Brush a pie pan with olive oil. Beat the eggs along with the milk, salt, and pepper. Stir in all of

the remaining ingredients. Pour the egg mixture into the pan. Cook for 20 minutes.

108.   Breakfast Tater Tot Casserole

Servings:4
Cooking Time: 17 To 18 Minutes
Ingredients:
- 4 eggs
- 1 cup milk
- Salt and pepper, to taste
- 12 ounces (340 g) ground chicken sausage
- 1 pound (454 g) frozen tater tots, thawed
- ¾ cup grated Cheddar cheese
- Cooking spray

Directions:
1. Whisk together the eggs and milk in a medium bowl. Season with salt and pepper to taste and stir until mixed. Set aside.
2. Place a skillet over medium-high heat and spritz with cooking spray. Place the ground sausage in the skillet and break it into smaller pieces with a spatula or spoon. Cook for 3 to 4 minutes until the sausage starts to brown, stirring occasionally. Remove from heat and set aside.
3. Coat the baking pan with cooking spray. Arrange the tater tots in the baking pan.
4. Slide the baking pan into Rack Position 1, select Convection Bake, set temperature to 400ºF (205ºC) and set time to 14 minutes.
5. After 6 minutes, remove the pan from the oven. Stir the tater tots and add the egg mixture and cooked sausage. Return the pan to the oven and continue cooking.
6. After 6 minutes, remove the pan from the oven. Scatter the cheese on top of the tater tots. Return the pan to the oven and continue to cook for another 2 minutes.
7. When done, the cheese should be bubbly and melted.
8. Let the mixture cool for 5 minutes and serve warm.

109.   Turkey Breakfast Sausage Patties

Servings:4
Cooking Time: 10 Minutes
Ingredients:
- 1 tablespoon chopped fresh thyme
- 1 tablespoon chopped fresh sage
- 1¼ teaspoons kosher salt
- 1 teaspoon chopped fennel seeds
- ¾ teaspoon smoked paprika
- ½ teaspoon onion powder
- ½ teaspoon garlic powder
- ⅛ teaspoon crushed red pepper flakes
- ⅛ teaspoon freshly ground black pepper
- 1 pound (454 g) 93% lean ground turkey

- ½ cup finely minced sweet apple (peeled)

Directions:
1. Thoroughly combine the thyme, sage, salt, fennel seeds, paprika, onion powder, garlic powder, red pepper flakes, and black pepper in a medium bowl.
2. Add the ground turkey and apple and stir until well incorporated. Divide the mixture into 8 equal portions and shape into patties with your hands, each about ¼ inch thick and 3 inches in diameter.
3. Place the patties in the air fryer basket in a single layer.
4. Put the air fryer basket on the baking pan and slide into Rack Position 2, select Air Fry, set temperature to 400ºF (205ºC), and set time to 10 minutes.
5. Flip the patties halfway through the cooking time.
6. When cooking is complete, the patties should be nicely browned and cooked through. Remove from the oven to a plate and serve warm.

110.   Bourbon Vanilla French Toast

Servings:4
Cooking Time: 6 Minutes
Ingredients:
- 2 large eggs
- 2 tablespoons water
- ⅔ cup whole or 2% milk
- 1 tablespoon butter, melted
- 2 tablespoons bourbon
- 1 teaspoon vanilla extract
- 8 (1-inch-thick) French bread slices
- Cooking spray

Directions:
1. Spray the baking pan with cooking spray.
2. Beat the eggs with the water in a shallow bowl until combined. Add the milk, melted butter, bourbon, and vanilla and stir to mix well.
3. Dredge 4 slices of bread in the batter, turning to coat both sides evenly. Transfer the bread slices to the baking pan.
4. Slide the baking pan into Rack Position 1, select Convection Bake, set temperature to 320ºF (160ºC) and set time to 6 minutes.
5. Flip the slices halfway through the cooking time.
6. When cooking is complete, the bread slices should be nicely browned.
7. Remove from the oven to a plate and serve warm.

111.   Zucchini Squash Pita Sandwiches Recipe

Servings:x
Cooking Time:x
Ingredients:
- 1 small Zucchini Squash, (5-6 ounces)

- Salt and Pepper, to taste
- 2 Whole Wheat Pitas
- 1/2 cup Hummus
- 1 1/2 cups Fresh Spinach, (2 handfuls)
- 1/2 cup Diced Red Bell Pepper, (about half a large pepper)
- 1/2 cup Chopped Red Onion, (about 1/4 a large onion)
- 2 teaspoons Olive Oil
- 1/4 teaspoon Dried Oregano
- 1/4 teaspoon Dried Thyme
- 1/4 teaspoon Garlic Powder
- 2 tablespoons Crumbled Feta Cheese, (about 1 ounce)

Directions:
1. Adjust the cooking rack to the lowest placement and preheat toaster oven to 425°F on the BAKE setting.
2. While the oven preheats, quarter the zucchini lengthwise and then cut into 1/2-inch thick pieces. Cut the bell pepper and onion into 1-inch thick pieces.
3. Add the vegetables to a roasting pan. Drizzle with oil and sprinkle over the oregano, garlic powder, and salt and pepper, to taste. Toss to combine.
4. Roast vegetables for 10 minutes. Carefully remove the pan and stir. Return pan to oven and continue cooking until the vegetables have softened and started to brown, about 5 minutes more. Remove from the toaster oven and set aside.
5. Reduce the temperature to 375°F and warm the pitas by placing them directly on the cooking rack for 1 to 2 minutes.
6. Spread warm pitas with hummus. Layer with spinach, roasted vegetables, and crumbled feta.

112. Thai Pork Sliders

Servings: 6 Sliders
Cooking Time: 14 Minutes
Ingredients:
- 1 pound (454 g) ground pork
- 1 tablespoon Thai curry paste
- 1½ tablespoons fish sauce
- ¼ cup thinly sliced scallions, white and green parts
- 2 tablespoons minced peeled fresh ginger
- 1 tablespoon light brown sugar
- 1 teaspoon ground black pepper
- 6 slider buns, split open lengthwise, warmed
- Cooking spray

Directions:
1. Spritz the air fryer basket with cooking spray.
2. Combine all the ingredients, except for the buns in a large bowl. Stir to mix well.
3. Divide and shape the mixture into six balls, then bash the balls into six 3-inch-diameter patties.

4. Arrange the patties in the basket and spritz with cooking spray.
5. Put the air fryer basket on the baking pan and slide into Rack Position 2, select Air Fry, set temperature to 375ºF (190ºC) and set time to 14 minutes.
6. Flip the patties halfway through the cooking time.
7. When cooked, the patties should be well browned.
8. Assemble the buns with patties to make the sliders and serve immediately.

113. Healthy Bran Muffins

Servings: 12
Cooking Time: 20 Minutes
Ingredients:
- 2 eggs
- 1 cup milk
- 1 1/2 cups wheat bran
- 1/4 cup molasses
- 1/4 cup white sugar
- 1/4 cup brown sugar
- 1/4 cup shortening
- 1/2 cup raisins
- 1/4 tsp cinnamon
- 1/2 tsp baking soda
- 1 1/2 tsp baking powder
- 1 cup flour
- 1/2 tsp salt

Directions:
1. Fit the oven with the rack in position
2. Line a 12-cup muffin tray with cupcake liners and set aside.
3. In a bowl, mix flour, raisins, cinnamon, baking soda, baking powder, flour, and salt.
4. In a separate bowl, beat sugar and shortening using a hand mixer until fluffy.
5. Add eggs and molasses and beat until well combined. Add bran and milk and stir well.
6. Add flour mixture and mix until just combined.
7. Pour mixture into the prepared muffin tray.
8. Set to bake at 400 F for 25 minutes. After 5 minutes place the muffin tray in the preheated oven.
9. Serve and enjoy.
- **Nutrition Info:** Calories 178 Fat 5.9 g Carbohydrates 31 g Sugar 15.5 g Protein 4 g Cholesterol 29 mg

114. Rice, Shrimp, And Spinach Frittata

Servings:4
Cooking Time: 16 Minutes
Ingredients:
- 4 eggs
- Pinch salt
- ½ cup cooked rice
- ½ cup chopped cooked shrimp
- ½ cup baby spinach
- ½ cup grated Monterey Jack cheese

- Nonstick cooking spray

Directions:
1. Spritz the baking pan with nonstick cooking spray.
2. Whisk the eggs and salt in a small bowl until frothy.
3. Place the cooked rice, shrimp, and baby spinach in the baking pan. Pour in the whisked eggs and scatter the cheese on top.
4. Slide the baking pan into Rack Position 1, select Convection Bake, set temperature to 320ºF (160ºC) and set time to 16 minutes.
5. When cooking is complete, the frittata should be golden and puffy.
6. Let the frittata cool for 5 minutes before slicing to serve.

115. White Chocolate & Vanilla Brownies With Walnuts

Servings:6
Cooking Time: 35 Minutes
Ingredients:
- 6 oz dark chocolate
- 6 oz butter
- ¾ cup white sugar
- 3 eggs
- 2 tsp vanilla extract
- ¾ cup flour
- ¼ cup cocoa powder
- 1 cup chopped walnuts
- 1 cup white chocolate chips

Directions:
1. Line a baking pan with parchment paper. In a saucepan, melt chocolate and butter over low heat. Do not stop stirring until you obtain a smooth mixture. Let cool slightly, whisk in eggs and vanilla. Sift flour and cocoa and stir to mix well.
2. Sprinkle the walnuts over and add the white chocolate into the batter. Pour the batter into the pan and cook for 20 minutes in the oven at 340 F on Bake function.

116. Sweet Breakfast Casserole

Servings: 4
Cooking Time: 30 Minutes
Ingredients:
- 3 tablespoons brown sugar
- 4 tablespoons margarine
- 2 tablespoons white sugar
- 1/2 tsp. cinnamon powder
- 1/2 cup flour
- For the casserole:
- 2 eggs
- 2 tablespoons white sugar
- 2 and 1/2 cups white flour
- 1 tsp. baking soda
- 1 tsp. baking powder
- 2 eggs
- 1/2 cup milk
- 2 cups margarine milk

- 4 tablespoons margarine
- Zest from 1 lemon, grated
- 1 and 2/3 cup blueberries

Directions:
1. In a bowl, mix eggs with 2 tablespoons white sugar, 2 and 1/2 cups white flour, baking powder, baking soda, 2 eggs, milk, margarine milk, 4 tablespoons margarine, lemon zest and blueberries, stir and pour into a pan that fits your air fryer.
2. In another bowls, mix 3 tablespoons brown sugar with 2 tablespoons white sugar, 4 tablespoons margarine, 1/2 cup flour and cinnamon, stir until you obtain a crumble and spread over blueberries mix.
3. Place in preheated air fryer and bake at 300 °F for 30 minutes.
4. Divide among plates and serve for breakfast.
- **Nutrition Info:** Calories 101 Fat 9.4 g Carbohydrates 0.3 g Sugar 0.2 g Protein 7 g Cholesterol 21 mg

117. Delicious Pumpkin Bread

Servings: 12
Cooking Time: 55 Minutes
Ingredients:
- 2 eggs
- 1/4 cup olive oil
- 1/2 cup milk
- 1 cup of sugar
- 1 cup pumpkin puree
- 1 tsp cinnamon
- 1/2 tsp baking soda
- 2 tsp baking powder
- 2 cups flour
- 1/2 tsp salt

Directions:
1. Fit the oven with the rack in position
2. In a bowl, mix flour, baking soda, salt, and baking powder.
3. In a separate bowl, whisk eggs with oil, milk, sugar, and pumpkin puree.
4. Add flour mixture into the egg mixture and mix until well combined.
5. Pour mixture into the greased loaf pan.
6. Set to bake at 350 F for 60 minutes. After 5 minutes place the loaf pan in the preheated oven.
7. Slice and serve.
- **Nutrition Info:** Calories 198 Fat 5.4 g Carbohydrates 35.3 g Sugar 17.9 g Protein 3.6 g Cholesterol 28 mg

118. Fruit Oatmeal With Coconut Flakes

Servings:x
Cooking Time:x
Ingredients:
- 2 cups old fashioned rolled oats
- 1 tsp vanilla extract
- 1 cup blueberries
- 1 cup raspberries

- 1 tsp baking powder
- 2 tsp brown sugar
- ½ tsp cinnamon
- ¼ cup unsweetened coconut flakes
- 2 cups low fat milk
- 2 egg whites

Directions:
1. Preheat oven to 350°F.
2. Combine oats, baking powder, brown sugar, cinnamon and coconut
3. flakes in a greased oven.
4. Add milk, egg whites and vanilla and stir well.
5. Add fruits and combine gently so as not to break up fruit.
6. Cook for 30-35 minutes until set and golden brown.

119. Wheat &seed Bread

Servings: 4
Cooking Time: 18 Minutes
Ingredients:
- 31/2 ounces of flour
- 1 tsp. of yeast
- 1 tsp. of salt
- 3 &1/2 ounces of wheat flour ¼ cup of pumpkin seeds

Directions:
1. Mix the wheat flour, yeast, salt, seeds and the plain flour together in a large bowl. Stir in ¾ cup of lukewarm water and keep stirring until dough becomes soft.
2. Knead for another 5 minutes until the dough becomes elastic and smooth. Mold into a ball and cover with a plastic bag. Set aside for 30 minutes for it to rise.
3. Heat your air fryer to 392°F.
4. Transfer the dough into a small pizza pan and place in the air fryer. Bake for 18 minutes until golden. Remove and place on a wire rack to cool.
- **Nutrition Info:** Calories 116 Fat 9.4 g Carbohydrates 0.3 g Sugar 0.2 g Protein 6 g Cholesterol 21 mg

120. Eggs In Bell Pepper Rings

Servings:4
Cooking Time: 7 Minutes
Ingredients:
- 1 large red, yellow, or orange bell pepper, cut into four ¾-inch rings
- 4 eggs
- Salt and freshly ground black pepper, to taste
- 2 teaspoons salsa
- Cooking spray

Directions:
1. Coat the baking pan lightly with cooking spray.
2. Put 4 bell pepper rings in the prepared baking pan. Crack one egg into each bell pepper ring and sprinkle with salt and

pepper. Top each egg with ½ teaspoon of salsa.
3. Put the air fryer basket on the baking pan and slide into Rack Position 2, select Air Fry, set temperature to 350ºF (180ºC) and set time to 7 minutes.
4. When done, the eggs should be cooked to your desired doneness.
5. Remove the rings from the pan to a plate and serve warm.

121. Italian Sausage & Egg Taquitos

Servings: 4
Cooking Time: 15 Minutes
Ingredients:
- 3 eggs, scrambled
- 6 oz. hot Italian sausage, cooked & crumbled
- ¼ cup sun dried tomatoes, drain & slice thin
- 1 avocado, halved, pitted, peeled & chopped
- 1 cup sharp cheddar cheese, grated
- 12 corn tortillas, softened

Directions:
1. Line the baking pan with parchment paper.
2. In a large bowl, place all ingredients and toss to mix.
3. One at a time, place a tortilla on a cutting board and add some of the filling mixture. Start at one side and roll tortilla over filling. Place seam side down on prepared pan. Repeat with remaining tortillas and filling.
4. Set to air fry at 425°F for 20 minutes. After 5 minutes, place the pan in position 2 of the oven and cook until taquitos are crisp and the cheese has melted. Serve immediately.
- **Nutrition Info:** Calories 682, Total Fat 36g, Saturated Fat 13g, Total Carbs 39g, Net Carbs 31g, Protein 23g, Sugar 2g, Fiber 8g, Sodium 590mg, Potassium 674mg, Phosphorus 532mg

122. Smoked Sausage Breakfast Mix

Servings: 4
Cooking Time: 30 Minutes
Ingredients:
- 1 and 1/2 pounds smoked sausage, diced and browned
- A pinch of salt and black pepper
- 1 and 1/2 cups grits
- 4 and 1/2 cups water
- 16 ounces cheddar cheese, shredded
- 1 cup milk
- ¼ tsp. garlic powder
- 1 and 1/2 tsp.s thyme, diced
- Cooking spray
- 4 eggs, whisked

Directions:
1. Put the water in a pot, bring to a boil over medium heat, add grits, stir, cover, cook for 5 minutes and take off heat.

2. Add cheese, stir until it melts and mix with milk, thyme, salt, pepper, garlic powder and eggs and whisk really well.
3. Heat up your air fryer at 300 °F, grease with cooking spray and add browned sausage.
4. Add grits mix, spread and cook for 25 minutes.
5. Divide among plates and serve for breakfast.
- **Nutrition Info:** Calories 113 Fat 8.2 g Carbohydrates 0.3 g Protein 5.4 g

123.   Mediterranean Spinach Frittata

Servings: 6
Cooking Time: 20 Minutes
Ingredients:
- 6 eggs
- 1/2 cup frozen spinach, drained the excess liquid
- 1/4 cup feta cheese, crumbled
- 1/4 cup olives, chopped
- 1/4 cup kalamata olives, chopped
- 1/2 cup tomatoes, diced
- 1/2 tsp garlic powder
- 1 tsp oregano
- 1/4 cup milk
- 1/2 tsp pepper
- 1/4 tsp salt

Directions:
1. Fit the oven with the rack in position
2. Spray 9-inch pie pan with cooking spray and set aside.
3. In a bowl, whisk eggs with oregano, garlic powder, milk, pepper, and salt until well combined.
4. Add olives, feta cheese, tomatoes, and spinach and mix well.
5. Pour egg mixture into the prepared pie pan.
6. Set to bake at 400 F for 25 minutes. After 5 minutes place the pie pan in the preheated oven.
7. Serve and enjoy.
- **Nutrition Info:** Calories 103 Fat 7.2 g Carbohydrates 2.9 g Sugar 1.5 g Protein 7.2 g Cholesterol 170 mg

124.   Crispy Chicken Egg Rolls

Servings:4
Cooking Time: 23 To 24 Minutes
Ingredients:
- 1 pound (454 g) ground chicken
- 2 teaspoons olive oil
- 2 garlic cloves, minced
- 1 teaspoon grated fresh ginger
- 2 cups white cabbage, shredded
- 1 onion, chopped
- ¼ cup soy sauce
- 8 egg roll wrappers
- 1 egg, beaten
- Cooking spray

Directions:
1. Spritz the air fryer basket with cooking spray.
2. Heat olive oil in a saucepan over medium heat. Sauté the garlic and ginger in the olive oil for 1 minute, or until fragrant. Add the ground chicken to the saucepan. Sauté for 5 minutes, or until the chicken is cooked through. Add the cabbage, onion and soy sauce and sauté for 5 to 6 minutes, or until the vegetables become soft. Remove the saucepan from the heat.
3. Unfold the egg roll wrappers on a clean work surface. Divide the chicken mixture among the wrappers and brush the edges of the wrappers with the beaten egg. Tightly roll up the egg rolls, enclosing the filling. Arrange the rolls in the pan.
4. Put the air fryer basket on the baking pan and slide into Rack Position 2, select Air Fry, set temperature to 370ºF (188ºC) and set time to 12 minutes.
5. Flip the rolls halfway through the cooking time.
6. When cooked, the rolls will be crispy and golden brown.
7. Transfer to a platter and let cool for 5 minutes before serving.

LUNCH RECIPES

125. Kalamta Mozarella Pita Melts

Servings: 2
Cooking Time: 5 Minutes
Ingredients:
- 2 (6-inch) whole wheat pitas
- 1 teaspoon extra-virgin olive oil
- 1 cup grated part-skim mozzarella cheese
- 1/4 small red onion
- 1/4 cup pitted Kalamata olives
- 2 tablespoons chopped fresh herbs such as parsley, basil, or oregano

Directions:
1. Start by preheating toaster oven to 425°F.
2. Brush the pita on both sides with oil and warm in the oven for one minute.
3. Dice onions and halve olives.
4. Sprinkle mozzarella over each pita and top with onion and olive.
5. Return to the oven for another 5 minutes or until the cheese is melted.
6. Sprinkle herbs over the pita and serve.
- **Nutrition Info:** Calories: 387, Sodium: 828 mg, Dietary Fiber: 7.4 g, Total Fat: 16.2 g, Total Carbs: 42.0 g, Protein: 23.0 g.

126. Okra And Green Beans Stew

Servings: 4
Cooking Time: 12 Minutes
Ingredients:
- 1 lb. green beans; halved
- 4 garlic cloves; minced
- 1 cup okra
- 3 tbsp. tomato sauce
- 1 tbsp. thyme; chopped.
- Salt and black pepper to taste.

Directions:
1. In a pan that fits your air fryer, mix all the ingredients, toss, introduce the pan in the air fryer and cook at 370°F for 15 minutes
2. Divide the stew into bowls and serve.
- **Nutrition Info:** Calories: 183; Fat: 5g; Fiber: 2g; Carbs: 4g; Protein: 8g

127. Cheddar & Cream Omelet

Servings: 2
Cooking Time: 8 Minutes
Ingredients:
- 4 eggs
- ¼ cup cream
- Salt and ground black pepper, as required
- ¼ cup Cheddar cheese, grated

Directions:
1. In a bowl, add the eggs, cream, salt, and black pepper and beat well.
2. Place the egg mixture into a small baking pan.
3. Press "Power Button" of Air Fry Oven and turn the dial to select the "Air Fry" mode.
4. Press the Time button and again turn the dial to set the cooking time to 8 minutes.
5. Now push the Temp button and rotate the dial to set the temperature at 350 degrees F.
6. Press "Start/Pause" button to start.
7. When the unit beeps to show that it is preheated, open the lid.
8. Arrange pan over the "Wire Rack" and insert in the oven.
9. After 4 minutes, sprinkle the omelet with cheese evenly.
10. Cut the omelet into 2 portions and serve hot.
11. Cut into equal-sized wedges and serve hot.
- **Nutrition Info:** Calories: 202 Cal Total Fat: 15.1 g Saturated Fat: 6.8 g Cholesterol: 348 mg Sodium: 298 mg Total Carbs: 1.8 g Fiber: 0 g Sugar: 1.4 g Protein: 14.8 g

128. Vegetarian Philly Sandwich

Servings: 2
Cooking Time: 20 Minutes
Ingredients:
- 2 tablespoons olive oil
- 8 ounces sliced portabello mushrooms
- 1 vidalia onion, thinly sliced
- 1 green bell pepper, thinly sliced
- 1 red bell pepper, thinly sliced
- Salt and pepper
- 4 slices 2% provolone cheese
- 4 rolls

Directions:
1. Preheat toaster oven to 475°F.
2. Heat the oil in a medium sauce pan over medium heat.
3. Sauté mushrooms about 5 minutes, then add the onions and peppers and sauté another 10 minutes.
4. Slice rolls lengthwise and divide the vegetables into each roll.
5. Add the cheese and toast until the rolls start to brown and the cheese melts.
- **Nutrition Info:** Calories: 645, Sodium: 916 mg, Dietary Fiber: 7.2 g, Total Fat: 33.3 g, Total Carbs: 61.8 g, Protein: 27.1 g.

129. Persimmon Toast With Sour Cream & Cinnamon

Servings: 1
Cooking Time: 5 Minutes
Ingredients:
- 1 slice of wheat bread
- 1/2 persimmon
- Sour cream to taste
- Sugar to taste
- Cinnamon to taste

Directions:

1. Spread a thin layer of sour cream across the bread.
2. Slice the persimmon into 1/4 inch pieces and lay them across the bread.
3. Sprinkle cinnamon and sugar over persimmon.
4. Toast in toaster oven until bread and persimmon begin to brown.
- **Nutrition Info:** Calories: 89, Sodium: 133 mg, Dietary Fiber: 2.0 g, Total Fat: 1.1 g, Total Carbs: 16.5 g, Protein: 3.8 g.

130. Perfect Size French Fries

Servings: 1
Cooking Time: 30 Minutes
Ingredients:
- 1 medium potato
- 1 tablespoon olive oil
- Salt and pepper to taste

Directions:
1. Start by preheating your oven to 425°F.
2. Clean the potato and cut it into fries or wedges.
3. Place fries in a bowl of cold water to rinse.
4. Lay the fries on a thick sheet of paper towels and pat dry.
5. Toss in a bowl with oil, salt, and pepper.
6. Bake for 30 minutes.
- **Nutrition Info:** Calories: 284, Sodium: 13 mg, Dietary Fiber: 4.7 g, Total Fat: 14.2 g, Total Carbs: 37.3 g, Protein: 4.3 g.

131. Chicken Legs With Dilled Brussels Sprouts

Servings: 2
Cooking Time: 10 Minutes
Ingredients:
- 2 chicken legs
- 1/2 teaspoon paprika
- 1/2 teaspoon kosher salt
- 1/2 teaspoon black pepper
- 1/2 pound Brussels sprouts
- 1 teaspoon dill, fresh or dried

Directions:
1. Start by preheating your Air Fryer to 370 degrees F.
2. Now, season your chicken with paprika, salt, and pepper. Transfer the chicken legs to the cooking basket. Cook for 10 minutes.
3. Flip the chicken legs and cook an additional 10 minutes. Reserve.
4. Add the Brussels sprouts to the cooking basket; sprinkle with dill. Cook at 380 degrees F for 15 minutes, shaking the basket halfway through.
5. Serve with the reserved chicken legs.
- **Nutrition Info:** 365 Calories; 21g Fat; 3g Carbs; 36g Protein; 2g Sugars; 3g Fiber

132. Herbed Duck Legs

Servings: 2
Cooking Time: 30 Minutes
Ingredients:
- ½ tablespoon fresh thyme, chopped
- ½ tablespoon fresh parsley, chopped
- 2 duck legs
- 1 garlic clove, minced
- 1 teaspoon five spice powder
- Salt and black pepper, as required

Directions:
1. Preheat the Air fryer to 340 degree F and grease an Air fryer basket.
2. Mix the garlic, herbs, five spice powder, salt, and black pepper in a bowl.
3. Rub the duck legs with garlic mixture generously and arrange into the Air fryer basket.
4. Cook for about 25 minutes and set the Air fryer to 390 degree F.
5. Cook for 5 more minutes and dish out to serve hot.
- **Nutrition Info:** Calories: 138, Fat: 4.5g, Carbohydrates: 1g, Sugar: 0g, Protein: 25g, Sodium: 82mg

133. Skinny Black Bean Flautas

Servings: 10
Cooking Time: 25 Minutes
Ingredients:
- 2 (15-ounce) cans black beans
- 1 cup shredded cheddar
- 1 (4-ounce) can diced green chilies
- 2 teaspoons taco seasoning
- 10 (8-inch) whole wheat flour tortillas
- Olive oil

Directions:
1. Start by preheating toaster oven to 350°F.
2. Drain black beans and mash in a medium bowl with a fork.
3. Mix in cheese, chilies, and taco seasoning until all ingredients are thoroughly combined.
4. Evenly spread the mixture over each tortilla and wrap tightly.
5. Brush each side lightly with olive oil and place on a baking sheet.
6. Bake for 12 minutes, turn, and bake for another 13 minutes.
- **Nutrition Info:** Calories: 367, Sodium: 136 mg, Dietary Fiber: 14.4 g, Total Fat: 2.8 g, Total Carbs: 64.8 g, Protein: 22.6 g.

134. Spanish Chicken Bake

Servings: 4
Cooking Time: 25 Minutes
Ingredients:
- ½ onion, quartered

- ½ red onion, quartered
- ½ lb. potatoes, quartered
- 4 garlic cloves
- 4 tomatoes, quartered
- 1/8 cup chorizo
- ¼ teaspoon paprika powder
- 4 chicken thighs, boneless
- ¼ teaspoon dried oregano
- ½ green bell pepper, julienned
- Salt
- Black pepper

Directions:
1. Toss chicken, veggies, and all the Ingredients: in a baking tray.
2. Press "Power Button" of Air Fry Oven and turn the dial to select the "Bake" mode.
3. Press the Time button and again turn the dial to set the cooking time to 25 minutes.
4. Now push the Temp button and rotate the dial to set the temperature at 425 degrees F.
5. Once preheated, place the baking pan inside and close its lid.
6. Serve warm.
- **Nutrition Info:** Calories 301 Total Fat 8.9 g Saturated Fat 4.5 g Cholesterol 57 mg Sodium 340 mg Total Carbs 24.7 g Fiber 1.2 g Sugar 1.3 g Protein 15.3 g

135. Rosemary Lemon Chicken

Servings: 8
Cooking Time: 45 Minutes
Ingredients:
- 4-lb. chicken, cut into pieces
- Salt and black pepper, to taste
- Flour for dredging 3 tablespoons olive oil
- 1 large onion, sliced
- Peel of ½ lemon
- 2 large garlic cloves, minced
- 1 1/2 teaspoons rosemary leaves
- 1 tablespoon honey
- 1/4 cup lemon juice
- 1 cup chicken broth

Directions:
1. Dredges the chicken through the flour then place in the baking pan.
2. Whisk broth with the rest of the Ingredients: in a bowl.
3. Pour this mixture over the dredged chicken in the pan.
4. Press "Power Button" of Air Fry Oven and turn the dial to select the "Bake" mode.
5. Press the Time button and again turn the dial to set the cooking time to 45 minutes.
6. Now push the Temp button and rotate the dial to set the temperature at 400 degrees F.
7. Once preheated, place the baking pan inside and close its lid.
8. Baste the chicken with its sauce every 15 minutes.

9. Serve warm.
- **Nutrition Info:** Calories 405 Total Fat 22.7 g Saturated Fat 6.1 g Cholesterol 4 mg Sodium 227 mg Total Carbs 26.1 g Fiber 1.4 g Sugar 0.9 g Protein 45.2 g

136. Spicy Green Crusted Chicken

Servings: 6
Cooking Time: 40 Minutes
Ingredients:
- 6 eggs, beaten
- 6 teaspoons parsley
- 4 teaspoons thyme
- 1 pound chicken pieces
- 6 teaspoons oregano
- Salt and freshly ground black pepper, to taste
- 4 teaspoons paprika

Directions:
1. Preheat the Air fryer to 360 degree F and grease an Air fryer basket.
2. Whisk eggs in a bowl and mix all the ingredients in another bowl except chicken pieces.
3. Dip the chicken in eggs and then coat generously with the dry mixture.
4. Arrange half of the chicken pieces in the Air fryer basket and cook for about 20 minutes.
5. Repeat with the remaining mixture and dish out to serve hot.
- **Nutrition Info:** Calories: 218, Fat: 10.4g, Carbohydrates: 2.6g, Sugar: 0.6g, Protein: 27.9g, Sodium: 128mg

137. Onion Omelet

Servings: 2
Cooking Time: 15 Minutes
Ingredients:
- 4 eggs
- ¼ teaspoon low-sodium soy sauce
- Ground black pepper, as required
- 1 teaspoon butter
- 1 medium yellow onion, sliced
- ¼ cup Cheddar cheese, grated

Directions:
1. In a skillet, melt the butter over medium heat and cook the onion and cook for about 8-10 minutes.
2. Remove from the heat and set aside to cool slightly.
3. Meanwhile, in a bowl, add the eggs, soy sauce and black pepper and beat well.
4. Add the cooked onion and gently, stir to combine.
5. Place the zucchini mixture into a small baking pan.
6. Press "Power Button" of Air Fry Oven and turn the dial to select the "Air Fry" mode.

7. Press the Time button and again turn the dial to set the cooking time to 5 minutes.
8. Now push the Temp button and rotate the dial to set the temperature at 355 degrees F.
9. Press "Start/Pause" button to start.
10. When the unit beeps to show that it is preheated, open the lid.
11. Arrange pan over the "Wire Rack" and insert in the oven.
12. Cut the omelet into 2 portions and serve hot.
- **Nutrition Info:** Calories: 222 Cal Total Fat: 15.4 g Saturated Fat: 6.9 g Cholesterol: 347 mg Sodium: 264 mg Total Carbs: 6.1 g Fiber: 1.2 g Sugar: 3.1 g Protein: 15.3 g

138. Saucy Chicken With Leeks

Servings: 6
Cooking Time: 10 Minutes
Ingredients:
- 2 leeks, sliced
- 2 large-sized tomatoes, chopped
- 3 cloves garlic, minced
- ½ teaspoon dried oregano
- 6 chicken legs, boneless and skinless
- ½ teaspoon smoked cayenne pepper
- 2 tablespoons olive oil
- A freshly ground nutmeg

Directions:
1. In a mixing dish, thoroughly combine all ingredients, minus the leeks. Place in the refrigerator and let it marinate overnight.
2. Lay the leeks onto the bottom of an Air Fryer cooking basket. Top with the chicken legs.
3. Roast chicken legs at 375 degrees F for 18 minutes, turning halfway through. Serve with hoisin sauce.
- **Nutrition Info:** 390 Calories; 16g Fat; 2g Carbs; 59g Protein; 8g Sugars; 4g Fiber

139. Roasted Fennel, Ditalini, And Shrimp

Servings: 4
Cooking Time: 30 Minutes
Ingredients:
- 1 pound extra large, thawed, tail-on shrimp
- 1 teaspoon fennel seeds
- 1 teaspoon salt
- 1 fennel bulb, halved and sliced crosswise
- 4 garlic cloves, chopped
- 2 tablespoons olive oil
- 1/2 teaspoon freshly ground black pepper
- Grated zest of 1 lemon
- 1/2 pound whole wheat ditalini

Directions:
1. Start by preheating toaster oven to 450°F.

2. Toast the seeds in a medium pan over medium heat for about 5 minutes, then toss with shrimp.
3. Add water and 1/2 teaspoon salt to the pan and bring the mixture to a boil.
4. Reduce heat and simmer for 30 minutes.
5. Combine fennel, garlic, oil, pepper, and remaining salt in a roasting pan.
6. Roast for 20 minutes, then add shrimp mixture and roast for another 5 minutes or until shrimp are cooked.
7. While the fennel is roasting, cook pasta per the directions on the package, drain, and set aside.
8. Remove the shrimp mixture and mix in pasta, roast for another 5 minutes.
- **Nutrition Info:** Calories: 420, Sodium: 890 mg, Dietary Fiber: 4.2 g, Total Fat: 10.2 g, Total Carbs: 49.5 g, Protein: 33.9 g.

140. Eggplant And Leeks Stew

Servings: 4
Cooking Time: 12 Minutes
Ingredients:
- 2 big eggplants, roughly cubed
- ½ bunch cilantro; chopped.
- 1 cup veggie stock
- 2 garlic cloves; minced
- 3 leeks; sliced
- 2 tbsp. olive oil
- 1 tbsp. hot sauce
- 1 tbsp. sweet paprika
- 1 tbsp. tomato puree
- Salt and black pepper to taste.

Directions:
1. In a pan that fits the air fryer, mix all the ingredients, toss, introduce in the fryer and cook at 380°F for 20 minutes
2. Divide the stew into bowls and serve for lunch.
- **Nutrition Info:** Calories: 183; Fat: 4g; Fiber: 2g; Carbs: 4g; Protein: 12g

141. Basic Roasted Tofu

Servings: 4
Cooking Time: 45 Minutes
Ingredients:
- 1 or more (16-ounce) containers extra-firm tofu
- 1 tablespoon sesame oil
- 1 tablespoon soy sauce
- 1 tablespoon rice vinegar
- 1 tablespoon water

Directions:
1. Start by drying the tofu: first pat dry with paper towels, then lay on another set of paper towels or a dish towel.
2. Put a plate on top of the tofu then put something heavy on the plate (like a large

can of vegetables). Leave it there for at least 20 minutes.
3. While tofu is being pressed, whip up marinade by combining oil, soy sauce, vinegar, and water in a bowl and set aside.
4. Cut the tofu into squares or sticks. Place the tofu in the marinade for at least 30 minutes.
5. Preheat toaster oven to 350°F. Line a pan with parchment paper and add as many pieces of tofu as you can, giving each piece adequate space.
6. Bake 20–45 minutes; tofu is done when the outside edges look golden brown. Time will vary depending on tofu size and shape.
- **Nutrition Info:** Calories: 114, Sodium: 239 mg, Dietary Fiber: 1.1 g, Total Fat: 8.1 g, Total Carbs: 2.2 g, Protein: 9.5 g.

142.   Green Bean Casserole(2)

Servings: 4
Cooking Time: 12 Minutes
Ingredients:
- 1 lb. fresh green beans, edges trimmed
- ½ oz. pork rinds, finely ground
- 1 oz. full-fat cream cheese
- ½ cup heavy whipping cream.
- ¼ cup diced yellow onion
- ½ cup chopped white mushrooms
- ½ cup chicken broth
- 4 tbsp. unsalted butter.
- ¼ tsp. xanthan gum

Directions:
1. In a medium skillet over medium heat, melt the butter. Sauté the onion and mushrooms until they become soft and fragrant, about 3–5 minutes.
2. Add the heavy whipping cream, cream cheese and broth to the pan. Whisk until smooth. Bring to a boil and then reduce to a simmer. Sprinkle the xanthan gum into the pan and remove from heat
3. Chop the green beans into 2-inch pieces and place into a 4-cup round baking dish. Pour the sauce mixture over them and stir until coated. Top the dish with ground pork rinds. Place into the air fryer basket
4. Adjust the temperature to 320 Degrees F and set the timer for 15 minutes. Top will be golden and green beans fork tender when fully cooked. Serve warm.
- **Nutrition Info:** Calories: 267; Protein: 6g; Fiber: 2g; Fat: 24g; Carbs: 7g

143.   Boneless Air Fryer Turkey Breasts

Servings: 4
Cooking Time: 50 Minutes
Ingredients:
- 3 lb boneless breast

- ¼ cup mayonnaise
- 2 tsp poultry seasoning
- 1 tsp salt
- ½ tsp garlic powder
- ¼ tsp black pepper

Directions:
1. Choose the Air Fry option on the Instant Pot Duo Crisp Air fryer. Set the temperature to 360°F and push start. The preheating will start.
2. Season your boneless turkey breast with mayonnaise, poultry seasoning, salt, garlic powder, and black pepper.
3. Once preheated, Air Fry the turkey breasts on 360°F for 1 hour, turning every 15 minutes or until internal temperature has reached a temperature of 165°F.
- **Nutrition Info:** Calories 558, Total Fat 18g, Total Carbs 1g, Protein 98g

144.   Chicken And Celery Stew

Servings: 6
Cooking Time: 12 Minutes
Ingredients:
- 1 lb. chicken breasts, skinless; boneless and cubed
- 4 celery stalks; chopped.
- ½ cup coconut cream
- 2 red bell peppers; chopped.
- 2 tsp. garlic; minced
- 1 tbsp. butter, soft
- Salt and black pepper to taste.

Directions:
1. Grease a baking dish that fits your air fryer with the butter, add all the ingredients in the pan and toss them.
2. Introduce the dish in the fryer, cook at 360°F for 30 minutes, divide into bowls and serve
- **Nutrition Info:** Calories: 246; Fat: 12g; Fiber: 2g; Carbs: 6g; Protein: 12g

145.   Fried Chicken Tacos

Servings: 4
Cooking Time: 10 Minutes
Ingredients:
- Chicken
- 1 lb. chicken tenders or breast chopped into 2-inch pieces
- 1 tsp garlic powder
- ½ tsp onion powder
- 1 large egg
- 1 ½ tsp salt
- 1 tsp paprika
- 3 Tbsp buttermilk
- ¾ cup All-purpose flour
- 3 Tbsp corn starch
- ½ tsp black pepper

- ½ tsp cayenne pepper
- oil for spraying
- Coleslaw
- ¼ tsp red pepper flakes
- 2 cups coleslaw mix
- 1 Tbsp brown sugar
- ½ tsp salt
- 2 Tbsp apple cider vinegar
- 1 Tbsp water
- Spicy Mayo
- ½ tsp salt
- ¼ cup mayonnaise
- 1 tsp garlic powder
- 2 Tbsp hot sauce
- 1 Tbsp buttermilk
- Tortilla wrappers

Directions:
1. Take a large bowl and mix together coleslaw mix, water, brown sugar, salt, apple cider vinegar, and red pepper flakes. Set aside.
2. Take another small bowl and combine mayonnaise, hot sauce, buttermilk, garlic powder, and salt. Set this mixture aside.
3. Select the Instant Pot Duo Crisp Air Fryer option, adjust the temperature to 360°F and push start. Preheating will start.
4. Create a clear station by placing two large flat pans side by side. Whisk together egg and buttermilk with salt and pepper in one of them. In the second, whisk flour, corn starch, black pepper, garlic powder, onion powder, salt, paprika, and cayenne pepper.
5. Cut the chicken tenders into 1-inch pieces. Season all pieces with a little salt and pepper.
6. Once the Instant Pot Duo Crisp Air Fryer is preheated, remove the tray and lightly spray it with oil. Coat your chicken with egg mixture while shaking off any excess egg, followed by the flour mixture, and place it on the tray and tray in the basket, making sure your chicken pieces don't overlap.
7. Close the Air Fryer lid, and cook on 360°F for 10 minutes
8. while flipping and spraying halfway through cooking.
9. Once the chicken is done, remove and place chicken into warmed tortilla shells. Top with coleslaw and spicy mayonnaise.
- **Nutrition Info:** Calories 375, Total Fat 15g, Total Carbs 31g, Protein 29g

146. Amazing Mac And Cheese

Servings:
Cooking Time: 12 Minutes
Ingredients:
- 1 cup cooked macaroni
- 1/2 cup warm milk

- 1 tablespoon parmesan cheese
- 1 cup grated cheddar cheese
- salt and pepper; to taste

Directions:
1. Preheat the Air Fryer to 350 - degrees Fahrenheit. Stir all of the ingredients; except Parmesan, in a baking dish.
2. Place the dish inside the Air Fryer and cook for 10 minutes. Top with the Parmesan cheese.

147. Lemon Pepper Turkey

Servings: 6
Cooking Time: 45 Minutes
Ingredients:
- 3 lbs. turkey breast
- 2 tablespoons oil
- 1 tablespoon Worcestershire sauce
- 1 teaspoon lemon pepper
- 1/2 teaspoon salt

Directions:
1. Whisk everything in a bowl and coat the turkey liberally.
2. Place the turkey in the Air fryer basket.
3. Press "Power Button" of Air Fry Oven and turn the dial to select the "Air Fry" mode.
4. Press the Time button and again turn the dial to set the cooking time to 45 minutes.
5. Now push the Temp button and rotate the dial to set the temperature at 375 degrees F.
6. Once preheated, place the air fryer basket inside and close its lid.
7. Serve warm.
- **Nutrition Info:** Calories 391 Total Fat 2.8 g Saturated Fat 0.6 g Cholesterol 330 mg Sodium 62 mg Total Carbs 36.5 g Fiber 9.2 g Sugar 4.5 g Protein 6.6

148. Butter Fish With Sake And Miso

Servings: 4
Cooking Time: 11 Minutes
Ingredients:
- 4 (7-ounce) pieces of butter fish
- 1/3 cup sake
- 1/3 cup mirin
- 2/3 cup sugar
- 1 cup white miso

Directions:
1. Start by combining sake, mirin, and sugar in a sauce pan and bring to a boil.
2. Allow to boil for 5 minutes, then reduce heat and simmer for another 10 minutes.
3. Remove from heat completely and mix in miso.
4. Marinate the fish in the mixture for as long as possible, up to 3 days if possible.
5. Preheat toaster oven to 450°F and bake fish for 8 minutes.

6. Switch your setting to Broil and broil another 2-3 minutes, until the sauce is caramelized.
- **Nutrition Info:** Calories: 529, Sodium: 2892 mg, Dietary Fiber: 3.7 g, Total Fat: 5.8 g, Total Carbs: 61.9 g, Protein: 53.4 g.

149. Dijon And Swiss Croque Monsieur

Servings: 2
Cooking Time: 13 Minutes
Ingredients:
- 4 slices white bread
- 2 tablespoons unsalted butter
- 1 tablespoon all-purpose flour
- 1/2 cup whole milk
- 3/4 cups shredded Swiss cheese
- 1/4 teaspoon freshly ground black pepper
- 1/8 teaspoon salt
- 1 tablespoon Dijon mustard
- 4 slices ham

Directions:
1. Start by cutting crusts off bread and placing them on a pan lined with parchment paper.
2. Melt 1 tablespoon of butter in a sauce pan, then dab the top sides of each piece of bread with butter.
3. Toast bread inoven for 3-5 minutes until each piece is golden brown.
4. Melt the second tablespoon of butter in the sauce pan and add the flour, mix together until they form a paste.
5. Add the milk and continue to mix until the sauce begins to thicken.
6. Remove from heat and mix in 1 tablespoon of Swiss cheese, salt, and pepper; continue stirring until cheese is melted.
7. Flip the bread over in the pan so the untoasted side is facing up.
8. Set two slices aside and spread Dijon on the other two slices.
9. Add ham and sprinkle 1/4 cup Swiss over each piece.
10. Broil for about 3 minutes.
11. Top the sandwiches off with the other slices of bread, soft-side down.
12. Top with sauce and sprinkle with remaining Swiss. Toast for another 5 minutes or until the cheese is golden brown.
13. Serve immediately.
- **Nutrition Info:** Calories: 452, Sodium: 1273 mg, Dietary Fiber: 1.6 g, Total Fat: 30.5 g, Total Carbs: 19.8 g, Protein: 24.4 g.

150. Lemon Chicken Breasts

Servings: 4
Cooking Time: 30 Minutes
Ingredients:
- 1/4 cup olive oil

- 3 tablespoons garlic, minced
- 1/3 cup dry white wine
- 1 tablespoon lemon zest, grated
- 2 tablespoons lemon juice
- 1 1/2 teaspoons dried oregano, crushed
- 1 teaspoon thyme leaves, minced
- Salt and black pepper
- 4 skin-on boneless chicken breasts
- 1 lemon, sliced

Directions:
1. Whisk everything in a baking pan to coat the chicken breasts well.
2. Place the lemon slices on top of the chicken breasts.
3. Spread the mustard mixture over the toasted bread slices.
4. Press "Power Button" of Air Fry Oven and turn the dial to select the "Bake" mode.
5. Press the Time button and again turn the dial to set the cooking time to 30 minutes.
6. Now push the Temp button and rotate the dial to set the temperature at 370 degrees F.
7. Once preheated, place the baking pan inside and close its lid.
8. Serve warm.
- **Nutrition Info:** Calories 388 Total Fat 8 g Saturated Fat 1 g Cholesterol 153mg sodium 339 mg Total Carbs 8 g Fiber 1 g Sugar 2 g Protein 13 g

151. Easy Italian Meatballs

Servings: 4
Cooking Time: 13 Minutes
Ingredients:
- 2-lb. lean ground turkey
- ¼ cup onion, minced
- 2 cloves garlic, minced
- 2 tablespoons parsley, chopped
- 2 eggs
- 1½ cup parmesan cheese, grated
- ½ teaspoon red pepper flakes
- ½ teaspoon Italian seasoning Salt and black pepper to taste

Directions:
1. Toss all the meatball Ingredients: in a bowl and mix well.
2. Make small meatballs out this mixture and place them in the air fryer basket.
3. Press "Power Button" of Air Fry Oven and turn the dial to select the "Air Fry" mode.
4. Press the Time button and again turn the dial to set the cooking time to 13 minutes.
5. Now push the Temp button and rotate the dial to set the temperature at 350 degrees F.
6. Once preheated, place the air fryer basket inside and close its lid.
7. Flip the meatballs when cooked halfway through.
8. Serve warm.

- **Nutrition Info:** Calories 472 Total Fat 25.8 g Saturated Fat .4 g Cholesterol 268 mg Sodium 503 mg Total Carbs 1.7 g Fiber 0.3 g Sugar 0.6 g Protein 59.6 g

152. Easy Prosciutto Grilled Cheese

Servings: 1
Cooking Time: 5 Minutes
Ingredients:
- 2 slices muenster cheese
- 2 slices white bread
- Four thinly-shaved pieces of prosciutto
- 1 tablespoon sweet and spicy pickles

Directions:
1. Set toaster oven to the Toast setting.
2. Place one slice of cheese on each piece of bread.
3. Put prosciutto on one slice and pickles on the other.
4. Transfer to a baking sheet and toast for 4 minutes or until the cheese is melted.
5. Combine the sides, cut, and serve.
- **Nutrition Info:** Calories: 460, Sodium: 2180 mg, Dietary Fiber: 0 g, Total Fat: 25.2 g, Total Carbs: 11.9 g, Protein: 44.2 g.

153. Duck Breast With Figs

Servings: 2
Cooking Time: 45 Minutes
Ingredients:
- 1 pound boneless duck breast
- 6 fresh figs, halved
- 1 tablespoon fresh thyme, chopped
- 2 cups fresh pomegranate juice
- 2 tablespoons lemon juice
- 3 tablespoons brown sugar
- 1 teaspoon olive oil
- Salt and black pepper, as required

Directions:
1. Preheat the Air fryer to 400 degree F and grease an Air fryer basket.
2. Put the pomegranate juice, lemon juice, and brown sugar in a medium saucepan over medium heat.
3. Bring to a boil and simmer on low heat for about 25 minutes.
4. Season the duck breasts generously with salt and black pepper.
5. Arrange the duck breasts into the Air fryer basket, skin side up and cook for about 14 minutes, flipping once in between.
6. Dish out the duck breasts onto a cutting board for about 10 minutes.
7. Meanwhile, put the figs, olive oil, salt, and black pepper in a bowl until well mixed.
8. Set the Air fryer to 400 degree F and arrange the figs into the Air fryer basket.
9. Cook for about 5 more minutes and dish out in a platter.

10. Put the duck breast with the roasted figs and drizzle with warm pomegranate juice mixture.
11. Garnish with fresh thyme and serve warm.
- **Nutrition Info:** Calories: 699, Fat: 12.1g, Carbohydrates: 90g, Sugar: 74g, Protein: 519g, Sodium: 110mg

154. Roasted Delicata Squash With Kale

Servings: 2
Cooking Time: 10 Minutes
Ingredients:
- 1 medium delicata squash
- 1 bunch kale
- 1 clove garlic
- 2 tablespoons olive oil
- Salt and pepper

Directions:
1. Start by preheating toaster oven to 425°F.
2. Clean squash and cut off each end. Cut in half and remove the seeds. Quarter the halves.
3. Toss the squash in 1 tablespoon of olive oil.
4. Place the squash on a greased baking sheet and roast for 25 minutes, turning halfway through.
5. Rinse kale and remove stems. Chop garlic.
6. Heat the leftover oil in a medium skillet and add kale and salt to taste.
7. Sauté the kale until it darkens, then mix in the garlic.
8. Cook for another minute then remove from heat and add 2 tablespoons of water.
9. Remove squash from oven and lay it on top of the garlic kale.
10. Top with salt and pepper to taste and serve.
- **Nutrition Info:** Calories: 159, Sodium: 28 mg, Dietary Fiber: 1.8 g, Total Fat: 14.2 g, Total Carbs: 8.2 g, Protein: 2.6 g.

155. Parmigiano Reggiano And Prosciutto Toasts With Balsamic Glaze

Servings: 8
Cooking Time: 15 Minutes
Ingredients:
- 3 ounces thinly sliced prosciutto, cut crosswise into 1/4-inch-wide strips
- 1 (3-ounce) piece Parmigiano Reggiano cheese
- 1/2 cup balsamic vinegar
- 1 medium red onion, thinly sliced
- 1 loaf ciabatta, cut into 3/4-inch-thick slices
- 1 tablespoon extra-virgin olive oil
- 1 clove garlic
- Black pepper to taste

Directions:

1. Preheat toaster oven to 350°F.
2. Place onion in a bowl of cold water and let sit for 10 minutes.
3. Bring vinegar to a boil, then reduce heat and simmer for 5 minutes.
4. Remove from heat completely and set aside to allow the vinegar to thicken.
5. Drain the onion.
6. Brush the tops of each bun with oil, rub with garlic, and sprinkle with pepper.
7. Use a vegetable peeler to make large curls of Parmigiano Reggiano cheese and place them on the bun.
8. Bake for 15 minutes or until the bread just starts to crisp.
9. Sprinkle prosciutto and onions on top, then drizzle vinegar and serve.
- **Nutrition Info:** Calories: 154, Sodium: 432 mg, Dietary Fiber: 1.0 g, Total Fat: 5.6 g, Total Carbs: 17.3 g, Protein: 8.1 g.

156. Chicken & Rice Casserole

Servings: 6
Cooking Time: 40 Minutes
Ingredients:
- 2 lbs. bone-in chicken thighs
- Salt and black pepper
- 1 teaspoon olive oil
- 5 cloves garlic, chopped
- 2 large onions, chopped
- 2 large red bell peppers, chopped
- 1 tablespoon sweet Hungarian paprika
- 1 teaspoon hot Hungarian paprika
- 2 tablespoons tomato paste
- 2 cups chicken broth
- 3 cups brown rice, thawed
- 2 tablespoons parsley, chopped
- 6 tablespoons sour cream

Directions:
1. Mix broth, tomato paste, and all the spices in a bowl.
2. Add chicken and mix well to coat.
3. Spread the rice in a casserole dish and add chicken along with its marinade.
4. Top the casserole with the rest of the Ingredients:.
5. Press "Power Button" of Air Fry Oven and turn the dial to select the "Bake" mode.
6. Press the Time button and again turn the dial to set the cooking time to 40 minutes.
7. Now push the Temp button and rotate the dial to set the temperature at 350 degrees F.
8. Once preheated, place the baking pan inside and close its lid.
9. Serve warm.
- **Nutrition Info:** Calories 440 Total Fat 7.9 g Saturated Fat 1.8 g Cholesterol 5 mg Sodium 581 mg Total Carbs 21.8 g Sugar 7.1 g Fiber 2.6 g Protein 37.2 g

157. Simple Turkey Breast

Servings: 10
Cooking Time: 40 Minutes
Ingredients:
- 1: 8-poundsbone-in turkey breast
- Salt and black pepper, as required
- 2 tablespoons olive oil

Directions:
1. Preheat the Air fryer to 360 degree F and grease an Air fryer basket.
2. Season the turkey breast with salt and black pepper and drizzle with oil.
3. Arrange the turkey breast into the Air Fryer basket, skin side down and cook for about 20 minutes.
4. Flip the side and cook for another 20 minutes.
5. Dish out in a platter and cut into desired size slices to serve.
- **Nutrition Info:** Calories: 719, Fat: 35.9g, Carbohydrates: 0g, Sugar: 0g, Protein: 97.2g, Sodium: 386mg

158. Sweet Potato And Parsnip Spiralized Latkes

Servings: 12
Cooking Time: 20 Minutes
Ingredients:
- 1 medium sweet potato
- 1 large parsnip
- 4 cups water
- 1 egg + 1 egg white
- 2 scallions
- 1/2 teaspoon garlic powder
- 1/2 teaspoon sea salt
- 1/2 teaspoon ground pepper

Directions:
1. Start by spiralizing the sweet potato and parsnip and chopping the scallions, reserving only the green parts.
2. Preheat toaster oven to 425°F.
3. Bring 4 cups of water to a boil. Place all of your noodles in a colander and pour the boiling water over the top, draining well.
4. Let the noodles cool, then grab handfuls and place them in a paper towel; squeeze to remove as much liquid as possible.
5. In a large bowl, beat egg and egg white together. Add noodles, scallions, garlic powder, salt, and pepper, mix well.
6. Prepare a baking sheet; scoop out 1/4 cup of mixture at a time and place on sheet.
7. Slightly press down each scoop with your hands, then bake for 20 minutes, flipping halfway through.
- **Nutrition Info:** Calories: 24, Sodium: 91 mg, Dietary Fiber: 1.0 g, Total Fat: 0.4 g, Total Carbs: 4.3 g, Protein: 0.9 g.

159.   Ground Chicken Meatballs

Servings: 4
Cooking Time: 10 Minutes
Ingredients:
- 1-lb. ground chicken
- 1/3 cup panko
- 1 teaspoon salt
- 2 teaspoons chives
- 1/2 teaspoon garlic powder
- 1 teaspoon thyme
- 1 egg

Directions:
1. Toss all the meatball Ingredients: in a bowl and mix well.
2. Make small meatballs out this mixture and place them in the air fryer basket.
3. Press "Power Button" of Air Fry Oven and turn the dial to select the "Air Fry" mode.
4. Press the Time button and again turn the dial to set the cooking time to 10 minutes.
5. Now push the Temp button and rotate the dial to set the temperature at 350 degrees F.
6. Once preheated, place the air fryer basket inside and close its lid.
7. Serve warm.
- **Nutrition Info:** Calories 453 Total Fat 2.4 g Saturated Fat 3 g Cholesterol 21 mg Sodium 216 mg Total Carbs 18 g Fiber 2.3 g Sugar 1.2 g Protein 23.2 g

160.   Roasted Beet Salad With Oranges & Beet Greens

Servings: 6
Cooking Time: 1-1/2 Hours
Ingredients:
- 6 medium beets with beet greens attached
- 2 large oranges
- 1 small sweet onion, cut into wedges
- 1/3 cup red wine vinegar
- 1/4 cup extra-virgin olive oil
- 2 garlic cloves, minced
- 1/2 teaspoon grated orange peel

Directions:
1. Start by preheating toaster oven to 400°F.
2. Trim leaves from beets and chop, then set aside.
3. Pierce beets with a fork and place in a roasting pan.
4. Roast beets for 1-1/2 hours.
5. Allow beets to cool, peel, then cut into 8 wedges and put into a bowl.
6. Place beet greens in a sauce pan and cover with just enough water to cover. Heat until water boils, then immediately remove from heat.
7. Drain greens and press to remove liquid from greens, then add to beet bowl.
8. Remove peel and pith from orange and segment, adding each segment to the bowl.
9. Add onion to beet mixture. In a separate bowl mix together vinegar, oil, garlic and orange peel.
10. Combine both bowls and toss, sprinkle with salt and pepper.
11. Let stand for an hour before serving.
- **Nutrition Info:** Calories: 214, Sodium: 183 mg, Dietary Fiber: 6.5 g, Total Fat: 8.9 g, Total Carbs: 32.4 g, Protein: 4.7 g.

161.   Creamy Green Beans And Tomatoes

Servings: 4
Cooking Time: 20 Minutes
Ingredients:
- 1 pound green beans, trimmed and halved
- ½ pound cherry tomatoes, halved
- 2 tablespoons olive oil
- 1 teaspoon oregano, dried
- 1 teaspoon basil, dried
- Salt and black pepper to the taste
- 1 cup heavy cream
- ½ tablespoon cilantro, chopped

Directions:
1. In your air fryer's pan, combine the green beans with the tomatoes and the other Ingredients., toss and cook at 360 degrees F for 20 minutes.
2. Divide the mix between plates and serve.
- **Nutrition Info:** Calories 174, fat 5, fiber 7, carbs 11, protein 4

162.   Coriander Potatoes

Servings: 4
Cooking Time: 25 Minutes
Ingredients:
- 1 pound gold potatoes, peeled and cut into wedges
- Salt and black pepper to the taste
- 1 tablespoon tomato sauce
- 2 tablespoons coriander, chopped
- ½ teaspoon garlic powder
- 1 teaspoon chili powder
- 1 tablespoon olive oil

Directions:
1. In a bowl, combine the potatoes with the tomato sauce and the other Ingredients:, toss, and transfer to the air fryer's basket.
2. Cook at 370 degrees F for 25 minutes, divide between plates and serve as a side dish.
- **Nutrition Info:** Calories 210, fat 5, fiber 7, carbs 12, protein 5

163.   Coriander Artichokes(3)

Servings: 4

Cooking Time: 12 Minutes
Ingredients:
- 12 oz. artichoke hearts
- 1 tbsp. lemon juice
- 1 tsp. coriander, ground
- ½ tsp. cumin seeds
- ½ tsp. olive oil
- Salt and black pepper to taste.

Directions:
1. In a pan that fits your air fryer, mix all the ingredients, toss, introduce the pan in the fryer and cook at 370°F for 15 minutes
2. Divide the mix between plates and serve as a side dish.
- **Nutrition Info:** Calories: 200; Fat: 7g; Fiber: 2g; Carbs: 5g; Protein: 8g

164. Turkey Meatloaf

Servings: 4
Cooking Time: 20 Minutes
Ingredients:
- 1 pound ground turkey
- 1 cup kale leaves, trimmed and finely chopped
- 1 cup onion, chopped
- ½ cup fresh breadcrumbs
- 1 cup Monterey Jack cheese, grated
- 2 garlic cloves, minced
- ¼ cup salsa verde
- 1 teaspoon red chili powder
- ½ teaspoon ground cumin
- ½ teaspoon dried oregano, crushed
- Salt and ground black pepper, as required

Directions:
1. Preheat the Air fryer to 400 degree F and grease an Air fryer basket.
2. Mix all the ingredients in a bowl and divide the turkey mixture into 4 equal-sized portions.
3. Shape each into a mini loaf and arrange the loaves into the Air fryer basket.
4. Cook for about 20 minutes and dish out to serve warm.
- **Nutrition Info:** Calories: 435, Fat: 23.1g, Carbohydrates: 18.1g, Sugar: 3.6g, Protein: 42.2g, Sodium: 641mg

165. Roasted Garlic(2)

Servings: 12 Cloves
Cooking Time: 12 Minutes
Ingredients:
- 1 medium head garlic
- 2 tsp. avocado oil

Directions:
1. Remove any hanging excess peel from the garlic but leave the cloves covered. Cut off ¼ of the head of garlic, exposing the tips of the cloves

2. Drizzle with avocado oil. Place the garlic head into a small sheet of aluminum foil, completely enclosing it. Place it into the air fryer basket. Adjust the temperature to 400 Degrees F and set the timer for 20 minutes. If your garlic head is a bit smaller, check it after 15 minutes
3. When done, garlic should be golden brown and very soft
4. To serve, cloves should pop out and easily be spread or sliced. Store in an airtight container in the refrigerator up to 5 days.
5. You may also freeze individual cloves on a baking sheet, then store together in a freezer-safe storage bag once frozen.
- **Nutrition Info:** Calories: 11; Protein: 2g; Fiber: 1g; Fat: 7g; Carbs: 0g

166. Barbecue Air Fried Chicken

Servings: 10
Cooking Time: 26 Minutes
Ingredients:
- 1 teaspoon Liquid Smoke
- 2 cloves Fresh Garlic smashed
- 1/2 cup Apple Cider Vinegar
- 3 pounds Chuck Roast well-marbled with intramuscular fat
- 1 Tablespoon Kosher Salt
- 1 Tablespoon Freshly Ground Black Pepper
- 2 teaspoons Garlic Powder
- 1.5 cups Barbecue Sauce
- 1/4 cup Light Brown Sugar + more for sprinkling
- 2 Tablespoons Honey optional and in place of 2 TBL sugar

Directions:
1. Add meat to the Instant Pot Duo Crisp Air Fryer Basket, spreading out the meat.
2. Select the option Air Fry.
3. Close the Air Fryer lid and cook at 300 degrees F for 8 minutes. Pause the Air Fryer and flip meat over after 4 minutes.
4. Remove the lid and baste with more barbecue sauce and sprinkle with a little brown sugar.
5. Again Close the Air Fryer lid and set the temperature at 400°F for 9 minutes. Watch meat though the lid and flip it over after 5 minutes.
- **Nutrition Info:** Calories 360, Total Fat 16g, Total Carbs 27g, Protein 27g

167. Roasted Grape And Goat Cheese Crostinis

Servings: 10
Cooking Time: 5 Minutes
Ingredients:
- 1 pound seedless red grapes
- 1 teaspoon chopped rosemary

- 4 tablespoons olive oil
- 1 rustic French baguette
- 1 cup sliced shallots
- 2 tablespoons unsalted butter
- 8 ounces goat cheese
- 1 tablespoon honey

Directions:
1. Start by preheating toaster oven to 400°F.
2. Toss grapes, rosemary, and 1 tablespoon of olive oil in a large bowl.
3. Transfer to a roasting pan and roast for 20 minutes.
4. Remove the pan from the oven and set aside to cool.
5. Slice the baguette into 1/2-inch-thick pieces.
6. Brush each slice with olive oil and place on baking sheet.
7. Bake for 8 minutes, then remove from oven and set aside.
8. In a medium skillet add butter and one tablespoon of olive oil.
9. Add shallots and sauté for about 10 minutes.
10. Mix goat cheese and honey in a medium bowl, then add contents of shallot pan and mix thoroughly.
11. Spread shallot mixture onto baguette, top with grapes, and serve.
- **Nutrition Info:** Calories: 238, Sodium: 139 mg, Dietary Fiber: 0.6 g, Total Fat: 16.3 g, Total Carbs: 16.4 g, Protein: 8.4 g.

168.   Turkey And Broccoli Stew

Servings: 4
Cooking Time: 12 Minutes
Ingredients:
- 1 broccoli head, florets separated
- 1 turkey breast, skinless; boneless and cubed
- 1 cup tomato sauce
- 1 tbsp. parsley; chopped.
- 1 tbsp. olive oil
- Salt and black pepper to taste.

Directions:
1. In a baking dish that fits your air fryer, mix the turkey with the rest of the ingredients except the parsley, toss, introduce the dish in the fryer, bake at 380°F for 25 minutes
2. Divide into bowls, sprinkle the parsley on top and serve.
- **Nutrition Info:** Calories: 250; Fat: 11g; Fiber: 2g; Carbs: 6g; Protein: 12g

169.   Spice-roasted Almonds

Servings: 32
Cooking Time: 10 Minutes
Ingredients:
- 1 tablespoon chili powder
- 1 tablespoon olive oil
- 1/2 teaspoon salt

- 1/2 teaspoon ground cumin
- 1/2 teaspoon ground coriander
- 1/4 teaspoon ground cinnamon
- 1/4 teaspoon black pepper
- 2 cups whole almonds

Directions:
1. Start by preheating toaster oven to 350°F.
2. Mix olive oil, chili powder, coriander, cinnamon, cumin, salt, and pepper.
3. Add almonds and toss together.
4. Transfer to a baking pan and bake for 10 minutes.
- **Nutrition Info:** Calories: 39, Sodium: 37 mg, Dietary Fiber: 0.8 g, Total Fat: 3.5 g, Total Carbs: 1.4 g, Protein: 1.3 g.

170.   Parmesan Chicken Meatballs

Servings: 4
Cooking Time: 12 Minutes
Ingredients:
- 1-lb. ground chicken
- 1 large egg, beaten
- ½ cup Parmesan cheese, grated
- ½ cup pork rinds, ground
- 1 teaspoon garlic powder
- 1 teaspoon paprika
- 1 teaspoon kosher salt
- ½ teaspoon pepper
- Crust:
- ½ cup pork rinds, ground

Directions:
1. Toss all the meatball Ingredients: in a bowl and mix well.
2. Make small meatballs out this mixture and roll them in the pork rinds.
3. Place the coated meatballs in the air fryer basket.
4. Press "Power Button" of Air Fry Oven and turn the dial to select the "Bake" mode.
5. Press the Time button and again turn the dial to set the cooking time to 12 minutes.
6. Now push the Temp button and rotate the dial to set the temperature at 400 degrees F.
7. Once preheated, place the air fryer basket inside and close its lid.
8. Serve warm.
- **Nutrition Info:** Calories 529 Total Fat 17 g Saturated Fat 3 g Cholesterol 65 mg Sodium 391 mg Total Carbs 55 g Fiber 6 g Sugar 8 g Protein 41g

171.   Turmeric Mushroom(3)

Servings: 4
Cooking Time: 12 Minutes
Ingredients:
- 1 lb. brown mushrooms
- 4 garlic cloves; minced
- ¼ tsp. cinnamon powder
- 1 tsp. olive oil

- ½ tsp. turmeric powder
- Salt and black pepper to taste.

Directions:
1. In a bowl, combine all the ingredients and toss.
2. Put the mushrooms in your air fryer's basket and cook at 370°F for 15 minutes
3. Divide the mix between plates and serve as a side dish.
- **Nutrition Info:** Calories: 208; Fat: 7g; Fiber: 3g; Carbs: 5g; Protein: 7g

172. Coconut Shrimp With Dip

Servings: 4
Cooking Time: 9 Minutes
Ingredients:
- 1 lb large raw shrimp peeled and deveined with tail on
- 2 eggs beaten
- ¼ cup Panko Breadcrumbs
- 1 tsp salt
- ¼ tsp black pepper
- ½ cup All-Purpose Flour
- ½ cup unsweetened shredded coconut
- Oil for spraying

Directions:
1. Clean and dry the shrimp. Set it aside.
2. Take 3 bowls. Put flour in the first bowl. Beat eggs in the second bowl. Mix coconut, breadcrumbs, salt, and black pepper in the third bowl.
3. Select the Air Fry option and adjust the temperature to 390°F. Push start and preheating will start.
4. Dip each shrimp in flour followed by the egg and then coconut mixture, ensuring shrimp is covered on all sides during each dip.
5. Once the preheating is done, place shrimp in a single layer on greased tray in the basket of the Instant Pot Duo Crisp Air Fryer.
6. Spray the shrimp with oil lightly, and then close the Air Fryer basket lid. Cook for around 4 minutes.
7. After 4 minutes
8. open the Air Fryer basket lid and flip the shrimp over. Respray the shrimp with oil, close the Air Fryer basket lid, and cook for five more minutes.
9. Remove shrimp from the basket and serve with Thai Sweet Chili Sauce.
- **Nutrition Info:** Calories 279, Total Fat 11g, Total Carbs 17g, Protein 28g

173. Chicken Caprese Sandwich

Servings: 2
Cooking Time: 3 Minutes
Ingredients:

- 2 leftover chicken breasts, or pre-cooked breaded chicken
- 1 large ripe tomato
- 4 ounces mozzarella cheese slices
- 4 slices of whole grain bread
- 1/4 cup olive oil
- 1/3 cup fresh basil leaves
- Salt and pepper to taste

Directions:
1. Start by slicing tomatoes into thin slices.
2. Layer tomatoes then cheese over two slices of bread and place on a greased baking sheet.
3. Toast in the toaster oven for about 2 minutes or until the cheese is melted.
4. Heat chicken while the cheese melts.
5. Remove from oven, sprinkle with basil, and add chicken.
6. Drizzle with oil and add salt and pepper.
7. Top with other slice of bread and serve.
- **Nutrition Info:** Calories: 808, Sodium: 847 mg, Dietary Fiber: 5.2 g, Total Fat: 43.6 g, Total Carbs: 30.7 g, Protein: 78.4 g.

174. Zucchini Stew

Servings: 4
Cooking Time: 12 Minutes
Ingredients:
- 8 zucchinis, roughly cubed
- ¼ cup tomato sauce
- 1 tbsp. olive oil
- ½ tsp. basil; chopped.
- ¼ tsp. rosemary; dried
- Salt and black pepper to taste.

Directions:
1. Grease a pan that fits your air fryer with the oil, add all the ingredients, toss, introduce the pan in the fryer and cook at 350°F for 12 minutes
2. Divide into bowls and serve.
- **Nutrition Info:** Calories: 200; Fat: 6g; Fiber: 2g; Carbs: 4g; Protein: 6g

175. Herb-roasted Chicken Tenders

Servings: 2
Cooking Time: 10 Minutes
Ingredients:
- 7 ounces chicken tenders
- 1 tablespoon olive oil
- 1/2 teaspoon Herbes de Provence
- 2 tablespoons Dijon mustard
- 1 tablespoon honey
- Salt and pepper

Directions:
1. Start by preheating toaster oven to 450°F.
2. Brush bottom of pan with 1/2 tablespoon olive oil.
3. Season the chicken with herbs, salt, and pepper.

4. Place the chicken in a single flat layer in the pan and drizzle the remaining olive oil over it.
5. Bake for about 10 minutes.
6. While the chicken is baking, mix together the mustard and honey for a tasty condiment.
- **Nutrition Info:** Calories: 297, Sodium: 268 mg, Dietary Fiber: 0.8 g, Total Fat: 15.5 g, Total Carbs: 9.6 g, Protein: 29.8 g.

176. Greek Lamb Meatballs

Servings: 12
Cooking Time: 12 Minutes
Ingredients:
- 1 pound ground lamb
- ½ cup breadcrumbs
- ¼ cup milk
- 2 egg yolks
- 1 teaspoon ground coriander
- 1 teaspoon ground cumin
- 3 garlic cloves, minced
- 1 teaspoon dried oregano
- ½ teaspoon salt
- ½ teaspoon black pepper
- 1 lemon, juiced and zested
- ¼ cup fresh parsley, chopped
- ½ cup crumbled feta cheese
- Olive oil, for shaping
- Tzatziki, for dipping

Directions:
1. Combine all ingredients except olive oil in a large mixing bowl and mix until fully incorporated.
2. Form 12 meatballs, about 2 ounces each. Use olive oil on your hands so they don't stick to the meatballs. Set aside.
3. Select the Broil function on the COSORI Air Fryer Toaster Oven, set time to 12 minutes, then press Start/Cancel to preheat.
4. Place the meatballs on the food tray, then insert the tray at top position in the preheated air fryer toaster oven. Press Start/Cancel.
5. Take out the meatballs when done and serve with a side of tzatziki.
- **Nutrition Info:** Calories: 129 kcal Total Fat: 6.4 g Saturated Fat: 0 g Cholesterol: 0 mg Sodium: 0 mg Total Carbs: 4.9 g Fiber: 0 g Sugar: 0 g Protein: 12.9 g

177. Deviled Chicken

Servings: 8
Cooking Time: 40 Minutes
Ingredients:
- 2 tablespoons butter
- 2 cloves garlic, chopped
- 1 cup Dijon mustard
- 1/2 teaspoon cayenne pepper
- 1 1/2 cups panko breadcrumbs
- 3/4 cup Parmesan, freshly grated
- 1/4 cup chives, chopped
- 2 teaspoons paprika
- 8 small bone-in chicken thighs, skin removed

Directions:
1. Toss the chicken thighs with crumbs, cheese, chives, butter, and spices in a bowl and mix well to coat.
2. Transfer the chicken along with its spice mix to a baking pan.
3. Press "Power Button" of Air Fry Oven and turn the dial to select the "Air Fry" mode.
4. Press the Time button and again turn the dial to set the cooking time to 40 minutes.
5. Now push the Temp button and rotate the dial to set the temperature at 350 degrees F.
6. Once preheated, place the baking pan inside and close its lid.
7. Serve warm.
- **Nutrition Info:** Calories 380 Total Fat 20 g Saturated Fat 5 g Cholesterol 151 mg Sodium 686 mg Total Carbs 33 g Fiber 1 g Sugar 1.2 g Protein 21 g

178. Bbq Chicken Breasts

Servings: 4
Cooking Time: 15 Minutes
Ingredients:
- 4 boneless skinless chicken breast about 6 oz each
- 1-2 Tbsp bbq seasoning

Directions:
1. Cover both sides of chicken breast with the BBQ seasoning. Cover and marinate the in the refrigerator for 45 minutes.
2. Choose the Air Fry option and set the temperature to 400°F. Push start and let it preheat for 5 minutes.
3. Upon preheating, place the chicken breast in the Instant Pot Duo Crisp Air Fryer basket, making sure they do not overlap. Spray with oil.
4. Cook for 13-14 minutes
5. flipping halfway.
6. Remove chicken when the chicken reaches an internal temperature of 160°F. Place on a plate and allow to rest for 5 minutes before slicing.
- **Nutrition Info:** Calories 131, Total Fat 3g, Total Carbs 2g, Protein 24g

179. Buttermilk Brined Turkey Breast

Servings: 8
Cooking Time: 20 Minutes
Ingredients:
- ¾ cup brine from a can of olives

- 3½ pounds boneless, skinless turkey breast
- 2 fresh thyme sprigs
- 1 fresh rosemary sprig
- ½ cup buttermilk

Directions:
1. Preheat the Air fryer to 350 degree F and grease an Air fryer basket.
2. Mix olive brine and buttermilk in a bowl until well combined.
3. Place the turkey breast, buttermilk mixture and herb sprigs in a resealable plastic bag.
4. Seal the bag and refrigerate for about 12 hours.
5. Remove the turkey breast from bag and arrange the turkey breast into the Air fryer basket.
6. Cook for about 20 minutes, flipping once in between.
7. Dish out the turkey breast onto a cutting board and cut into desired size slices to serve.
- **Nutrition Info:** Calories: 215, Fat: 3.5g, Carbohydrates: 9.4g, Sugar: 7.7g, Protein: 34.4g, Sodium: 2000mg

180. Chicken Potato Bake

Servings: 4
Cooking Time: 25 Minutes
Ingredients:
- 4 potatoes, diced
- 1 tablespoon garlic, minced
- 1.5 tablespoons olive oil
- 1/8 teaspoon salt
- 1/8 teaspoon pepper
- 1.5 lbs. boneless skinless chicken
- 3/4 cup mozzarella cheese, shredded
- parsley chopped

Directions:
1. Toss chicken and potatoes with all the spices and oil in a baking pan.
2. Drizzle the cheese on top of the chicken and potato.
3. Press "Power Button" of Air Fry Oven and turn the dial to select the "Bake" mode.
4. Press the Time button and again turn the dial to set the cooking time to 25 minutes.
5. Now push the Temp button and rotate the dial to set the temperature at 375 degrees F.
6. Once preheated, place the baking pan inside and close its lid.
7. Serve warm.
- **Nutrition Info:** Calories 695 Total Fat 17.5 g Saturated Fat 4.8 g Cholesterol 283 mg Sodium 355 mg Total Carbs 26.4 g Fiber 1.8 g Sugar 0.8 g Protein 117.4 g

181. Creamy Chicken Tenders

Servings: 8
Cooking Time: 20 Minutes

Ingredients:
- 2 pounds chicken tenders
- 1 cup feta cheese
- 4 tablespoons olive oil
- 1 cup cream
- Salt and black pepper, to taste

Directions:
1. Preheat the Air fryer to 340 degree F and grease an Air fryer basket.
2. Season the chicken tenders with salt and black pepper.
3. Arrange the chicken tenderloins in the Air fryer basket and drizzle with olive oil.\
4. Cook for about 15 minutes and set the Air fryer to 390 degree F.
5. Cook for about 5 more minutes and dish out to serve warm.
6. Repeat with the remaining mixture and dish out to serve hot.
- **Nutrition Info:** Calories: 344, Fat: 21.1g, Carbohydrates: 1.7g, Sugar: 1.4g, Protein: 35.7g, Sodium: 317mg

182. Lamb Gyro

Servings: 4
Cooking Time: 25 Minutes
Ingredients:
- 1 pound ground lamb
- ¼ red onion, minced
- ¼ cup mint, minced
- ¼ cup parsley, minced
- 2 cloves garlic, minced
- ½ teaspoon salt
- ⅛ teaspoon rosemary
- ½ teaspoon black pepper
- 4 slices pita bread
- ¾ cup hummus
- 1 cup romaine lettuce, shredded
- ½ onion sliced
- 1 Roma tomato, diced
- ½ cucumber, skinned and thinly sliced
- 12 mint leaves, minced
- Tzatziki sauce, to taste

Directions:
1. Mix ground lamb, red onion, mint, parsley, garlic, salt, rosemary, and black pepper until fully incorporated.
2. Select the Broil function on the COSORI Air Fryer Toaster Oven, set time to 25 minutes and temperature to 450°F, then press Start/Cancel to preheat.
3. Line the food tray with parchment paper and place ground lamb on top, shaping it into a patty 1-inch-thick and 6 inches in diameter.
4. Insert the food tray at top position in the preheated air fryer toaster oven, then press Start/Cancel.
5. Remove when done and cut into thin slices.

6. Assemble each gyro starting with pita bread, then hummus, lamb meat, lettuce, onion, tomato, cucumber, and mint leaves, then drizzle with tzatziki.
7. Serve immediately.
- **Nutrition Info:** Calories: 409 kcal Total Fat: 14.6 g Saturated Fat: 0 g Cholesterol: 0 mg Sodium: 0 mg Total Carbs: 29.9 g Fiber: 0 g Sugar: 0 g Protein: 39.4 g

183. Ranch Chicken Wings

Servings: 3
Cooking Time: 10 Minutes
Ingredients:
- 1/4 cup almond meal
- 1/4 cup flaxseed meal
- 2 tablespoons butter, melted
- 6 tablespoons parmesan cheese, preferably freshly grated
- 1 tablespoon Ranch seasoning mix
- 2 tablespoons oyster sauce
- 6 chicken wings, bone-in

Directions:
1. Start by preheating your Air Fryer to 370 degrees F.
2. In a resealable bag, place the almond meal, flaxseed meal, butter, parmesan, Ranch seasoning mix, andoyster sauce. Add the chicken wings and shake to coat on all sides.
3. Arrange the chicken wings in the Air Fryer basket. Spritz the chicken wings with a nonstick cooking spray.
4. Cook for 11 minutes. Turn them over and cook an additional 11 minutes. Serve warm with your favorite dipping sauce, if desired. Enjoy!
- **Nutrition Info:** 285 Calories; 22g Fat; 3g Carbs; 12g Protein; 5g Sugars; 6g Fiber

184. Moroccan Pork Kebabs

Servings: 4
Cooking Time: 45 Minutes
Ingredients:
- 1/4 cup orange juice
- 1 tablespoon tomato paste
- 1 clove chopped garlic
- 1 tablespoon ground cumin
- 1/8 teaspoon ground cinnamon
- 4 tablespoons olive oil
- 1-1/2 teaspoons salt
- 3/4 teaspoon black pepper
- 1-1/2 pounds boneless pork loin
- 1 small eggplant
- 1 small red onion
- Pita bread (optional)
- 1/2 small cucumber
- 2 tablespoons chopped fresh mint
- Wooden skewers

Directions:
1. Start by placing wooden skewers in water to soak.
2. Cut pork loin and eggplant into 1- to 1-1/2-inch chunks.
3. Preheat toaster oven to 425°F.
4. Cut cucumber and onions into pieces and chop the mint.
5. In a large bowl, combine the orange juice, tomato paste, garlic, cumin, cinnamon, 2 tablespoons of oil, 1 teaspoon of salt, and 1/2 teaspoon of pepper.
6. Add the pork to this mixture and refrigerate for at least 30 minutes, but up to 8 hours.
7. Mix together vegetables, remaining oil, and salt and pepper.
8. Skewer the vegetables and bake for 20 minutes.
9. Add the pork to the skewers and bake for an additional 25 minutes.
10. Remove ingredients from skewers and sprinkle with mint; serve with flatbread if using.
- **Nutrition Info:** Calories: 465, Sodium: 1061 mg, Dietary Fiber: 5.6 g, Total Fat: 20.8 g, Total Carbs: 21.9 g, Protein: 48.2 g.

185. Turkey Meatballs With Manchego Cheese

Servings: 4
Cooking Time: 10 Minutes
Ingredients:
- 1 pound ground turkey
- 1/2 pound ground pork
- 1 egg, well beaten
- 1 teaspoon dried basil
- 1 teaspoon dried rosemary
- 1/4 cup Manchego cheese, grated
- 2 tablespoons yellow onions, finely chopped
- 1 teaspoon fresh garlic, finely chopped
- Sea salt and ground black pepper, to taste

Directions:
1. In a mixing bowl, combine all the ingredients until everything is well incorporated.
2. Shape the mixture into 1-inch balls.
3. Cook the meatballs in the preheated Air Fryer at 380 degrees for 7 minutes. Shake halfway through the cooking time. Work in batches.
4. Serve with your favorite pasta.
- **Nutrition Info:** 386 Calories; 24g Fat; 9g Carbs; 41g Protein; 3g Sugars; 2g Fiber

186. Okra Casserole

Servings: 4
Cooking Time: 12 Minutes
Ingredients:
- 2 red bell peppers; cubed

- 2 tomatoes; chopped.
- 3 garlic cloves; minced
- 3 cups okra
- ½ cup cheddar; shredded
- ¼ cup tomato puree
- 1 tbsp. cilantro; chopped.
- 1 tsp. olive oil
- 2 tsp. coriander, ground
- Salt and black pepper to taste.

Directions:

1. Grease a heat proof dish that fits your air fryer with the oil, add all the ingredients except the cilantro and the cheese and toss them really gently
2. Sprinkle the cheese and the cilantro on top, introduce the dish in the fryer and cook at 390°F for 20 minutes.
3. Divide between plates and serve for lunch.
- **Nutrition Info:** Calories: 221; Fat: 7g; Fiber: 2g; Carbs: 4g; Protein: 9g

DINNER RECIPES

187.   Summer Fish Packets

Servings: 2
Cooking Time: 20 Minutes
Ingredients:
- 2 snapper fillets
- 1 shallot, peeled and sliced
- 2 garlic cloves, halved
- 1 bell pepper, sliced
- 1 small-sized serrano pepper, sliced
- 1 tomato, sliced
- 1 tablespoon olive oil
- 1/4 teaspoon freshly ground black pepper
- 1/2 teaspoon paprika
- Sea salt, to taste
- 2 bay leaves

Directions:
1. Place two parchment sheets on a working surface. Place the fish in the center of one side of the parchment paper.
2. Top with the shallot, garlic, peppers, and tomato. Drizzle olive oil over the fish and vegetables. Season with black pepper, paprika, and salt. Add the bay leaves.
3. Fold over the other half of the parchment. Now, fold the paper around the edges tightly and create a half moon shape, sealing the fish inside.
4. Cook in the preheated Air Fryer at 390 degrees F for 15 minutes. Serve warm.
- **Nutrition Info:** 329 Calories; 8g Fat; 17g Carbs; 47g Protein; 4g Sugars; 8g Fiber

188.   Ham Rolls

Servings: 4
Cooking Time: 15 Minutes
Ingredients:
- 12-ounce refrigerated pizza crust, rolled into ¼ inch thickness
- 1/3 pound cooked ham, sliced
- ¾ cup Mozzarella cheese, shredded
- 3 cups Colby cheese, shredded
- 3-ounce roasted red bell peppers
- 1 tablespoon olive oil

Directions:
1. Preheat the Air fryer to 360 degree F and grease an Air fryer basket.
2. Arrange the ham, cheeses and roasted peppers over one side of dough and fold to seal.
3. Brush the dough evenly with olive oil and cook for about 15 minutes, flipping twice in between.
4. Dish out in a platter and serve warm.
- **Nutrition Info:** Calories: 594, Fat: 35.8g, Carbohydrates: 35.4g, Sugar: 2.8g, Protein: 33g, Sodium: 1545mg

189.   Homemade Pork Ratatouille

Servings: 4
Cooking Time: 25 Minutes
Ingredients:
- 4 pork sausages
- For ratatouille
- 1 pepper, chopped
- 2 zucchinis, chopped
- 1 eggplant, chopped
- 1 medium red onion, chopped
- 1 tbsp olive oil
- 1-ounce butterbean, drained
- 15 oz tomatoes, chopped
- 2 sprigs fresh thyme
- 1 tbsp balsamic vinegar
- 2 garlic cloves, minced
- 1 red chili, chopped

Directions:
1. Preheat your air fryer to 392 f. Mix pepper, eggplant, oil, onion, zucchinis, and add to the cooking basket. Roast for 20 minutes. Set aside to cool. Reduce air fryer temperature to 356 f. In a saucepan, mix prepared vegetables and the remaining ratatouille ingredients, and bring to a boil over medium heat.
2. Let the mixture simmer for 10 minutes; season with salt and pepper. Add sausages to your air fryer's basket and cook for 10-15 minutes. Serve the sausages with ratatouille.
- **Nutrition Info:** Calories: 232.3 Cal Total Fat: 11.5 g Saturated Fat: 4.0 g Cholesterol: 58.2 mg Sodium: 611 mg Total Carbs: 9.2 g Fiber: 1.7 g Sugar: 4.4 g Protein: 23.1 g

190.   Chicken Lasagna With Eggplants

Servings: 10
Cooking Time: 17 Minutes
Ingredients:
- 6 oz Cheddar cheese, shredded
- 7 oz Parmesan cheese, shredded
- 2 eggplants
- 1-pound ground chicken
- 1 teaspoon paprika
- 1 teaspoon salt
- ½ teaspoon cayenne pepper
- ½ cup heavy cream
- 2 teaspoon butter
- 4 oz chive stems, diced

Directions:
1. Take the air fryer basket tray and spread it with the butter.
2. Then peel the eggplants and slice them.
3. Separate the sliced eggplants into 3 parts.

4. Combine the ground chicken with the paprika, salt, cayenne pepper, and diced chives.
5. Mix the mixture up.
6. Separate the ground chicken mixture into 2 parts.
7. Make the layer of the first part of the sliced eggplant in the air fryer basket tray.
8. Then make the layer of the ground chicken mixture.
9. After this, sprinkle the ground chicken layer with the half of the shredded Cheddar cheese,
10. Then cover the cheese with the second part of the sliced eggplant.
11. The next step is to make the layer of the ground chicken and all shredded Cheddar cheese,
12. Cover the cheese layer with the last part of the sliced eggplants.
13. Then sprinkle the eggplants with shredded Parmesan cheese.
14. Pour the heavy cream and add butter.
15. Preheat the air fryer to 365 F.
16. Cook the lasagna for 17 minutes.
17. When the time is over – let the lasagna chill gently.
18. Serve it!
- **Nutrition Info:** calories 291, fat 17.6, fiber 4.6, carbs 7.8, protein 27.4

191. Veggie Stuffed Bell Peppers

Servings: 6
Cooking Time: 25 Minutes
Ingredients:
- 6 large bell peppers, tops and seeds removed
- 1 carrot, peeled and finely chopped
- 1 potato, peeled and finely chopped
- ½ cup fresh peas, shelled
- 1/3 cup cheddar cheese, grated
- 2 garlic cloves, minced
- Salt and black pepper, to taste

Directions:
1. Preheat the Air fryer to 350 ºF and grease an Air fryer basket.
2. Mix vegetables, garlic, salt and black pepper in a bowl.
3. Stuff the vegetable mixture in each bell pepper and arrange in the Air fryer pan.
4. Cook for about 20 minutes and top with cheddar cheese.
5. Cook for about 5 more minutes and dish out to serve warm.
- **Nutrition Info:** Calories: 101, Fat: 2.5g, Carbohydrates: 17.1g, Sugar: 7.4g, Protein: 4.1g, Sodium: 51mg

192. Creole Beef Meatloaf

Servings: 6
Cooking Time: 15 Minutes
Ingredients:
- 1 lb. ground beef
- 1/2 tablespoon butter
- 1 red bell pepper diced
- 1/3 cup red onion diced
- 1/3 cup cilantro diced
- 1/3 cup zucchini diced
- 1 tablespoon creole seasoning
- 1/2 teaspoon turmeric
- 1/2 teaspoon cumin
- 1/2 teaspoon coriander
- 2 garlic cloves minced
- Salt and black pepper to taste

Directions:
1. Mix the beef minced with all the meatball ingredients in a bowl.
2. Make small meatballs out of this mixture and place them in the Air fryer basket.
3. Press "Power Button" of Air Fry Oven and turn the dial to select the "Air Fry" mode.
4. Press the Time button and again turn the dial to set the cooking time to 15 minutes.
5. Now push the Temp button and rotate the dial to set the temperature at 370 degrees F.
6. Once preheated, place the Air fryer basket in the oven and close its lid.
7. Slice and serve warm.
- **Nutrition Info:** Calories: 331 Cal Total Fat: 2.5 g Saturated Fat: 0.5 g Cholesterol: 35 mg Sodium: 595 mg Total Carbs: 69 g Fiber: 12.2 g Sugar: 12.5 g Protein: 26.7 g

193. Curried Eggplant

Servings: 2
Cooking Time: 10 Minutes
Ingredients:
- 1 large eggplant, cut into ½-inch thick slices
- 1 garlic clove, minced
- ½ fresh red chili, chopped
- 1 tablespoon vegetable oil
- ¼ teaspoon curry powder
- Salt, to taste

Directions:
1. Preheat the Air fryer to 300 degree F and grease an Air fryer basket.
2. Mix all the ingredients in a bowl and toss to coat well.
3. Arrange the eggplant slices in the Air fryer basket and cook for about 10 minutes, tossing once in between.
4. Dish out onto serving plates and serve hot.
- **Nutrition Info:** Calories: 121, Fat: 7.3g, Carbohydrates: 14.2g, Sugar: 7g, Protein: 2.4g, Sodium: 83mg

194. One-pan Shrimp And Chorizo Mix Grill

Servings: 4
Cooking Time: 15 Minutes
Ingredients:
- 1 ½ pounds large shrimps, peeled and deveined
- Salt and pepper to taste
- 6 links fresh chorizo sausage
- 2 bunches asparagus spears, trimmed
- Lime wedges

Directions:
1. Place the instant pot air fryer lid on and preheat the instant pot at 390 degrees F.
2. Place the grill pan accessory in the instant pot.
3. Season the shrimps with salt and pepper to taste. Set aside.
4. Place the chorizo on the grill pan and the sausage.
5. Place the asparagus on top.
6. Close the air fryer lid and grill for 15 minutes.
7. Serve with lime wedges.
- **Nutrition Info:** Calories:124 ; Carbs: 9.4g; Protein: 8.2g; Fat: 7.1g

195. Pollock With Kalamata Olives And Capers

Servings: 3
Cooking Time: 20 Minutes
Ingredients:
- 2 tablespoons olive oil
- 1 red onion, sliced
- 2 cloves garlic, chopped
- 1 Florina pepper, deveined and minced
- 3 pollock fillets,skinless
- 2 ripe tomatoes, diced
- 12 Kalamata olives, pitted and chopped
- 2 tablespoons capers
- 1 teaspoon oregano
- 1 teaspoon rosemary
- Sea salt, to taste
- 1/2 cup white wine

Directions:
1. Start by preheating your Air Fryer to 360 degrees F. Heat the oil in a baking pan. Once hot, sauté the onion, garlic, and pepper for 2 to 3 minutes or until fragrant.
2. Add the fish fillets to the baking pan. Top with the tomatoes, olives, and capers. Sprinkle with the oregano, rosemary, and salt. Pour in white wine and transfer to the cooking basket.
3. Turn the temperature to 395 degrees F and bake for 10 minutes. Taste for seasoning and serve on individual plates, garnished

with some extra Mediterranean herbs if desired. Enjoy!
- **Nutrition Info:** 480 Calories; 37g Fat; 9g Carbs; 49g Protein; 5g Sugars; 2g Fiber

196. Cheesy Shrimp

Servings: 4
Cooking Time: 20 Minutes
Ingredients:
- 2/3 cup Parmesan cheese, grated
- 2 pounds shrimp, peeled and deveined
- 4 garlic cloves, minced
- 2 tablespoons olive oil
- 1 teaspoon dried basil
- ½ teaspoon dried oregano
- 1 teaspoon onion powder
- ½ teaspoon red pepper flakes, crushed
- Ground black pepper, as required
- 2 tablespoons fresh lemon juice

Directions:
1. Preheat the Air fryer to 350 degree F and grease an Air fryer basket.
2. Mix Parmesan cheese, garlic, olive oil, herbs, and spices in a large bowl.
3. Arrange half of the shrimp into the Air fryer basket in a single layer and cook for about 10 minutes.
4. Dish out the shrimps onto serving plates and drizzle with lemon juice to serve hot.
- **Nutrition Info:** Calories: 386, Fat: 14.2g, Carbohydrates: 5.3g, Sugar: 0.4g, Protein: 57.3g, Sodium: 670mg

197. Rice Flour Coated Shrimp

Servings: 3
Cooking Time: 20 Minutes
Ingredients:
- 3 tablespoons rice flour
- 1 pound shrimp, peeled and deveined
- 2 tablespoons olive oil
- 1 teaspoon powdered sugar
- Salt and black pepper, as required

Directions:
1. Preheat the Air fryer to 325 ºF and grease an Air fryer basket.
2. Mix rice flour, olive oil, sugar, salt, and black pepper in a bowl.
3. Stir in the shrimp and transfer half of the shrimp to the Air fryer basket.
4. Cook for about 10 minutes, flipping once in between.
5. Dish out the mixture onto serving plates and repeat with the remaining mixture.
- **Nutrition Info:** Calories: 299, Fat: 12g, Carbohydrates: 11.1g, Sugar: 0.8g, Protein: 35g, Sodium: 419mg

198. Cheese Zucchini Boats

Servings: 2

Cooking Time: 20 Minutes
Ingredients:
- 2 medium zucchinis
- ¼ cup full-fat ricotta cheese
- ¼ cup shredded mozzarella cheese
- ¼ cup low-carb, no-sugar-added pasta sauce.
- 2 tbsp. grated vegetarian Parmesan cheese
- 1 tbsp. avocado oil
- ¼ tsp. garlic powder.
- ½ tsp. dried parsley.
- ¼ tsp. dried oregano.

Directions:
1. Cut off 1-inch from the top and bottom of each zucchini.
2. Slice zucchini in half lengthwise and use a spoon to scoop out a bit of the inside, making room for filling. Brush with oil and spoon 2 tbsp. pasta sauce into each shell
3. Take a medium bowl, mix ricotta, mozzarella, oregano, garlic powder and parsley
4. Spoon the mixture into each zucchini shell. Place stuffed zucchini shells into the air fryer basket.
5. Adjust the temperature to 350 Degrees F and set the timer for 20 minutes
6. To remove from the fryer basket, use tongs or a spatula and carefully lift out. Top with Parmesan. Serve immediately.
- **Nutrition Info:** Calories: 215; Protein: 15g; Fiber: 7g; Fat: 19g; Carbs: 3g

199. Buttered Scallops

Servings: 2
Cooking Time: 4 Minutes
Ingredients:
- ¾ pound sea scallops, cleaned and patted very dry
- 1 tablespoon butter, melted
- ½ tablespoon fresh thyme, minced
- Salt and black pepper, as required

Directions:
1. Preheat the Air fryer to 390 degree F and grease an Air fryer basket.
2. Mix scallops, butter, thyme, salt, and black pepper in a bowl.
3. Arrange scallops in the Air fryer basket and cook for about 4 minutes.
4. Dish out the scallops in a platter and serve hot.
- **Nutrition Info:** Calories: 202, Fat: 7.1g, Carbohydrates: 4.4g, Sugar: 0g, Protein: 28.7g, Sodium: 393mg

200. Fish Cakes With Horseradish Sauce

Servings: 4
Cooking Time: 20 Minutes

Ingredients:
- Halibut Cakes:
- 1 pound halibut
- 2 tablespoons olive oil
- 1/2 teaspoon cayenne pepper
- 1/4 teaspoon black pepper
- Salt, to taste
- 2 tablespoons cilantro, chopped
- 1 shallot, chopped
- 2 garlic cloves, minced
- 1 cup Romano cheese, grated
- 1 egg, whisked
- 1 tablespoon Worcestershire sauce
- Mayo Sauce:
- 1 teaspoon horseradish, grated
- 1/2 cup mayonnaise

Directions:
1. Start by preheating your Air Fryer to 380 degrees F. Spritz the Air Fryer basket with cooking oil.
2. Mix all ingredients for the halibut cakes in a bowl; knead with your hands until everything is well incorporated.
3. Shape the mixture into equally sized patties. Transfer your patties to the Air Fryer basket. Cook the fish patties for 10 minutes, turning them over halfway through.
4. Mix the horseradish and mayonnaise. Serve the halibut cakes with the horseradish mayo.
- **Nutrition Info:** 532 Calories; 32g Fat; 3g Carbs; 28g Protein; 3g Sugars; 6g Fiber

201. Cheese And Garlic Stuffed Chicken Breasts

Servings: 2
Cooking Time: 20 Minutes
Ingredients:
- 1/2 cup Cottage cheese 2 eggs, beaten
- 2 medium-sized chicken breasts, halved
- 2 tablespoons fresh coriander, chopped 1tsp. fine sea salt
- Seasoned breadcrumbs
- 1/3 tsp. freshly ground black pepper, to savor 3 cloves garlic, finely minced

Directions:
1. Firstly, flatten out the chicken breast using a meat tenderizer.
2. In a medium-sized mixing dish, combine the Cottage cheese with the garlic, coriander, salt, and black pepper.
3. Spread 1/3 of the mixture over the first chicken breast. Repeat with the remaining ingredients. Roll the chicken around the filling; make sure to secure with toothpicks.
4. Now, whisk the egg in a shallow bowl. In another shallow bowl, combine the salt,

ground black pepper, and seasoned breadcrumbs.

5. Coat the chicken breasts with the whisked egg; now, roll them in the breadcrumbs.
6. Cook in the air fryer cooking basket at 365 °F for 22 minutes. Serve immediately.
- **Nutrition Info:** 424 Calories; 24.5g Fat; 7.5g Carbs; 43.4g Protein; 5.3g Sugars

202. Easy Marinated London Broil

Servings: 4
Cooking Time: 20 Minutes
Ingredients:
- For the marinade:
- 2 tablespoons Worcestershire sauce
- 2 garlic cloves, minced
- 1 tablespoon oil
- 2 tablespoons rice vinegar
- London Broil:
- 2 pounds London broil
- 2 tablespoons tomato paste
- Sea salt and cracked black pepper, to taste
- 1 tablespoon mustard

Directions:
1. Combine all the marinade ingredients in a mixing bowl; add the London boil to the bowl. Cover and let it marinate for 3 hours.
2. Preheat the Air Fryer to 400 degrees F. Spritz the Air Fryer grill pan with cooking oil.
3. Grill the marinated London broil in the preheated Air Fryer for 18 minutes. Turn London broil over, top with the tomato paste, salt, black pepper, and mustard.
4. Continue to grill an additional 10 minutes. Serve immediately.
- **Nutrition Info:** 517 Calories; 21g Fat; 5g Carbs; 70g Protein; 4g Sugars; 7g Fiber

203. Zucchini Muffins

Servings: 8
Cooking Time: 20 Minutes
Ingredients:
- 6 eggs
- 4 drops stevia 1/4 cup Swerve
- 1/3 cup coconut oil, melted 1 cup zucchini, grated
- 3/4 cup coconut flour 1/4 tsp ground nutmeg 1 tsp ground cinnamon 1/2 tsp baking soda

Directions:
1. Preheat the air fryer to 325 F.
2. Add all ingredients except zucchini in a bowl and mix well.
3. Add zucchini and stir well.
4. Pour batter into the silicone muffin molds and place into the air fryer basket.
5. Cook muffins for 20 minutes.
6. Serve and enjoy.

- **Nutrition Info:** Calories 136 Fat 12 g Carbohydrates 1 g Sugar 0.6 g Protein 4 g Cholesterol 123 mg

204. Adobe Turkey Chimichangas

Servings: 4
Cooking Time: 15 Minutes
Ingredients:
- 1 pound thickly-sliced smoked turkey from deli counter, chopped
- 1 tablespoon chili powder
- 2 cups shredded slaw cabbage
- 1 to 2 chipotles in adobo sauce
- 1 cup tomato sauce
- 3 chopped scallions
- Salt and pepper
- 4 (12-inch) flour tortillas
- 1-1/2 cups pepper jack cheese
- 2 tablespoons olive oil
- 1 cup sour cream
- 2 tablespoons chopped cilantro

Directions:
1. Start by preheating toaster oven to 400°F.
2. In a medium bowl mix together turkey and chili powder.
3. Add cabbage, chipotles, tomato sauce, and scallions; mix well.
4. Season cabbage mixture with salt and pepper and turn a few times.
5. Warm tortillas in a microwave or on a stove top.
6. Lay cheese flat in each tortilla and top with turkey mixture.
7. Fold in the top and bottom of the tortilla, then roll to close.
8. Brush baking tray with oil, then place chimichangas on tray and brush with oil.
9. Bake for 15 minutes or until tortilla is golden brown.
10. Top with sour cream and cilantro and serve.
- **Nutrition Info:** Calories: 638, Sodium: 1785 mg, Dietary Fiber: 4.2 g, Total Fat: 44.0 g, Total Carbs: 23.9 g, Protein: 38.4 g.

205. Herbed Carrots

Servings: 8
Cooking Time: 14 Minutes
Ingredients:
- 6 large carrots, peeled and sliced lengthwise
- 2 tablespoons olive oil
- ½ tablespoon fresh oregano, chopped
- ½ tablespoon fresh parsley, chopped
- Salt and black pepper, to taste
- 2 tablespoons olive oil, divided
- ½ cup fat-free Italian dressing
- Salt, to taste

Directions:
1. Preheat the Air fryer to 360-degree F and grease an Air fryer basket.

2. Mix the carrot slices and olive oil in a bowl and toss to coat well.
3. Arrange the carrot slices in the Air fryer basket and cook for about 12 minutes.
4. Dish out the carrot slices onto serving plates and sprinkle with herbs, salt and black pepper.
5. Transfer into the Air fryer basket and cook for 2 more minutes.
6. Dish out and serve hot.
- **Nutrition Info:** Calories: 93, Fat: 7.2g, Carbohydrates: 7.3g, Sugar: 3.8g, Protein: 0.7g, Sodium: 252mg

206. Cod With Avocado Mayo Sauce

Servings: 2
Cooking Time: 20 Minutes
Ingredients:
- 2 cod fish fillets
- 1 egg
- Sea salt, to taste
- 2 teaspoons olive oil
- 1/2 avocado, peeled, pitted, and mashed
- 1 tablespoon mayonnaise
- 3 tablespoons sour cream
- 1/2 teaspoon yellow mustard
- 1 teaspoon lemon juice
- 1 garlic clove, minced
- 1/4 teaspoon black pepper
- 1/4 teaspoon salt
- 1/4 teaspoon hot pepper sauce

Directions:
1. Start by preheating your Air Fryer to 360 degrees F. Spritz the Air Fryer basket with cooking oil.
2. Pat dry the fish fillets with a kitchen towel. Beat the egg in a shallow bowl. Add in the salt and olive oil.
3. Dip the fish into the egg mixture, making sure to coat thoroughly. Cook in the preheated Air Fryer approximately 12 minutes.
4. Meanwhile, make the avocado sauce by mixing the remaining ingredients in a bowl. Place in your refrigerator until ready to serve.
5. Serve the fish fillets with chilled avocado sauce on the side.
- **Nutrition Info:** 344 Calories; 27g Fat; 8g Carbs; 21g Protein; 8g Sugars; 7g Fiber

207. Broccoli With Olives

Servings: 4
Cooking Time: 19 Minutes
Ingredients:
- 2 pounds broccoli, stemmed and cut into 1-inch florets
- 1/3 cup Kalamata olives, halved and pitted
- ¼ cup Parmesan cheese, grated
- 2 tablespoons olive oil
- Salt and ground black pepper, as required
- 2 teaspoons fresh lemon zest, grated

Directions:
1. Preheat the Air fryer to 400 ºF and grease an Air fryer basket.
2. Boil the broccoli for about 4 minutes and drain well.
3. Mix broccoli, oil, salt, and black pepper in a bowl and toss to coat well.
4. Arrange broccoli into the Air fryer basket and cook for about 15 minutes.
5. Stir in the olives, lemon zest and cheese and dish out to serve.
- **Nutrition Info:** Calories: 169, Fat: 10.2g, Carbohydrates: 16g, Sugar: 3.9g, Protein: 8.5g, Sodium: 254mg

208. Tomato Stuffed Pork Roll

Servings: 4
Cooking Time: 15 Minutes
Ingredients:
- 1 scallion, chopped
- ¼ cup sun-dried tomatoes, chopped finely
- 2 tablespoons fresh parsley, chopped
- 4: 6-ouncepork cutlets, pounded slightly
- Salt and freshly ground black pepper, to taste
- 2 teaspoons paprika
- ½ tablespoon olive oil

Directions:
1. Preheat the Air fryer to 390 degree F and grease an Air fryer basket.
2. Mix scallion, tomatoes, parsley, salt and black pepper in a bowl.
3. Coat each cutlet with tomato mixture and roll up the cutlet, securing with cocktail sticks.
4. Coat the rolls with oil and rub with paprika, salt and black pepper.
5. Arrange the rolls in the Air fryer basket and cook for about 15 minutes, flipping once in between.
6. Dish out in a platter and serve warm.
- **Nutrition Info:** Calories: 244, Fat: 14.5g, Carbohydrates: 20.1g, Sugar: 1.7g, Protein: 8.2g, Sodium: 670mg

209. Sesame Seeds Bok Choy

Servings: 4
Cooking Time: 6 Minutes
Ingredients:
- 4 bunches baby bok choy, bottoms removed and leaves separated
- 1 teaspoon sesame seeds
- Olive oil cooking spray
- 1 teaspoon garlic powder

Directions:

1. Preheat the Air fryer to 325 ºF and grease an Air fryer basket.
2. Arrange the bok choy leaves into the Air fryer basket and spray with the cooking spray.
3. Sprinkle with garlic powder and cook for about 6 minutes, shaking twice in between.
4. Dish out in the bok choy onto serving plates and serve garnished with sesame seeds.
- **Nutrition Info:** Calories: 26, Fat: 0.7g, Carbohydrates: 4g, Sugar: 1.9g, Protein: 2.5g, Sodium: 98mg

210. Lemony Green Beans

Servings: 3
Cooking Time: 12 Minutes
Ingredients:
- 1 pound green beans, trimmed and halved
- 1 teaspoon butter, melted
- 1 tablespoon fresh lemon juice
- ¼ teaspoon garlic powder

Directions:
1. Preheat the Air fryer to 400 ºF and grease an Air fryer basket.
2. Mix all the ingredients in a bowl and toss to coat well.
3. Arrange the green beans into the Air fryer basket and cook for about 12 minutes.
4. Dish out in a serving plate and serve hot.
- **Nutrition Info:** Calories: 60, Fat: 1.5g, Carbohydrates: 11.1g, Sugar: 2.3g, Protein: 2.8g, Sodium: 70mg

211. Shrimp Scampi

Servings: 6
Cooking Time: 7 Minutes
Ingredients:
- 4 tablespoons salted butter
- 1 pound shrimp, peeled and deveined
- 2 tablespoons fresh basil, chopped
- 1 tablespoon fresh chives, chopped
- 1 tablespoon fresh lemon juice
- 1 tablespoon garlic, minced
- 2 teaspoons red pepper flakes, crushed
- 2 tablespoons dry white wine

Directions:
1. Preheat the Air fryer to 325 ºF and grease an Air fryer pan.
2. Heat butter, lemon juice, garlic, and red pepper flakes in a pan and return the pan to Air fryer basket.
3. Cook for about 2 minutes and stir in shrimp, basil, chives and wine.
4. Cook for about 5 minutes and dish out the mixture onto serving plates.
5. Serve hot.
- **Nutrition Info:** Calories: 250, Fat: 13.7g, Carbohydrates: 3.3g, Sugar: 0.3g, Protein: 26.3g, Sodium: 360mg

212. Marinated Cajun Beef

Servings: 2
Cooking Time: 20 Minutes
Ingredients:
- 1/3 cup beef broth
- 2 tablespoons Cajun seasoning, crushed
- 1/2 teaspoon garlic powder
- 3/4 pound beef tenderloins
- ½ tablespoon pear cider vinegar
- 1/3 teaspoon cayenne pepper
- 1 ½ tablespoon olive oil
- 1/2 teaspoon freshly ground black pepper
- 1 teaspoon salt

Directions:
1. Firstly, coat the beef tenderloins with salt, cayenne pepper, and black pepper.
2. Mix the remaining items in a medium-sized bowl; let the meat marinate for 40 minutes in this mixture.
3. Roast the beef for about 22 minutes at 385 degrees F, turning it halfway through the cooking time.
- **Nutrition Info:** 483 Calories; 23g Fat; 5g Carbs; 53g Protein; 6g Sugars; 4g Fiber

213. Easy Air Fryed Roasted Asparagus

Servings: 4
Cooking Time: 10 Minutes
Ingredients:
- 1 bunch fresh asparagus
- 1 ½ tsp herbs de provence
- Fresh lemon wedge (optional)
- 1 tablespoon olive oil or cooking spray
- Salt and pepper to taste

Directions:
1. Wash asparagus and trim off hard ends
2. Drizzle asparagus with olive oil and add seasonings
3. Place asparagus in air fryer and cook on 360F for 6 to 10 minutes
4. Drizzle squeezed lemon over roasted asparagus.
- **Nutrition Info:** Calories 46 protein 2g fat 3g net carbs 1g

214. Portuguese Bacalao Tapas

Servings: 4
Cooking Time: 26 Minutes
Ingredients:
- 1-pound codfish fillet, chopped
- 2 Yukon Gold potatoes, peeled and diced
- 2 tablespoon butter
- 1 yellow onion, thinly sliced
- 1 clove garlic, chopped, divided
- 1/4 cup chopped fresh parsley, divided
- 1/4 cup olive oil
- 3/4 teaspoon red pepper flakes

- freshly ground black pepper to taste
- 2 hard-cooked eggs, chopped
- 5 pitted green olives
- 5 pitted black olives

Directions:
1. Place the instant pot air fryer lid on, lightly grease baking pan of the instant pot with cooking spray. Add butter and place the baking pan in the instant pot.
2. Close the air fryer lid and melt butter at 360 ºF. Stir in onions and cook for 6 minutes until caramelized.
3. Stir in black pepper, red pepper flakes, half of the parsley, garlic, olive oil, diced potatoes, and chopped fish. For 10 minutes, cook on 360 ºF. Halfway through cooking time, stir well to mix.
4. Cook for 10 minutes at 390 ºF until tops are lightly browned.
5. Garnish with remaining parsley, eggs, black and green olives.
6. Serve and enjoy with chips.
- **Nutrition Info:** Calories: 691; Carbs: 25.2g; Protein: 77.1g; Fat: 31.3g

215. Pork Chops With Chicory Treviso

Servings: 2
Cooking Time: 0-15;
Ingredients:
- 4 pork chops
- 40g butter
- Flour to taste
- 1 chicory stalk
- Salt to taste

Directions:
1. Cut the chicory into small pieces. Place the butter and chicory in pieces on the basket of the air fryer previously preheated at 1800C and brown for 2 min.
2. Add the previously floured and salted pork slices (directly over the chicory), simmer for 6 minutes turning them over after 3 minutes.
3. Remove the slices and place them on a serving plate, covering them with the rest of the red chicory juice collected at the bottom of the basket.
- **Nutrition Info:** Calories 504, Fat 33, Carbohydrates 0g, Sugars 0g, Protein 42g, Cholesterol 130mg

216. Christmas Filet Mignon Steak

Servings: 6
Cooking Time: 20 Minutes
Ingredients:
- 1/3 stick butter, at room temperature
- 1/2 cup heavy cream

- 1/2 medium-sized garlic bulb, peeled and pressed
- 6 filet mignon steaks
- 2 teaspoons mixed peppercorns, freshly cracked
- 1 ½ tablespoons apple cider
- A dash of hot sauce
- 1 ½ teaspoons sea salt flakes

Directions:
1. Season the mignon steaks with the cracked peppercorns and salt flakes. Roast the mignon steaks in the preheated Air Fryer for 24 minutes at 385 degrees F, turning once. Check for doneness and set aside, keeping it warm.
2. In a small nonstick saucepan that is placed over a moderate flame, mash the garlic to a smooth paste. Whisk in the rest of the above ingredients. Whisk constantly until it has a uniform consistency.
3. To finish, lay the filet mignon steaks on serving plates; spoon a little sauce onto each filet mignon.
- **Nutrition Info:** 452 Calories; 32g Fat; 8g Carbs; 26g Protein; 6g Sugars; 1g Fiber

217. Pork Chops With Keto Gravy

Servings: 4
Cooking Time: 17 Minutes
Ingredients:
- 1-pound pork chops
- 1 teaspoon kosher salt
- ½ teaspoon ground cinnamon
- 1 teaspoon ground white pepper
- 1 cup heavy cream
- 6 oz. white mushrooms
- 1 tablespoon butter
- ½ teaspoon ground ginger
- 1 teaspoon ground turmeric
- 4 oz chive stems
- 1 garlic clove, chopped

Directions:
1. Sprinkle the pork chops with the kosher salt, ground cinnamon, ground white pepper, and ground turmeric.
2. Preheat the air fryer to 375 F.
3. Pour the heavy cream in the air fryer basket tray.
4. Then slice the white mushrooms and add them in the heavy cream.
5. After this, add butter, ground ginger, chopped chives, and chopped garlic.
6. Cook the gravy for 5 minutes.
7. Then stir the cream gravy and add the pork chops.
8. Cook the pork chops at 400 F for 12 minutes.

9. When the time is over stir the pork chops gently and transfer them to the serving plates.
10. Enjoy!
- **Nutrition Info:** calories 518, fat 42.4, fiber 1.5, carbs 6.2, protein 28

218. Shrimp Casserole Louisiana Style

Servings: 2
Cooking Time: 35 Minutes
Ingredients:
- 3/4 cup uncooked instant rice
- 3/4 cup water
- 1/2 pound small shrimp, peeled and deveined
- 1 tablespoon butter
- 1/2 (4 ounces) can sliced mushrooms, drained
- 1/2 (8 ounces) container sour cream
- 1/3 cup shredded Cheddar cheese

Directions:
1. Place the instant pot air fryer lid on, lightly grease baking pan of the instant pot with cooking spray. Add rice, water, mushrooms, and butter. Cover with foil and place the baking pan in the instant pot.
2. Close the air fryer lid and cook at 360 ºF for 20 minutes.
3. Open foil cover, stir in shrimps, return foil and let it rest for 5 minutes.
4. Remove foil completely and stir in sour cream. Mix well and evenly spread rice. Top with cheese.
5. Cook for 7 minutes at 390 ºF until tops are lightly browned.
6. Serve and enjoy.
- **Nutrition Info:** Calories: 569; Carbs: 38.5g; Protein: 31.8g; Fat: 31.9g

219. Roasted Butternut Squash With Brussels Sprouts & Sweet Potato Noodles

Servings: 2
Cooking Time: 15 Minutes
Ingredients:
- Squash:
- 3 cups chopped butternut squash
- 2 teaspoons extra light olive oil
- 1/8 teaspoon sea salt
- Veggies:
- 5-6 Brussels sprouts
- 5 fresh shiitake mushrooms
- 2 cloves garlic
- 1/2 teaspoon black sesame seeds
- 1/2 teaspoon white sesame seeds
- A few sprinkles ground pepper
- A small pinch red pepper flakes

- 1 tablespoon extra light olive oil
- 1 teaspoon sesame oil
- 1 teaspoon onion powder
- 1 teaspoon garlic powder
- 1/4 teaspoon sea salt
- Noodles:
- 1 bundle sweet potato vermicelli
- 2-3 teaspoons low-sodium soy sauce

Directions:
1. Start by soaking potato vermicelli in water for at least 2 hours.
2. Preheat toaster oven to 375°F.
3. Place squash on a baking sheet with edges, then drizzle with olive oil and sprinkle with salt and pepper. Mix together well on pan.
4. Bake the squash for 30 minutes, mixing and flipping half way through.
5. Remove the stems from the mushrooms and chop the Brussels sprouts.
6. Chop garlic and mix the veggies.
7. Drizzle sesame and olive oil over the mixture, then add garlic powder, onion powder, sesame seeds, red pepper flakes, salt, and pepper.
8. Bake veggie mix for 15 minutes.
9. While the veggies bake, put noodles in a small sauce pan and add just enough water to cover.
10. Bring water to a rolling boil and boil noodles for about 8 minutes.
11. Drain noodles and combine with squash and veggies in a large bowl.
12. Drizzle with soy sauce, sprinkle with sesame seeds, and serve.
- **Nutrition Info:** Calories: 409, Sodium: 1124 mg, Dietary Fiber: 12.2 g, Total Fat: 15.6 g, Total Carbs: 69.3 g, Protein: 8.8 g.

220. Fried Spicy Tofu

Servings: 4
Cooking Time: 20 Minutes
Ingredients:
- 16 ounces firm tofu, pressed and cubed
- 1 tablespoon vegan oyster sauce
- 1 tablespoon tamari sauce
- 1 teaspoon cider vinegar
- 1 teaspoon pure maple syrup
- 1 teaspoon sriracha
- 1/2 teaspoon shallot powder
- 1/2 teaspoon porcini powder
- 1 teaspoon garlic powder
- 1 tablespoon sesame oil
- 2 tablespoons golden flaxseed meal

Directions:
1. Toss the tofu with the oyster sauce, tamari sauce, vinegar, maple syrup, sriracha, shallot powder, porcini powder, garlic powder, and sesame oil. Let it marinate for 30 minutes.

2. Toss the marinated tofu with the flaxseed meal.
3. Cook at 360 degrees F for 10 minutes; turn them over and cook for 12 minutes more.
- **Nutrition Info:** 173 Calories; 13g Fat; 5g Carbs; 12g Protein; 8g Sugars; 1g Fiber

221. Smoked Sausage And Bacon Shashlik

Servings: 4
Cooking Time: 20 Minutes
Ingredients:
- 1 pound smoked Polish beef sausage, sliced
- 1 tablespoon mustard
- 1 tablespoon olive oil
- 2 tablespoons Worcestershire sauce
- 2 bell peppers, sliced
- Salt and ground black pepper, to taste

Directions:
1. Toss the sausage with the mustard, olive, and Worcestershire sauce. Thread sausage and peppers onto skewers.
2. Sprinkle with salt and black pepper.
3. Cook in the preheated Air Fryer at 360 degrees Ffor 11 minutes. Brush the skewers with the reserved marinade.
- **Nutrition Info:** 422 Calories; 36g Fat; 9g Carbs; 18g Protein; 6g Sugars; 7g Fiber

222. Tasty Sausage Bacon Rolls

Servings: 4
Cooking Time: 1 Hour 44 Minutes
Ingredients:
- Sausage:
- 8 bacon strips
- 8 pork sausages
- Relish:
- 8 large tomatoes
- 1 clove garlic, peeled
- 1 small onion, peeled
- 3 tbsp chopped parsley
- A pinch of salt
- A pinch of pepper
- 2 tbsp sugar
- 1 tsp smoked paprika
- 1 tbsp white wine vinegar

Directions:
1. Start with the relish; add the tomatoes, garlic, and onion in a food processor. Blitz them for 10 seconds until the mixture is pulpy. Pour the pulp into a saucepan, add the vinegar, salt, pepper, and place it over medium heat.
2. Bring to simmer for 10 minutes; add the paprika and sugar. Stir with a spoon and simmer for 10 minutes until pulpy and thick. Turn off the heat, transfer the relish to a bowl and chill it for an hour. In 30 minutes

after putting the relish in the refrigerator, move on to the sausages. Wrap each sausage with a bacon strip neatly and stick in a bamboo skewer at the end of the sausage to secure the bacon ends.
3. Open the Air Fryer, place 3 to 4 wrapped sausages in the fryer basket and cook for 12 minutes at 350 F. Ensure that the bacon is golden and crispy before removing them. Repeat the cooking process for the remaining wrapped sausages. Remove the relish from the refrigerator. Serve the sausages and relish with turnip mash.
- **Nutrition Info:** 346 Calories; 11g Fat; 4g Carbs; 32g Protein; 1g Sugars; 1g Fiber

223. Vegetable Cane

Servings: 4
Cooking Time: More Than 60 Minutes;
Ingredients:
- 2 calf legs
- 4 carrots
- 4 medium potatoes
- 1 clove garlic
- 300ml Broth
- Leave to taste
- Pepper to taste

Directions:
1. Place the ears, garlic, and half of the broth in the greased basket.
2. Set the temperature to 1800C.
3. Cook the stems for 40 minutes, turning them in the middle of cooking.
4. Add the vegetables in pieces, salt, pepper, pour the rest of the broth and cook for another 50 minutes (time may vary depending on the size of the hocks).
5. Mix the vegetables and the ears 2 to 3 times during cooking.
- **Nutrition Info:** Calories 7.9, Fat 0.49g, Carbohydrate 0.77g, Sugar 0.49g, Protein 0.08mg, Cholesterol 0mg

224. Salsa Stuffed Eggplants

Servings: 2
Cooking Time: 25 Minutes
Ingredients:
- 1 large eggplant
- 8 cherry tomatoes, quartered
- ½ tablespoon fresh parsley
- 2 teaspoons olive oil, divided
- 2 teaspoons fresh lemon juice, divided
- 2 tablespoons tomato salsa
- Salt and black pepper, as required

Directions:
1. Preheat the Air fryer to 390 degree F and grease an Air fryer basket.
2. Arrange the eggplant into the Air fryer basket and cook for about 15 minutes.

3. Cut the eggplant in half lengthwise and drizzle evenly with one teaspoon of oil.
4. Set the Air fryer to 355 degree F and arrange the eggplant into the Air fryer basket, cut-side up.
5. Cook for another 10 minutes and dish out in a bowl.
6. Scoop out the flesh from the eggplant and transfer into a bowl.
7. Stir in the tomatoes, salsa, parsley, salt, black pepper, remaining oil, and lemon juice.
8. Squeeze lemon juice on the eggplant halves and stuff with the salsa mixture to serve.
- **Nutrition Info:** Calories: 192, Fat: 6.1g, Carbohydrates: 33.8g, Sugar: 20.4g, Protein: 6.9g, Sodium: 204mg

225. Garlic Lamb Shank

Servings: 5
Cooking Time: 24 Minutes
Ingredients:
- 17 oz. lamb shanks
- 2 tablespoon garlic, peeled
- 1 teaspoon kosher salt
- 1 tablespoon dried parsley
- 4 oz chive stems, chopped
- ½ cup chicken stock
- 1 teaspoon butter
- 1 teaspoon dried rosemary
- 1 teaspoon nutmeg
- ½ teaspoon ground black pepper

Directions:
1. Chop the garlic roughly.
2. Make the cuts in the lamb shank and fill the cuts with the chopped garlic.
3. Then sprinkle the lamb shank with the kosher salt, dried parsley, dried rosemary, nutmeg, and ground black pepper.
4. Stir the spices on the lamb shank gently.
5. Then put the butter and chicken stock in the air fryer basket tray.
6. Preheat the air fryer to 380 F.
7. Put the chives in the air fryer basket tray.
8. Add the lamb shank and cook the meat for 24 minutes.
9. When the lamb shank is cooked – transfer it to the serving plate and sprinkle with the remaining liquid from the cooked meat.
10. Enjoy!
- **Nutrition Info:** calories 205, fat 8.2, fiber 0.8, carbs 3.8, protein 27.2

226. Coconut Crusted Shrimp

Servings: 3
Cooking Time: 40 Minutes
Ingredients:
- 8 ounces coconut milk
- ½ cup sweetened coconut, shredded
- ½ cup panko breadcrumbs
- 1 pound large shrimp, peeled and deveined
- Salt and black pepper, to taste

Directions:
1. Preheat the Air fryer to 350-degree F and grease an Air fryer basket.
2. Place the coconut milk in a shallow bowl.
3. Mix coconut, breadcrumbs, salt, and black pepper in another bowl.
4. Dip each shrimp into coconut milk and finally, dredge in the coconut mixture.
5. Arrange half of the shrimps into the Air fryer basket and cook for about 20 minutes.
6. Dish out the shrimps onto serving plates and repeat with the remaining mixture to serve.
- **Nutrition Info:** Calories: 408, Fats: 23.7g, Carbohydrates: 11.7g, Sugar: 3.4g, Proteins: 31g, Sodium: 253mg

227. Salmon Casserole

Servings: 8
Cooking Time: 12 Minutes
Ingredients:
- 7 oz Cheddar cheese, shredded
- ½ cup cream
- 1-pound salmon fillet
- 1 tablespoon dried dill
- 1 teaspoon dried parsley
- 1 teaspoon salt
- 1 teaspoon ground coriander
- ½ teaspoon ground black pepper
- 2 green pepper, chopped
- 4 oz chive stems, diced
- 7 oz bok choy, chopped
- 1 tablespoon olive oil

Directions:
1. Sprinkle the salmon fillet with the dried dill, dried parsley, ground coriander, and ground black pepper.
2. Massage the salmon fillet gently and leave it for 5 minutes to make the fish soaks the spices.
3. Meanwhile, sprinkle the air fryer casserole tray with the olive oil inside.
4. After this, cut the salmon fillet into the cubes.
5. Separate the salmon cubes into 2 parts.
6. Then place the first part of the salmon cubes in the casserole tray.
7. Sprinkle the fish with the chopped bok choy, diced chives, and chopped green pepper.
8. After this, place the second part of the salmon cubes over the vegetables.
9. Then sprinkle the casserole with the shredded cheese and heavy cream.
10. Preheat the air fryer to 380 F.
11. Cook the salmon casserole for 12 minutes.
12. When the dish is cooked – it will have a crunchy light brown crust

13. Serve it and enjoy!
- **Nutrition Info:** calories 216, fat 14.4, fiber 1.1, carbs 4.3, protein 18.2

228. Asparagus Frittata

Servings: 4
Cooking Time: 10 Minutes
Ingredients:
- 6 eggs
- 3 mushrooms, sliced
- 10 asparagus, chopped 1/4 cup half and half
- 2 tsp butter, melted
- 1 cup mozzarella cheese, shredded 1 tsp pepper
- 1 tsp salt

Directions:
1. Toss mushrooms and asparagus with melted butter and add into the air fryer basket.
2. Cook mushrooms and asparagus at 350 F for 5 minutes. Shake basket twice.
3. Meanwhile, in a bowl, whisk together eggs, half and half, pepper, and salt.
4. Transfer cook mushrooms and asparagus into the air fryer baking dish.
5. Pour egg mixture over mushrooms and asparagus.
6. Place dish in the air fryer and cook at 350 F for 5 minutes or until eggs are set.
7. Slice and serve.
- **Nutrition Info:** Calories 211 Fat 13 g Carbohydrates 4 g Sugar 1 g Protein 16 g Cholesterol 272 mg

229. Red Hot Chili Fish Curry

Servings: 4
Cooking Time: 20 Minutes
Ingredients:
- 2 tablespoons sunflower oil
- 1 pound fish, chopped
- 2 red chilies, chopped
- 1 tablespoon coriander powder
- 1 teaspoon red curry paste
- 1 cup coconut milk
- Salt and white pepper, to taste
- 1/2 teaspoon fenugreek seeds
- 1 shallot, minced
- 1 garlic clove, minced
- 1 ripe tomato, pureed

Directions:
1. Preheat your Air Fryer to 380 degrees F; brush the cooking basket with 1 tablespoon of sunflower oil.
2. Cook your fish for 10 minutes on both sides. Transfer to the baking pan that is previously greased with the remaining tablespoon of sunflower oil.
3. Add the remaining ingredients and reduce the heat to 350 degrees F. Continue to cook

an additional 10 to 12 minutes or until everything is heated through. Enjoy!
- **Nutrition Info:** 298 Calories; 18g Fat; 4g Carbs; 23g Protein; 7g Sugars; 7g Fiber

230. Lamb Skewers

Servings: 4
Cooking Time: 20 Minutes
Ingredients:
- 2 lb. lamb meat; cubed
- 2 red bell peppers; cut into medium pieces
- ¼ cup olive oil
- 2 tbsp. lemon juice
- 1 tbsp. oregano; dried
- 1 tbsp. red vinegar
- 1 tbsp. garlic; minced
- ½ tsp. rosemary; dried
- A pinch of salt and black pepper

Directions:
1. Take a bowl and mix all the ingredients and toss them well.
2. Thread the lamb and bell peppers on skewers, place them in your air fryer's basket and cook at 380°F for 10 minutes on each side. Divide between plates and serve with a side salad
- **Nutrition Info:** Calories: 274; Fat: 12g; Fiber: 3g; Carbs: 6g; Protein: 16g

231. Rich Meatloaf With Mustard And Peppers

Servings: 5
Cooking Time: 20 Minutes
Ingredients:
- 1 pound beef, ground
- 1/2 pound veal, ground
- 1 egg
- 4 tablespoons vegetable juice
- 1/2 cup pork rinds
- 2 bell peppers, chopped
- 1 onion, chopped
- 2 garlic cloves, minced
- 2 tablespoons tomato paste
- 2 tablespoons soy sauce
- 1 (1-ouncepackage ranch dressing mix
- Sea salt, to taste
- 1/2 teaspoon ground black pepper, to taste
- 7 ounces tomato puree
- 1 tablespoon Dijon mustard

Directions:
1. Start by preheating your Air Fryer to 330 degrees F.
2. In a mixing bowl, thoroughly combine the ground beef, veal, egg, vegetable juice, pork rinds, bell peppers, onion, garlic, tomato paste, soy sauce, ranch dressing mix, salt, and ground black pepper.

3. Mix until everything is well incorporated and press into a lightly greased meatloaf pan.
4. Cook approximately 25 minutes in the preheated Air Fryer. Whisk the tomato puree with the mustard and spread the topping over the top of your meatloaf.
5. Continue to cook 2 minutes more. Let it stand on a cooling rack for 6 minutes before slicing and serving. Enjoy!
- **Nutrition Info:** 398 Calories; 24g Fat; 9g Carbs; 32g Protein; 3g Sugars; 6g Fiber

232.   Shrimp Kebabs

Servings: 2
Cooking Time: 10 Minutes
Ingredients:
- ¾ pound shrimp, peeled and deveined
- 1 tablespoon fresh cilantro, chopped
- Wooden skewers, presoaked
- 2 tablespoons fresh lemon juice
- 1 teaspoon garlic, minced
- ½ teaspoon paprika
- ½ teaspoon ground cumin
- Salt and ground black pepper, as required

Directions:
1. Preheat the Air fryer to 350 degree F and grease an Air fryer basket.
2. Mix lemon juice, garlic, and spices in a bowl.
3. Stir in the shrimp and mix to coat well.
4. Thread the shrimp onto presoaked wooden skewers and transfer to the Air fryer basket.
5. Cook for about 10 minutes, flipping once in between.
6. Dish out the mixture onto serving plates and serve garnished with fresh cilantro.
- **Nutrition Info:** Calories: 212, Fat: 3.2g, Carbohydrates: 3.9g, Sugar: 0.4g, Protein: 39.1g, Sodium: 497mg

233.   Salmon With Crisped Topped Crumbs

Servings: 2
Cooking Time: 15 Minutes
Ingredients:
- 1-1/2 cups soft bread crumbs
- 2 tablespoons minced fresh parsley
- 1 tablespoon minced fresh thyme or 1 teaspoon dried thyme
- 2 garlic cloves, minced
- 1 teaspoon grated lemon zest
- 1/2 teaspoon salt
- 1/4 teaspoon lemon-pepper seasoning
- 1/4 teaspoon paprika
- 1 tablespoon butter, melted
- 2 salmon fillets (6 ounces each)

Directions:

1. In a medium bowl mix well bread crumbs, fresh parsley thyme, garlic, lemon zest, salt, lemon-pepper seasoning, and paprika.
2. Place the instant pot air fryer lid on, lightly grease baking pan of the instant pot with cooking spray. Add salmon fillet with skin side down. Evenly sprinkle crumbs on tops of salmon and place the baking pan in the instant pot.
3. Close the air fryer lid and cook at 390 ºF for 10 minutes.
4. Let it rest for 5 minutes.
5. Serve and enjoy.
- **Nutrition Info:** Calories: 331; Carbs: 9.0g; Protein: 31.0g; Fat: 19.0g

234.   Roasted Garlic Zucchini Rolls

Servings: 4
Cooking Time: 20 Minutes
Ingredients:
- 2 medium zucchinis
- ½ cup full-fat ricotta cheese
- ¼ white onion; peeled. And diced
- 2 cups spinach; chopped
- ¼ cup heavy cream
- ½ cup sliced baby portobello mushrooms
- ¾ cup shredded mozzarella cheese, divided.
- 2 tbsp. unsalted butter.
- 2 tbsp. vegetable broth.
- ½ tsp. finely minced roasted garlic
- ¼ tsp. dried oregano.
- ⅛ tsp. xanthan gum
- ¼ tsp. salt
- ½ tsp. garlic powder.

Directions:
1. Using a mandoline or sharp knife, slice zucchini into long strips lengthwise. Place strips between paper towels to absorb moisture. Set aside
2. In a medium saucepan over medium heat, melt butter. Add onion and sauté until fragrant. Add garlic and sauté 30 seconds.
3. Pour in heavy cream, broth and xanthan gum. Turn off heat and whisk mixture until it begins to thicken, about 3 minutes.
4. Take a medium bowl, add ricotta, salt, garlic powder and oregano and mix well. Fold in spinach, mushrooms and ½ cup mozzarella
5. Pour half of the sauce into a 6-inch round baking pan. To assemble the rolls, place two strips of zucchini on a work surface. Spoon 2 tbsp. of ricotta mixture onto the slices and roll up. Place seam side down on top of sauce. Repeat with remaining ingredients
6. Pour remaining sauce over the rolls and sprinkle with remaining mozzarella. Cover with foil and place into the air fryer basket. Adjust the temperature to 350 Degrees F and set the timer for 20 minutes. In the last

5 minutes, remove the foil to brown the cheese. Serve immediately.
- **Nutrition Info:** Calories: 245; Protein: 15g; Fiber: 8g; Fat: 19g; Carbs: 1g

235. Creamy Tuna Cakes

Servings: 4
Cooking Time: 15 Minutes
Ingredients:
- 2: 6-ouncescans tuna, drained
- 1½ tablespoon almond flour
- 1½ tablespoons mayonnaise
- 1 tablespoon fresh lemon juice
- 1 teaspoon dried dill
- 1 teaspoon garlic powder
- ½ teaspoon onion powder
- Pinch of salt and ground black pepper

Directions:
1. Preheat the Air fryer to 400-degree F and grease an Air fryer basket.
2. Mix the tuna, mayonnaise, almond flour, lemon juice, dill, and spices in a large bowl.
3. Make 4 equal-sized patties from the mixture and arrange in the Air fryer basket.
4. Cook for about 10 minutes and flip the sides.
5. Cook for 5 more minutes and dish out the tuna cakes in serving plates to serve warm.
- **Nutrition Info:** Calories: 200, Fat: 10.1g, Carbohydrates: 2.9g, Sugar: 0.8g, Protein: 23.4g, Sodium: 122mg

236. Broccoli Crust Pizza

Servings: 4
Cooking Time: 20 Minutes
Ingredients:
- 3 cups riced broccoli, steamed and drained well
- ½ cup shredded mozzarella cheese
- ½ cup grated vegetarian Parmesan cheese.
- 1 large egg.
- 3 tbsp. low-carb Alfredo sauce

Directions:
1. Take a large bowl, mix broccoli, egg and Parmesan.
2. Cut a piece of parchment to fit your air fryer basket. Press out the pizza mixture to fit on the parchment, working in two batches if necessary. Place into the air fryer basket. Adjust the temperature to 370 Degrees F and set the timer for 5 minutes.
3. When the timer beeps, the crust should be firm enough to flip. If not, add 2 additional minutes. Flip crust.
4. Top with Alfredo sauce and mozzarella. Return to the air fryer basket and cook an additional 7 minutes or until cheese is golden and bubbling. Serve warm.
- **Nutrition Info:** Calories: 136; Protein: 9g; Fiber: 3g; Fat: 6g; Carbs:7g

237. Salmon Steak Grilled With Cilantro Garlic Sauce

Servings: 2
Cooking Time: 15 Minutes
Ingredients:
- 2 salmon steaks
- Salt and pepper to taste
- 2 tablespoons vegetable oil
- 2 cloves of garlic, minced
- 1 cup cilantro leaves
- ½ cup Greek yogurt
- 1 teaspoon honey

Directions:
1. Place the instant pot air fryer lid on and preheat the instant pot at 390 degrees F.
2. Place the grill pan accessory in the instant pot.
3. Season the salmon steaks with salt and pepper. Brush with oil.
4. Place on the grill pan, close the air fryer lid and grill for 15 minutes and make sure to flip halfway through the cooking time.
5. In a food processor, mix the garlic, cilantro leaves, yogurt, and honey. Season with salt and pepper to taste. Pulse until smooth.
6. Serve the salmon steaks with the cilantro sauce.
- **Nutrition Info:** Calories: 485; Carbs: 6.3g; Protein: 47.6g; Fat: 29.9g

238. Beef, Olives And Tomatoes

Servings: 4
Cooking Time: 35 Minutes
Ingredients:
- 2pounds beef stew meat, cubed
- 1cup black olives, pitted and halved
- 1cup cherry tomatoes, halved
- 1tablespoon smoked paprika
- 3tablespoons olive oil
- 1teaspoon coriander, ground
- Salt and black pepper to the taste

Directions:
1. In the air fryer's pan, mix the beef with the olives and the other ingredients, toss and cook at 390 degrees F for 35 minutes.
2. Divide between plates and serve.
- **Nutrition Info:** Calories 291, Fat 12, Fiber 9, Carbs 20, Protein 26

239. Sage Sausages Balls

Servings: 4
Cooking Time: 20 Minutes
Ingredients:
- 3 ½ oz sausages, sliced
- Salt and black pepper to taste
- 1 cup onion, chopped
- 3 tbsp breadcrumbs
- ½ tsp garlic puree

- 1 tsp sage

Directions:

1. Preheat your air fryer to 340 f. In a bowl, mix onions, sausage meat, sage, garlic puree, salt and pepper. Add breadcrumbs to a plate. Form balls using the mixture and roll them in breadcrumbs. Add onion balls in your air fryer's cooking basket and cook for 15 minutes. Serve and enjoy!
- **Nutrition Info:** Calories: 162 Cal Total Fat: 12.1 g Saturated Fat: 0 g Cholesterol: 25 mg Sodium: 324 mg Total Carbs: 7.3 g Fiber: 0 g Sugar: 0 g Protein: 6 g

240. Baked Egg And Veggies

Servings: 2
Cooking Time: 20 Minutes
Ingredients:

- 1 cup fresh spinach; chopped
- 1 small zucchini, sliced lengthwise and quartered
- 1 medium Roma tomato; diced
- ½ medium green bell pepper; seeded and diced
- 2 large eggs.
- 2 tbsp. salted butter
- ¼ tsp. garlic powder.
- ¼ tsp. onion powder.
- ½ tsp. dried basil
- ¼ tsp. dried oregano.

Directions:

1. Grease two (4-inchramekins with 1 tbsp. butter each.
2. Take a large bowl, toss zucchini, bell pepper, spinach and tomatoes. Divide the mixture in two and place half in each ramekin.
3. Crack an egg on top of each ramekin and sprinkle with onion powder, garlic powder, basil and oregano. Place into the air fryer basket. Adjust the temperature to 330 Degrees F and set the timer for 10 minutes. Serve immediately.
- **Nutrition Info:** Calories: 150; Protein: 3g; Fiber: 2g; Fat: 10g; Carbs: 6g

241. Greek Souvlaki With Eggplant

Servings: 4
Cooking Time: 20 Minutes
Ingredients:

- 1 ½ pounds beef stew meat cubes
- 1/4 cup mayonnaise
- 1/4 cup sour cream
- 1 tablespoon yellow mustard
- 1 tablespoon Worcestershire sauce
- 1 cup pearl onions
- 1 small-sized eggplant, 1 ½-inch cubes
- Sea salt and ground black pepper, to taste

Directions:

1. In a mixing bowl, toss all ingredients until everything is well coated.
2. Place in your refrigerator, cover, and let it marinate for 1 hour.
3. Soak wooden skewers in water for 15 minutes
4. Thread the beef cubes, pearl onions and eggplant onto skewers. Cook in preheated Air Fryer at 395 degrees F for 12 minutes, flipping halfway through the cooking time. Serve warm.
- **Nutrition Info:** 372 Calories; 22g Fat; 2g Carbs; 33g Protein; 6g Sugars; 7g Fiber

242. Indian Meatballs With Lamb

Servings: 8
Cooking Time: 14 Minutes
Ingredients:

- 1 garlic clove
- 1 tablespoon butter
- 4 oz chive stems
- ¼ tablespoon turmeric
- 1/3 teaspoon cayenne pepper
- 1 teaspoon ground coriander
- ¼ teaspoon bay leaf
- 1 teaspoon salt
- 1-pound ground lamb
- 1 egg
- 1 teaspoon ground black pepper

Directions:

1. Peel the garlic clove and mince it
2. Combine the minced garlic with the ground lamb.
3. Then sprinkle the meat mixture with the turmeric, cayenne pepper, ground coriander, bay leaf, salt, and ground black pepper.
4. Beat the egg in the forcemeat.
5. Then grate the chives and add them in the lamb forcemeat too.
6. Mix it up to make the smooth mass.
7. Then preheat the air fryer to 400 F.
8. Put the butter in the air fryer basket tray and melt it.
9. Then make the meatballs from the lamb mixture and place them in the air fryer basket tray.
10. Cook the dish for 14 minutes.
11. Stir the meatballs twice during the cooking.
12. Serve the cooked meatballs immediately.
13. Enjoy!
- **Nutrition Info:** calories 134, fat 6.2, fiber 0.4, carbs 1.8, protein 16.9

243. Clam With Lemons On The Grill

Servings: 6
Cooking Time: 6 Minutes
Ingredients:

- 4 pounds littleneck clams
- Salt and pepper to taste
- 1 clove of garlic, minced
- ½ cup parsley, chopped
- 1 teaspoon crushed red pepper flakes
- 5 tablespoons olive oil
- 1 loaf crusty bread, halved
- ½ cup Parmesan cheese, grated

Directions:
1. Place the instant pot air fryer lid on and preheat the instant pot at 390 degrees F.
2. Place the grill pan accessory in the instant pot.
3. Place the clams on the grill pan, close the air fryer lid and cook for 6 minutes.
4. Once the clams have opened, take them out and extract the meat.
5. Transfer the meat into a bowl and season with salt and pepper.
6. Stir in the garlic, parsley, red pepper flakes, and olive oil.
7. Serve on top of bread and sprinkle with Parmesan cheese.
- **Nutrition Info:** Calories: 341; Carbs: 26g; Protein:48.3g; Fat: 17.2g

244. Chili Pepper Lamb Chops

Servings: 6
Cooking Time: 10 Minutes
Ingredients:
- 21 oz. lamb chops
- 1 teaspoon chili pepper
- ½ teaspoon chili flakes
- 1 teaspoon onion powder
- 1 teaspoon garlic powder
- 1 teaspoon cayenne pepper
- 1 tablespoon olive oil
- 1 tablespoon butter
- ½ teaspoon lime zest

Directions:
1. Melt the butter and combine it with the olive oil.
2. Whisk the liquid and add chili pepper, chili flakes, onion powder, garlic powder, cayenne pepper, and lime zest.
3. Whisk it well
4. Then sprinkle the lamb chops with the prepared oily marinade.
5. Leave the meat for at least 5 minutes in the fridge.
6. Preheat the air fryer to 400 F.
7. Place the marinated lamb chops in the air fryer and cook them for 5 minutes.
8. After this, open the air fryer and turn the lamb chops into another side.
9. Cook the lamb chops for 5 minutes more.
10. When the meat is cooked – transfer it to the serving plates.
11. Enjoy!

- **Nutrition Info:** calories 227, fat 11.6, fiber 0.2, carbs 1, protein 28.1

245. Carrot Beef Cake

Servings: 10
Cooking Time: 60 Minutes
Ingredients:
- 3 eggs, beaten
- 1/2 cup almond milk
- 1-oz. onion soup mix
- 1 cup dry bread crumbs
- 2 cups shredded carrots
- 2 lbs. lean ground beef
- 1/2-lb. ground pork

Directions:
1. Thoroughly mix ground beef with carrots and all other ingredients in a bowl.
2. Grease a meatloaf pan with oil or butter and spread the minced beef in the pan.
3. Press "Power Button" of Air Fry Oven and turn the dial to select the "Bake" mode.
4. Press the Time button and again turn the dial to set the cooking time to 60 minutes.
5. Now push the Temp button and rotate the dial to set the temperature at 350 degrees F.
6. Once preheated, place the beef baking pan in the oven and close its lid.
7. Slice and serve.
- **Nutrition Info:** Calories: 212 Cal Total Fat: 11.8 g Saturated Fat: 2.2 g Cholesterol: 23 mg Sodium: 321 mg Total Carbs: 14.6 g Fiber: 4.4 g Sugar: 8 g Protein: 17.3 g

246. Bbq Pork Ribs

Servings: 2 To 3
Cooking Time: 5 Hrs 30 Minutes
Ingredients:
- 1 lb pork ribs
- 1 tsp soy sauce
- Salt and black pepper to taste
- 1 tsp oregano
- 1 tbsp + 1 tbsp maple syrup
- 3 tbsp barbecue sauce
- 2 cloves garlic, minced
- 1 tbsp cayenne pepper
- 1 tsp sesame oil

Directions:
1. Put the chops on a chopping board and use a knife to cut them into smaller pieces of desired sizes. Put them in a mixing bowl, add the soy sauce, salt, pepper, oregano, one tablespoon of maple syrup, barbecue sauce, garlic, cayenne pepper, and sesame oil. Mix well and place the pork in the fridge to marinate in the spices for 5 hours.
2. Preheat the Air Fryer to 350 F. Open the Air Fryer and place the ribs in the fryer basket. Slide the fryer basket in and cook for 15 minutes. Open the Air fryer, turn the ribs

using tongs, apply the remaining maple syrup with a brush, close the Air Fryer, and continue cooking for 10 minutes.

- **Nutrition Info:** 346 Calories; 11g Fat; 4g Carbs; 32g Protein; 1g Sugars; 1g Fiber

247. Morning Ham And Cheese Sandwich

Servings: 4
Cooking Time: 15 Minutes
Ingredients:

- 8 slices whole wheat bread
- 4 slices lean pork ham
- 4 slices cheese
- 8 slices tomato

Directions:

1. Preheat your air fryer to 360 f. Lay four slices of bread on a flat surface. Spread the slices with cheese, tomato, turkey and ham. Cover with the remaining slices to form sandwiches. Add the sandwiches to the air fryer cooking basket and cook for 10 minutes.

- **Nutrition Info:** Calories: 361 Cal Total Fat: 16.7 g Saturated Fat: 0 g Cholesterol: 0 mg

Sodium: 1320 mg Total Carbs: 32.5 g Fiber: 2.3 g Sugar: 5.13 g Protein: 19.3 g

248. Pesto & White Wine Salmon

Servings: 4
Cooking Time: 10 Minutes
Ingredients:

- 1-1/4 pounds salmon filet
- 2 tablespoons white wine
- 2 tablespoons pesto
- 1 lemon

Directions:

1. Cut the salmon into 4 pieces and place on a greased baking sheet.
2. Slice the lemon into quarters and squeeze 1 quarter over each piece of salmon.
3. Drizzle wine over salmon and set aside to marinate while preheating the toaster oven on broil.
4. Spread pesto over each piece of salmon.
5. Broil for at least 10 minutes, or until the fish is cooked to desired doneness and the pesto is browned.

- **Nutrition Info:** Calories: 236, Sodium: 111 mg, Dietary Fiber: 0.9 g, Total Fat: 12.1 g, Total Carbs: 3.3 g, Protein: 28.6 g.

249. Crispy Cracker Crusted Pork Chops

Servings: 3
Cooking Time: 30 Minutes
Ingredients:
- 3 pork chops, boneless
- 2 tbsp milk
- 1 egg, lightly beaten
- 1/2 cup crackers, crushed
- 4 tbsp parmesan cheese, grated
- Pepper
- Salt

Directions:
1. Fit the oven with the rack in position
2. In a shallow bowl, whisk egg and milk.
3. In a separate shallow dish, mix cheese, crackers, pepper, and salt.
4. Dip pork chops in egg then coat with cheese mixture.
5. Place coated pork chops in a baking pan.
6. Set to bake at 350 F for 35 minutes. After 5 minutes place the baking pan in the preheated oven.
7. Serve and enjoy.
- **Nutrition Info:** Calories 360 Fat 25.9 g Carbohydrates 7.2 g Sugar 0.8 g Protein 23.5 g Cholesterol 130 mg

250. Mushroom In Bacon-wrapped Filets Mignons

Servings:8
Cooking Time: 13 Minutes
Ingredients:
- 1 ounce (28 g) dried porcini mushrooms
- ½ teaspoon granulated white sugar
- ½ teaspoon salt
- ½ teaspoon ground white pepper
- 8 (4-ounce / 113-g) filets mignons or beef tenderloin steaks
- 8 thin-cut bacon strips

Directions:
1. Put the mushrooms, sugar, salt, and white pepper in a spice grinder and grind to combine.
2. On a clean work surface, rub the filets mignons with the mushroom mixture, then wrap each filet with a bacon strip. Secure with toothpicks if necessary.
3. Arrange the bacon-wrapped filets mignons in the basket, seam side down.
4. Put the air fryer basket on the baking pan and slide into Rack Position 2, select Air Fry, set temperature to 400ºF (205ºC) and set time to 13 minutes.
5. Flip the filets halfway through.

6. When cooking is complete, the filets should be medium rare.
7. Serve immediately.

251. Air Fryer Chicken Parmesan

Servings: 4
Cooking Time: 9 Minutes
Ingredients:
- ½ C. keto marinara
- 6 tbsp. mozzarella cheese
- 1 tbsp. melted ghee
- 2 tbsp. grated parmesan cheese
- 6 tbsp. gluten-free seasoned breadcrumbs
- 1 8-ounce chicken breasts

Directions:
1. Preparing the Ingredients. Ensure air fryer oven is preheated to 360 degrees. Spray the basket with olive oil.
2. Mix parmesan cheese and breadcrumbs together. Melt ghee.
3. Brush melted ghee onto the chicken and dip into breadcrumb mixture.
4. Place coated chicken in the air fryer oven and top with olive oil.
5. Air Frying. Set temperature to 360°F, and set time to 6 minutes. Cook 2 breasts for 6 minutes and top each breast with a tablespoon of sauce and 1½ tablespoons of mozzarella cheese. Cook another 3 minutes to melt cheese.
6. Keep cooked pieces warm as you repeat the process with remaining breasts.
- **Nutrition Info:** CALORIES: 251; FAT: 10G; PROTEIN:31G; SUGAR:0G

252. Simple & Healthy Baked Chicken Breasts

Servings: 6
Cooking Time: 20 Minutes
Ingredients:
- 6 chicken breasts, skinless & boneless
- 1/4 tsp paprika
- 1 tsp Italian seasoning
- 2 tbsp olive oil
- 1/4 tsp pepper
- 1/2 tsp seasoning salt

Directions:
1. Fit the oven with the rack in position
2. Brush chicken with oil and season with paprika, Italian seasoning, pepper, and salt.
3. Place chicken breasts into the baking dish.
4. Set to bake at 400 F for 25 minutes. After 5 minutes place the baking dish in the preheated oven.
5. Serve and enjoy.

- **Nutrition Info:** Calories 320 Fat 15.7 g Carbohydrates 0.2 g Sugar 0.1 g Protein 42.3 g Cholesterol 130 mg

253. Garlic Chicken

Servings: 6
Cooking Time: 40 Minutes
Ingredients:
- 2 lbs chicken thighs, skinless and boneless
- 10 garlic cloves, sliced
- 2 tbsp olive oil
- 2 tbsp fresh parsley, chopped
- 1 fresh lemon juice
- Pepper
- Salt

Directions:
1. Fit the oven with the rack in position
2. Place chicken in baking pan and season with pepper and salt.
3. Sprinkle parsley and garlic over the chicken. Drizzle with oil and lemon juice.
4. Set to bake at 450 F for 45 minutes. After 5 minutes place the baking pan in the preheated oven.
5. Serve and enjoy.
- **Nutrition Info:** Calories 337 Fat 16 g Carbohydrates 1.9 g Sugar 0.2 g Protein 44.2 g Cholesterol 135 mg

254. Meatballs(8)

Servings: 4
Cooking Time: 10 Minutes
Ingredients:
- 1 egg, lightly beaten
- 1 lb ground beef
- 1/4 cup onion, chopped
- 2 tbsp taco seasoning
- 1 tbsp garlic, minced
- 1/2 cup cheddar cheese, shredded
- 1/4 cup cilantro, chopped
- Pepper
- Salt

Directions:
1. Fit the oven with the rack in position 2.
2. Line the air fryer basket with parchment paper.
3. Add ground beef and remaining ingredients into the large bowl and mix until well combined.
4. Make small meatballs from meat mixture and place in the air fryer basket then place an air fryer basket in the baking pan.
5. Place a baking pan on the oven rack. Set to air fry at 400 F for 10 minutes.
6. Serve and enjoy.
- **Nutrition Info:** Calories 290 Fat 12.9 g Carbohydrates 1.7 g Sugar 0.5 g Protein 39.5 g Cholesterol 157 mg

255. Mexican Salsa Chicken

Servings: 6
Cooking Time: 30 Minutes
Ingredients:
- 4 chicken breasts, skinless & boneless
- 1/4 tsp cumin
- 1/4 tsp garlic powder
- 1 3/4 cups Mexican shredded cheese
- 12 oz salsa
- 1/4 tsp pepper
- 1/4 tsp salt

Directions:
1. Fit the oven with the rack in position
2. Place chicken breasts into the baking dish and season with cumin, garlic powder, pepper, and salt.
3. Pour salsa over chicken breasts.
4. Sprinkle shredded cheese on top of chicken.
5. Set to bake at 375 F for 35 minutes. After 5 minutes place the baking dish in the preheated oven.
6. Serve and enjoy.
- **Nutrition Info:** Calories 330 Fat 17.8 g Carbohydrates 6.1 g Sugar 1.8 g Protein 36.1 g Cholesterol 116 mg

256. Tasty Lemon Chicken

Servings: 1
Cooking Time: 15 Minutes
Ingredients:
- 1 chicken breast, boneless and skinless
- 1 fresh lemon juice
- 1 fresh lemon, sliced
- 1/2 tbsp Italian seasoning
- Pepper
- Salt

Directions:
1. Fit the oven with the rack in position
2. Season chicken with Italian season, pepper, and salt.
3. Place chicken breast in baking dish.
4. Pour lemon juice over chicken and arrange lemon slices on top of chicken.
5. Set to bake at 350 F for 20 minutes. After 5 minutes place the baking dish in the preheated oven.
6. Serve and enjoy.
- **Nutrition Info:** Calories 178 Fat 5.4 g Carbohydrates 7.2 g Sugar 3.1 g Protein 24.8 g Cholesterol 77 mg

257. Pork Neck With Salad

Servings: 2
Cooking Time: 12 Minutes
Ingredients:
- For Pork:
- 1 tablespoon soy sauce
- 1 tablespoon fish sauce

- ½ tablespoon oyster sauce
- ½ pound pork neck
- For Salad:
- 1 ripe tomato, sliced tickly
- 8-10 Thai shallots, sliced
- 1 scallion, chopped
- 1 bunch fresh basil leaves
- 1 bunch fresh cilantro leaves
- For Dressing:
- 3 tablespoons fish sauce
- 2 tablespoons olive oil
- 1 teaspoon apple cider vinegar
- 1 tablespoon palm sugar
- 2 bird eye chili
- 1 tablespoon garlic, minced

Directions:
1. Preparing the Ingredients. For pork in a bowl, mix together all ingredients except pork.
2. Add pork neck and coat with marinade evenly. Refrigerate for about 2-3 hours.
3. Preheat the air fryer oven to 340 degrees F.
4. Air Frying. Place the pork neck onto a grill pan. Cook for about 12 minutes.
5. Meanwhile, in a large salad bowl, mix together all salad ingredients.
6. In a bowl, add all dressing ingredients and beat till well combined.
7. Remove pork neck from Air fryer oven and cut into desired slices.
8. Place pork slices over salad.

258.   Pork Wonton Wonderful

Servings: 3
Cooking Time: 25 Minutes
Ingredients:
- 8 wanton wrappers (Leasa brand works great, though any will do)
- 4 ounces of raw minced pork
- 1 medium-sized green apple
- 1 cup of water, for wetting the wanton wrappers
- 1 tablespoon of vegetable oil
- ½ tablespoon of oyster sauce
- 1 tablespoon of soy sauce
- Large pinch of ground white pepper

Directions:
1. Preparing the Ingredients. Cover the basket of the air fryer oven with a lining of tin foil, leaving the edges uncovered to allow air to circulate through the basket. Preheat the air fryer oven to 350 degrees.
2. In a small mixing bowl, combine the oyster sauce, soy sauce, and white pepper, then add in the minced pork and stir thoroughly. Cover and set in the fridge to marinate for at least 15 minutes. Core the apple, and slice into small cubes – smaller than bite-sized chunks.

3. Add the apples to the marinating meat mixture, and combine thoroughly. Spread the wonton wrappers, and fill each with a large spoonful of the filling. Wrap the wontons into triangles, so that the wrappers fully cover the filling, and seal with a drop of the water.
4. Coat each filled and wrapped wonton thoroughly with the vegetable oil, to help ensure a nice crispy fry. Place the wontons on the foil-lined air-fryer rack/basket. Place the Rack on the middle-shelf of the air fryer oven.
5. Air Frying. Set the air fryer oven timer to 25 minutes. Halfway through cooking time, shake the handle of the air fryer rack/basket vigorously to jostle the wontons and ensure even frying. After 25 minutes, when the air fryer oven shuts off, the wontons will be crispy golden-brown on the outside and juicy and delicious on the inside. Serve directly from the Oven rack/basket and enjoy while hot.

259.   Delicious Pork Belly

Servings: 6
Cooking Time: 55 Minutes
Ingredients:
- 3 lbs pork belly, cut into 2-inch cubes
- 3 green onions stalk, chopped
- 1/4 tsp pepper
- 1 tbsp sesame oil
- 2 tbsp brown sugar
- 1/4 cup rice vinegar
- 1/4 cup soy sauce
- 1 tsp red chili flakes
- 1 tsp garlic, minced
- 1/4 tsp salt

Directions:
1. Fit the oven with the rack in position
2. Add all ingredients into the zip-lock bag, seal bag shake well and place in the refrigerator for 1 hour.
3. Place marinated pork belly cubes into the parchment-lined baking pan.
4. Set to bake at 400 F for 60 minutes. After 5 minutes place the baking pan in the preheated oven.
5. Turn pork belly cubes after 30 minutes.
6. Serve and enjoy.
- **Nutrition Info:** Calories 362 Fat 32.3 g Carbohydrates 5.5 g Sugar 3.3 g Protein 10.4 g Cholesterol 51 mg

260.   Chicken Burger Patties

Servings: 4
Cooking Time: 25 Minutes
Ingredients:
- 1 lb ground chicken

- 1 egg, lightly beaten
- 1 cup cheddar cheese, shredded
- 1 cup carrot, grated
- 1 cup cauliflower, grated
- 1/8 tsp red pepper flakes
- 2 garlic cloves, minced
- 1/2 cup onion, minced
- 3/4 cup breadcrumbs
- Pepper
- Salt

Directions:
1. Fit the oven with the rack in position
2. Add all ingredients into the bowl and mix until well combined.
3. Make small patties and place them in a parchment-lined baking pan.
4. Set to bake at 400 F for 30 minutes. After 5 minutes place the baking pan in the preheated oven.
5. Serve and enjoy.
- **Nutrition Info:** Calories 451 Fat 20 g Carbohydrates 20.9 g Sugar 4.1 g Protein 44.9 g Cholesterol 172 mg

261. Bacon-wrapped Chicken Breasts Rolls

Servings:4
Cooking Time: 15 Minutes
Ingredients:
- ¼ cup chopped fresh chives
- 2 tablespoons lemon juice
- 1 teaspoon dried sage
- 1 teaspoon fresh rosemary leaves
- ½ cup fresh parsley leaves
- 4 cloves garlic, peeled
- 1 teaspoon ground fennel
- 3 teaspoons sea salt
- ½ teaspoon red pepper flakes
- 4 (4-ounce / 113-g) boneless, skinless chicken breasts, pounded to ¼ inch thick
- 8 slices bacon
- Sprigs of fresh rosemary, for garnish
- Cooking spray

Directions:
1. Spritz the air fryer basket with cooking spray.
2. Put the chives, lemon juice, sage, rosemary, parsley, garlic, fennel, salt, and red pepper flakes in a food processor, then pulse to purée until smooth.
3. Unfold the chicken breasts on a clean work surface, then brush the top side of the chicken breasts with the sauce.
4. Roll the chicken breasts up from the shorter side, then wrap each chicken rolls with 2 bacon slices to cover. Secure with toothpicks.
5. Arrange the rolls in the basket.

6. Put the air fryer basket on the baking pan and slide into Rack Position 2, select Air Fry, set temperature to 340ºF (171ºC) and set time to 10 minutes.
7. Flip the rolls halfway through.
8. After 10 minutes, increase temperature to 390ºF (199ºC) and set time to 5 minutes.
9. When cooking is complete, the bacon should be browned and crispy.
10. Transfer the rolls to a large plate. Discard the toothpicks and spread with rosemary sprigs before serving.

262. Easy Pork Chops

Servings: 2
Cooking Time: 25 Minutes
Ingredients:
- 2 pork chops
- 2 tsp brown sugar
- 1 tsp smoked paprika
- Pepper
- Salt

Directions:
1. Fit the oven with the rack in position
2. Mix smoked paprika, brown sugar, pepper, and salt and rub all over pork chops.
3. Place pork chops in a baking pan.
4. Set to bake at 325 F for 30 minutes. After 5 minutes place the baking pan in the preheated oven.
5. Serve and enjoy.
- **Nutrition Info:** Calories 271 Fat 20 g Carbohydrates 3.6 g Sugar 3 g Protein 18.1 g Cholesterol 69 mg

263. Cheese Chicken Fries

Servings:x
Cooking Time:x
Ingredients:
- 1 lb. chicken (Cut in to long Oregano Fingers)
- ingredients for the marinade:
- 1 tbsp. olive oil
- 1 tsp. mixed herbs
- ½ tsp. red chili flakes
- A pinch of salt to taste
- 1 tbsp. lemon juice
- For the garnish:
- 1 cup melted cheddar cheese

Directions:
1. Take all the ingredients mentioned under the heading "For the marinade" and mix them well.
2. Cook the chicken Oregano Fingers and soak them in the marinade.
3. Pre heat the oven for around 5 minutes at 300 Fahrenheit. Take out the
4. basket of the fryer and place the chicken Oregano Fingers in them. Close the basket.

5. Now keep the fryer at 220 Fahrenheit for 20 or 25 minutes. In between the process, toss the fries twice or thrice so that they get cooked properly.
6. Towards the end of the cooking process (the last 2 minutes or so), sprinkle the cut coriander leaves on the fries. Add the melted cheddar cheese over the fries and serve hot.

264. Herb Turkey Tenderloin

Servings: 4
Cooking Time: 40 Minutes
Ingredients:
- 24 oz turkey tenderloin
- 1 tbsp dried rosemary
- 1 tbsp dried sage
- Pepper
- Salt

Directions:
1. Fit the oven with the rack in position
2. Rub turkey tenderloin with rosemary, sage, pepper, and salt.
3. Place turkey tenderloin into the baking pan.
4. Set to bake at 350 F for 45 minutes. After 5 minutes place the baking pan in the preheated oven.
5. Slice and serve.
- **Nutrition Info:** Calories 185 Fat 2.4 g Carbohydrates 0.9 g Sugar 0 g Protein 42.3 g Cholesterol 68 mg

265. Pheasant Chili

Servings:x
Cooking Time:x
Ingredients:
- 1 lb. cubed pheasant
- 2 ½ tsp. ginger-garlic paste
- 1 tsp. red chili sauce
- ¼ tsp. salt
- ¼ tsp. red chili powder/black pepper
- A few drops of edible orange food coloring
- For sauce:
- 2 tbsp. olive oil
- 1 ½ tsp. ginger garlic paste
- ½ tbsp. red chili sauce
- 2 tbsp. tomato ketchup
- 2 tsp. soya sauce
- 1-2 tbsp. honey
- ¼ tsp. Ajinomoto
- 1-2 tsp. red chili flakes

Directions:
1. Mix all the ingredients for the marinade and put the pheasant cubes inside and let it rest overnight. Mix the breadcrumbs, oregano and red chili flakes well and place the marinated Oregano Fingers on this mixture.
2. Cover it with plastic wrap and leave it till right before you serve to cook. Pre heat the oven at 160 degrees Fahrenheit for 5 minutes. Place the Oregano Fingers in the fry basket and close it. Let them cook at the same temperature for another 15 minutes or so. Toss the Oregano Fingers well so that they are cooked uniformly.

266. Air Fryer Chicken Tenders

Servings: 4
Cooking Time: 16 Minutes
Ingredients:
- 1 lb chicken tenders
- For rub:
- 1/2 tbsp dried thyme
- 1 tbsp garlic powder
- 1 tbsp paprika
- 1/2 tbsp onion powder
- 1/2 tsp cayenne pepper
- Pepper
- Salt

Directions:
1. Fit the oven with the rack in position 2.
2. In a bowl, add all rub ingredients and mix well.
3. Add chicken tenders into the bowl and coat well.
4. Place chicken tenders in the air fryer basket then place an air fryer basket in the baking pan.
5. Place a baking pan on the oven rack. Set to air fry at 370 F for 16 minutes.
6. Serve and enjoy.
- **Nutrition Info:** Calories 232 Fat 8.7 g Carbohydrates 3.6 g Sugar 1 g Protein 33.6 g Cholesterol 101 mg

267. Chipotle Pork Chops

Servings:4
Cooking Time: 35 Minutes
Ingredients:
- 4 pork chops
- 1 lime, juiced
- Salt and black pepper to taste
- 1 tsp garlic powder
- 2 cups white rice, cooked
- 1 can (14.5 oz) tomato sauce
- 1 onion, chopped
- 3 garlic cloves, minced
- ½ tsp dried oregano
- 1 tsp chipotle chili powder

Directions:
1. Season pork chops with salt, pepper, and garlic powder. In a bowl, mix onion, garlic, chipotle powder, oregano, and tomato sauce. Toss in the pork to coat. Let marinate for 1 hour.
2. Remove the chops from the mixture and place them in a greased baking dish. Select Bake function, adjust the temperature to

380 F, and press Start. Cook for 25 minutes. Serve with rice.

268. Delicious Coconut Chicken Casserole

Servings: 4
Cooking Time: 20 Minutes
Ingredients:
- 2 large eggs, beaten
- 2 tbsp garlic powder
- Salt and black pepper to taste
- ¾ cup breadcrumbs
- ¾ cup shredded coconut
- 1 pound chicken tenders

Directions:
1. Preheat your on Air Fry function to 400 F. Spray a baking sheet with cooking spray. In a deep dish, whisk garlic powder, eggs, pepper, and salt. In another bowl, mix the breadcrumbs and coconut. Dip your chicken tenders in egg mixture, then in the coconut mix; shake off any excess. Place the prepared chicken tenders in the greased basket and fit in the baking tray; cook for 12-14 minutes until golden brown. Serve.

269. Air Fry Chicken Drumsticks

Servings: 6
Cooking Time: 25 Minutes
Ingredients:
- 6 chicken drumsticks
- 1/2 tsp garlic powder
- 2 tbsp olive oil
- 1/2 tsp ground cumin
- 3/4 tsp paprika
- Pepper
- Salt

Directions:
1. Fit the oven with the rack in position 2.
2. Add chicken drumsticks and olive oil in a large bowl and toss well.
3. Sprinkle garlic powder, paprika, cumin, pepper, and salt over chicken drumsticks and toss until well coated.
4. Place chicken drumsticks in the air fryer basket then place an air fryer basket in the baking pan.
5. Place a baking pan on the oven rack. Set to air fry at 400 F for 25 minutes.
6. Serve and enjoy.
- **Nutrition Info:** Calories 120 Fat 7.4 g Carbohydrates 0.4 g Sugar 0.1 g Protein 12.8 g Cholesterol 40 mg

270. Spicy Pork Lettuce Wraps

Servings:4
Cooking Time: 12 Minutes
Ingredients:
- 1 (1-pound / 454-g) medium pork tenderloin, silver skin and external fat trimmed
- ²/₃ cup soy sauce, divided
- 1 teaspoon cornstarch
- 1 medium jalapeño, deseeded and minced
- 1 can diced water chestnuts
- ½ large red bell pepper, deseeded and chopped
- 2 scallions, chopped, white and green parts separated
- 1 head butter lettuce
- ½ cup roasted, chopped almonds
- ¼ cup coarsely chopped cilantro

Directions:
1. Cut the tenderloin into ¼-inch slices and place them in the baking pan. Baste with about 3 tablespoons of soy sauce. Stir the cornstarch into the remaining sauce and set aside.
2. Slide the baking pan into Rack Position 2, select Roast, set temperature to 375ºF (190ºC), and set time to 12 minutes.
3. After 5 minutes, remove from the oven. Place the pork slices on a cutting board. Place the jalapeño, water chestnuts, red pepper, and the white parts of the scallions in the baking pan and pour the remaining sauce over. Stir to coat the vegetables with the sauce. Return the pan to the oven and continue cooking.
4. While the vegetables cook, chop the pork into small pieces. Separate the lettuce leaves, discarding any tough outer leaves and setting aside the small inner leaves for another use. You'll want 12 to 18 leaves, depending on size and your appetites.
5. After 5 minutes, remove from the oven. Add the pork to the vegetables, stirring to combine. Return the pan to the oven and continue cooking for the remaining 2 minutes until the pork is warmed back up and the sauce has reduced slightly.
6. When cooking is complete, remove from the oven. Place the pork and vegetables in a medium serving bowl and stir in half the green parts of the scallions. To serve, spoon some pork and vegetables into each of the lettuce leaves. Top with the remaining scallion greens and garnish with the nuts and cilantro.

271. Meatballs(14)

Servings: 4
Cooking Time: 25 Minutes
Ingredients:
- 1 lb ground beef
- 1 tsp fresh rosemary, chopped
- 1 tbsp garlic, chopped

- 1/2 tsp pepper
- 1 tsp garlic powder
- 1 tsp onion powder
- 1/4 cup breadcrumbs
- 2 eggs
- 1 lb ground pork
- 1/2 tsp pepper
- 1 tsp sea salt

Directions:
1. Fit the oven with the rack in position
2. Add all ingredients into the mixing bowl and mix until well combined.
3. Make small balls from the meat mixture and place it into the parchment-lined baking pan.
4. Set to bake at 400 F for 30 minutes. After 5 minutes place the baking pan in the preheated oven.
5. Serve and enjoy.
- **Nutrition Info:** Calories 441 Fat 13.7 g Carbohydrates 7.2 g Sugar 1 g Protein 68.1 g Cholesterol 266 mg

272. Pineapple & Ginger Chicken Kabobs

Servings: 2
Cooking Time: 20 Minutes
Ingredients:
- 2 chicken breasts, cut into 2-inch pieces
- ½ cup soy sauce
- ½ cup pineapple juice
- ¼ cup sesame oil
- 4 cloves garlic, chopped
- 1 tbsp fresh ginger, grated
- 4 scallions, chopped
- 2 tbsp toasted sesame seeds
- A pinch of black pepper

Directions:
1. In a bowl, toss to coat all the ingredients except the chicken. Let sit for 10 minutes.
2. Preheat your oven on Air Fry function to 390 F. Remove the chicken pieces and pat them dry using paper towels. Thread the chicken pieces onto skewers and trim any fat. Place in the AirFryer basket and fit in the baking tray. Cook for 7-10 minutes, flipping once. Serve.

273. Chicken Schnitzel

Servings:4
Cooking Time: 5 Minutes
Ingredients:
- ½ cup all-purpose flour
- 1 teaspoon marjoram
- ½ teaspoon thyme
- 1 teaspoon dried parsley flakes
- ½ teaspoon salt
- 1 egg

- 1 teaspoon lemon juice
- 1 teaspoon water
- 1 cup bread crumbs
- 4 chicken tenders, pounded thin, cut in half lengthwise
- Cooking spray

Directions:
1. Spritz the air fryer basket with cooking spray.
2. Combine the flour, marjoram, thyme, parsley, and salt in a shallow dish. Stir to mix well.
3. Whisk the egg with lemon juice and water in a large bowl. Pour the bread crumbs in a separate shallow dish.
4. Roll the chicken halves in the flour mixture first, then in the egg mixture, and then roll over the bread crumbs to coat well. Shake the excess off.
5. Arrange the chicken halves in the basket and spritz with cooking spray on both sides.
6. Put the air fryer basket on the baking pan and slide into Rack Position 2, select Air Fry, set temperature to 390ºF (199ºC) and set time to 5 minutes.
7. Flip the halves halfway through.
8. When cooking is complete, the chicken halves should be golden brown and crispy.
9. Serve immediately.

274. Honey Garlic Pork Chops

Servings: 4
Cooking Time: 12 Minutes
Ingredients:
- 4 pork chops
- 2 tbsp lemon juice
- 1/4 cup honey
- 2 garlic cloves, minced
- 1 tbsp olive oil
- 1 tbsp sweet chili sauce
- Pepper
- Salt

Directions:
1. Fit the oven with the rack in position 2.
2. Season pork chops with pepper and salt and place in air fryer basket then place air fryer basket in baking pan.
3. Place a baking pan on the oven rack. Set to air fry at 400 F for 12 minutes.
4. Meanwhile, heat oil in a pan over medium heat.
5. Add garlic and sauté for 30 seconds.
6. Add remaining ingredients and stir well and cook for 3 minutes.
7. Place pork chops on serving dish.
8. Pour sauce over pork chops and serve.
- **Nutrition Info:** Calories 362 Fat 23.5 g Carbohydrates 19.6 g Sugar 19.1 g Protein 18.2 g Cholesterol 69 mg

275. Thai Curry Beef Meatballs

Servings:4
Cooking Time: 15 Minutes
Ingredients:
- 1 pound (454 g) ground beef
- 1 tablespoon sesame oil
- 2 teaspoons chopped lemongrass
- 1 teaspoon red Thai curry paste
- 1 teaspoon Thai seasoning blend
- Juice and zest of ½ lime
- Cooking spray

Directions:
1. Spritz the air fryer basket with cooking spray.
2. In a medium bowl, combine all the ingredients until well blended.
3. Shape the meat mixture into 24 meatballs and arrange them in the pan.
4. Put the air fryer basket on the baking pan and slide into Rack Position 2, select Air Fry, set temperature to 380ºF (193ºC) and set time to 15 minutes.
5. Flip the meatballs halfway through.
6. When cooking is complete, the meatballs should be browned.
7. Transfer the meatballs to plates. Let cool for 5 minutes before serving.

276. Garlic Butter Wings

Servings: 4
Cooking Time: 25 Minutes
Ingredients:
- 1 lb chicken wings
- 1 tsp garlic powder
- 1/4 tsp pepper
- 1/2 tsp Italian seasoning
- 1/2 tsp salt
- For sauce:
- 1 tbsp butter, melted
- 1/8 tsp garlic powder

Directions:
1. Fit the oven with the rack in position 2.
2. In a large bowl, toss chicken wings with Italian seasoning, garlic powder, pepper, and salt.
3. Arrange chicken wings in the air fryer basket then place an air fryer basket in the baking pan.
4. Place a baking pan on the oven rack. Set to air fry at 390 F for 25 minutes.
5. In a bowl, mix melted butter and garlic powder.
6. Add chicken wings and toss until well coated.
7. Serve and enjoy.
- **Nutrition Info:** Calories 246 Fat 11.5 g Carbohydrates 0.7 g Sugar 0.2 g Protein 33 g Cholesterol 109 mg

277. Roasted Pork Tenderloin

Servings: 4
Cooking Time: 1 Hour
Ingredients:
- 1 (3-pound) pork tenderloin
- 2 tablespoons extra-virgin olive oil
- 2 garlic cloves, minced
- 1 teaspoon dried basil
- 1 teaspoon dried oregano
- 1 teaspoon dried thyme
- Salt
- Pepper

Directions:
1. Preparing the Ingredients. Drizzle the pork tenderloin with the olive oil.
2. Rub the garlic, basil, oregano, thyme, and salt and pepper to taste all over the tenderloin.
3. Air Frying. Place the tenderloin in the air fryer oven. Cook for 45 minutes.
4. Use a meat thermometer to test for doneness
5. Open the air fryer oven and flip the pork tenderloin. Cook for an additional 15 minutes.
6. Remove the cooked pork from the air fryer oven and allow it to rest for 10 minutes before cutting.
- **Nutrition Info:** CALORIES: 283; FAT: 10G; PROTEIN:48

278. Minced Venison Grandma's Easy To Cook Wontons With Garlic Paste

Servings:x
Cooking Time:x
Ingredients:
- 1 ½ cup all-purpose flour
- ½ tsp. salt
- 2 tsp. soya sauce
- 5 tbsp. water
- 2 cups minced venison
- 2 tbsp. oil
- 2 tsp. ginger-garlic paste
- 2 tsp. vinegar

Directions:
1. Squeeze the dough and cover it with plastic wrap and set aside. Next, cook the ingredients for the filling and try to ensure that the venison is covered well with the sauce. Roll the dough and place the filling in the center.
2. Now, wrap the dough to cover the filling and pinch the edges together. Pre heat the oven at 200° F for 5 minutes.
3. Place the wontons in the fry basket and close it. Let them cook at the same temperature for another 20 minutes.

Recommended sides are chili sauce or ketchup.

279. Air Fried Beef Satay With Peanut Dipping Sauce

Servings:4
Cooking Time: 5 Minutes
Ingredients:
- 8 ounces (227 g) London broil, sliced into 8 strips
- 2 teaspoons curry powder
- ½ teaspoon kosher salt
- Cooking spray
- Peanut Dipping sauce:
- 2 tablespoons creamy peanut butter
- 1 tablespoon reduced-sodium soy sauce
- 2 teaspoons rice vinegar
- 1 teaspoon honey
- 1 teaspoon grated ginger
- Special Equipment:
- 4 bamboo skewers, cut into halves and soaked in water for 20 minutes to keep them from burning while cooking

Directions:
1. Spritz the air fryer basket with cooking spray.
2. In a bowl, place the London broil strips and sprinkle with the curry powder and kosher salt to season. Thread the strips onto the soaked skewers.
3. Arrange the skewers in the prepared basket and spritz with cooking spray.
4. Put the air fryer basket on the baking pan and slide into Rack Position 2, select Air Fry, set temperature to 360ºF (182ºC) and set time to 5 minutes.
5. Flip the beef halfway through the cooking time.
6. When cooking is complete, the beef should be well browned.
7. In the meantime, stir together the peanut butter, soy sauce, rice vinegar, honey, and ginger in a bowl to make the dipping sauce.
8. Transfer the beef to the serving dishes and let rest for 5 minutes. Serve with the peanut dipping sauce on the side.

280. Meatballs(3)

Servings: 4
Cooking Time: 20 Minutes
Ingredients:
- 1 lb ground beef
- 1/2 small onion, chopped
- 1 egg, lightly beaten
- 2 garlic cloves, minced
- 1 tbsp basil, chopped
- 1/4 cup parmesan cheese, grated
- 1/2 cup breadcrumbs

- 1 tbsp Italian parsley, chopped
- 1 tbsp rosemary, chopped
- 2 tbsp milk
- Pepper
- Salt

Directions:
1. Fit the oven with the rack in position
2. Add all ingredients into the mixing bowl and mix until well combined.
3. Make small balls from the meat mixture and place them into the baking pan.
4. Set to bake at 375 F for 25 minutes. After 5 minutes place the baking pan in the preheated oven.
5. Serve and enjoy.
- **Nutrition Info:** Calories 311 Fat 10.4 g Carbohydrates 12.3 g Sugar 1.7 g Protein 39.9 g Cholesterol 147 mg

281. Baked Lemon Pepper Chicken

Servings: 4
Cooking Time: 35 Minutes
Ingredients:
- 4 chicken thighs
- 1 tsp garlic powder
- 1/2 tsp onion powder
- 1 tbsp lemon pepper seasoning
- 2 tbsp fresh lemon juice
- 1/2 tsp paprika
- 2 tbsp olive oil
- 1 tsp salt

Directions:
1. Fit the oven with the rack in position
2. Add chicken in the mixing bowl.
3. Pour lemon juice and olive oil over chicken and coat well.
4. Mix lemon pepper seasoning, paprika, Italian seasoning, onion powder, garlic powder, and salt and rub all over the chicken thighs.
5. Place chicken in baking pan.
6. Set to bake at 400 F for 40 minutes. After 5 minutes place the baking pan in the preheated oven.
7. Serve and enjoy.
- **Nutrition Info:** Calories 184 Fat 11.6 g Carbohydrates 2.1 g Sugar 0.5 g Protein 17.8 g Cholesterol 53 mg

282. Crispy Parmesan Escallops

Servings:4
Cooking Time: 20 Minutes
Ingredients:
- 4 skinless chicken breasts
- 1 cup panko breadcrumbs
- ¼ cup Parmesan cheese, grated
- 3 fresh sage leaves, chopped
- 1 cup flour
- 2 eggs, beaten

Directions:

1. Place the chicken breasts between 2 sheets of cling film and beat well using a rolling pin to a ¼-inch thickness. In a bowl, mix Parmesan cheese, sage, and breadcrumbs.
2. Dip the chicken into the flour and then into the eggs. Finally, dredge into the breadcrumbs mixture. Transfer to the basket and cook in the for 14 minutes at 350 F on AirFry mode.

283. Cheesy Chicken Tenders

Servings: 4
Cooking Time: 30 Minutes
Ingredients:

- 1 large white meat chicken breast, approximately 5-6 ounces, sliced into strips
- 1 cup of breadcrumbs (Panko brand works well)
- 2 medium-sized eggs
- Pinch of salt and pepper
- 1 tablespoon of grated or powdered parmesan cheese

Directions:

1. Preparing the Ingredients. Cover the basket of the air fryer oven with a lining of tin foil, leaving the edges uncovered to allow air to circulate through the basket. Preheat the air fryer oven to 350 degrees. In a mixing bowl, beat the eggs until fluffy and until the yolks and whites are fully combined, and set aside. In a separate mixing bowl, combine the breadcrumbs, parmesan, salt, and pepper, and set aside. One by one, dip each piece of raw chicken into the bowl with dry ingredients, coating all sides; then submerge into the bowl with wet ingredients, then dip again into the dry ingredients. Lay the coated chicken pieces on the foil covering the Oven rack/basket, in a single flat layer. Place the Rack on the middle-shelf of the air fryer oven.
2. Air Frying. Set the air fryer oven timer for 15 minutes. After 15 minutes, the air fryer will turn off and the chicken should be mid-way cooked and the breaded coating starting to brown. Using tongs turn each piece of chicken over to ensure a full all over fry. Reset the air fryer oven to 320 degrees for another 15 minutes. After 15 minutes, when the air fryer shuts off, remove the fried chicken strips using tongs and set on a serving plate. Eat as soon as cool enough to handle, and enjoy!
- **Nutrition Info:** CALORIES: 278; FAT: 15G; PROTEIN:29G; SUGAR:7G

284. Flavorful Lemon Pepper Chicken

Servings: 4
Cooking Time: 25 Minutes
Ingredients:

- 4 chicken breasts, boneless & skinless
- 3 tbsp fresh lemon juice
- 2 tsp ground black pepper
- 5 tbsp olive oil
- 1/2 tsp sea salt

Directions:

1. Fit the oven with the rack in position
2. Heat 2 tablespoons of oil in a pan over medium-high heat. Brown chicken in a pan.
3. In a small bowl, mix lemon juice, remaining oil, pepper, and salt.
4. Place browned chicken into the baking dish. Pour lemon juice mixture over chicken.
5. Set to bake at 425 F for 30 minutes. After 5 minutes place the baking dish in the preheated oven.
6. Serve and enjoy.
- **Nutrition Info:** Calories 433 Fat 28.4 g Carbohydrates 0.9 g Sugar 0.3 g Protein 42.4 g Cholesterol 130 mg

285. Classic Walliser Schnitzel

Servings:2
Cooking Time: 14 Minutes
Ingredients:

- ½ cup pork rinds
- ½ tablespoon fresh parsley
- ½ teaspoon fennel seed
- ½ teaspoon mustard
- $^1/_3$ tablespoon cider vinegar
- 1 teaspoon garlic salt
- $^1/_3$ teaspoon ground black pepper
- 2 eggs
- 2 pork schnitzel, halved
- Cooking spray

Directions:

1. Spritz the air fryer basket with cooking spray.
2. Put the pork rinds, parsley, fennel seeds, and mustard in a food processor. Pour in the vinegar and sprinkle with salt and ground black pepper. Pulse until well combined and smooth.
3. Pour the pork rind mixture in a large bowl. Whisk the eggs in a separate bowl.
4. Dunk the pork schnitzel in the whisked eggs, then dunk in the pork rind mixture to coat well. Shake the excess off.
5. Arrange the schnitzel in the pan and spritz with cooking spray.
6. Put the air fryer basket on the baking pan and slide into Rack Position 2, select Air Fry,

set temperature to 350ºF (180ºC) and set time to 14 minutes.

7. After 7 minutes, remove from the oven. Flip the schnitzel. Return to the oven and continue cooking.
8. When cooking is complete, the schnitzel should be golden and crispy.
9. Serve immediately.

286. Flavorful Sirloin Steak

Servings: 2
Cooking Time: 14 Minutes
Ingredients:
- 1 lb sirloin steaks
- 1/2 tsp garlic powder
- 1/2 tsp onion powder
- 1/4 tsp smoked paprika
- 1 tsp olive oil
- Pepper
- Salt

Directions:
1. Fit the oven with the rack in position 2.
2. Line the air fryer basket with parchment paper.
3. Brush steak with olive oil and rub with garlic powder, onion powder, paprika, pepper, and salt.
4. Place the steak in the air fryer basket then places an air fryer basket in the baking pan.
5. Place a baking pan on the oven rack. Set to air fry at 400 F for 14 minutes.
6. Serve and enjoy.
- **Nutrition Info:** Calories 447 Fat 16.5 g Carbohydrates 1.2 g Sugar 0.4 g Protein 69 g Cholesterol 203 mg

287. Spiced Pork Chops

Servings: 4
Cooking Time: 16 Minutes
Ingredients:
- 4 pork chops, boneless
- 1/2 tsp granulated onion
- 1/2 tsp granulated garlic
- 1/4 tsp sugar
- 2 tsp olive oil
- 1/2 tsp celery seed
- 1/2 tsp parsley
- 1/2 tsp salt

Directions:
1. Fit the oven with the rack in position 2.
2. Brush pork chops with olive oil.
3. Mix celery seed, parsley, granulated onion, garlic, sugar, and salt and sprinkle over pork chops.
4. Place pork chops in the air fryer basket then place an air fryer basket in the baking pan.
5. Place a baking pan on the oven rack. Set to air fry at 350 F for 16 minutes.
6. Serve and enjoy.

- **Nutrition Info:** Calories 279 Fat 22.3 g Carbohydrates 0.6 g Sugar 0.3 g Protein 18.1 g Cholesterol 69 mg

288. Crispy Breaded Pork Chops

Servings: 8
Cooking Time: 15 Minutes
Ingredients:
- 1/8 tsp. pepper
- ¼ tsp. chili powder
- ½ tsp. onion powder
- ½ tsp. garlic powder
- 1 ¼ tsp. sweet paprika
- 2 tbsp. grated parmesan cheese
- 1/3 C. crushed cornflake crumbs
- ½ C. panko breadcrumbs
- 1 beaten egg
- 6 center-cut boneless pork chops

Directions:
1. Preparing the Ingredients. Ensure that your air fryer oven is preheated to 400 degrees. Spray the basket with olive oil.
2. With ½ teaspoon salt and pepper, season both sides of pork chops.
3. Combine ¾ teaspoon salt with pepper, chili powder, onion powder, garlic powder, paprika, cornflake crumbs, panko breadcrumbs, and parmesan cheese.
4. Beat egg in another bowl.
5. Dip pork chops into the egg and then crumb mixture.
6. Add pork chops to air fryer oven and spritz with olive oil.
7. Air Frying. Set temperature to 400°F, and set time to 12 minutes. Cook 12 minutes, making sure to flip over halfway through the cooking process.
8. Only add 3 chops in at a time and repeat the process with remaining pork chops.
- **Nutrition Info:** CALORIES: 378; FAT: 13G; PROTEIN:33G; SUGAR:1

289. Mustard Chicken Breasts

Servings:4
Cooking Time: 20 Minutes
Ingredients:
- ¼ cup flour
- 1 lb chicken breasts, sliced
- 1 tbsp Worcestershire sauce
- ¼ cup onions, chopped
- 1 ½ cups brown sugar
- ¼ cup yellow mustard
- ¾ cup water
- ½ cup ketchup

Directions:
1. Preheat on AirFry function to 360 F. In a bowl, mix sugar, water, ketchup, onions, mustard, Worcestershire sauce, salt, and pepper. Stir until the sugar dissolves.

2. Flour the chicken slices and then dip it in the mustard mixture. Let marinate for 10 minutes. Place the chicken in a greased baking dish and press Start. Cook for 15 minutes. Serve immediately.

290. Lamb Pops

Servings:x
Cooking Time:x
Ingredients:
- 1 cup cubed lamb
- 1 ½ tsp. garlic paste
- Salt and pepper to taste
- 1 tsp. dry oregano
- 1 tsp. dry basil
- ½ cup hung curd
- 1 tsp. lemon juice
- 1 tsp. red chili flakes

Directions:
1. Add the ingredients into a separate bowl and mix them well to get a consistent mixture. Dip the lamb pieces in the above mixture and leave them aside for some time. Pre heat the oven at 180° C for around 5 minutes.
2. Place the coated lamb pieces in the fry basket and close it properly. Let them cook at the same temperature for 20 more minutes.
3. Keep turning them over in the basket so that they are cooked properly. Serve with tomato ketchup.

291. Crispy Chicken Nuggets

Servings: 4
Cooking Time: 25 Minutes
Ingredients:
- 1 1/2 lbs chicken breast, boneless & cut into chunks
- 1/4 cup parmesan cheese, shredded
- 1/4 cup mayonnaise
- 1/2 tsp garlic powder
- 1/4 tsp salt

Directions:
1. Fit the oven with the rack in position 2.
2. In a bowl, mix mayonnaise, cheese, garlic powder, and salt.
3. Add chicken and mix until well coated.
4. Arrange coated chicken in the air fryer basket then place an air fryer basket in the baking pan.
5. Place a baking pan on the oven rack. Set to air fry at 400 F for 25 minutes.
6. Serve and enjoy.
- **Nutrition Info:** Calories 270 Fat 10.4 g Carbohydrates 4 g Sugar 1 g Protein 38.1 g Cholesterol 117 mg

292. Simple Pork Meatballs With Red Chili

Servings:4
Cooking Time: 15 Minutes
Ingredients:
- 1 pound (454 g) ground pork
- 2 cloves garlic, finely minced
- 1 cup scallions, finely chopped
- 1½ tablespoons Worcestershire sauce
- ½ teaspoon freshly grated ginger root
- 1 teaspoon turmeric powder
- 1 tablespoon oyster sauce
- 1 small sliced red chili, for garnish
- Cooking spray

Directions:
1. Spritz the air fryer basket with cooking spray.
2. Combine all the ingredients, except for the red chili in a large bowl. Toss to mix well.
3. Shape the mixture into equally sized balls, then arrange them in the basket and spritz with cooking spray.
4. Put the air fryer basket on the baking pan and slide into Rack Position 2, select Air Fry, set temperature to 350ºF (180ºC) and set time to 15 minutes.
5. After 7 minutes, remove from the oven. Flip the balls. Return to the oven and continue cooking.
6. When cooking is complete, the balls should be lightly browned.
7. Serve the pork meatballs with red chili on top.

293. Sweet Sticky Chicken Wings

Servings:4
Cooking Time: 20 Minutes
Ingredients:
- 16 chicken wings
- ¼ cup butter
- ¼ cup honey
- ½ tbsp salt
- 4 garlic cloves, minced
- ¾ cup potato starch

Directions:
1. Preheat on AirFry function to 370 F. Coat the wings with potato starch and place them in a greased baking dish. Press Start and cook for 5 minutes. Whisk the rest of the ingredients in a bowl. Pour the sauce over the wings and cook for another 10 minutes. Serve warm.

294. Garlic Lemony Chicken Breast

Servings:2
Cooking Time: 20 Minutes
Ingredients:
- 1 chicken breast

- 2 lemon, juiced and rind reserved
- 1 tbsp chicken seasoning
- 1 tbsp garlic puree
- A handful of peppercorns
- Salt and black pepper to taste

Directions:
1. Place a silver foil sheet on a flat surface. Add all seasonings alongside the lemon rind. Lay the chicken breast onto a chopping board and trim any fat and little bones; season.
2. Rub the chicken seasoning on both sides. Place on the foil sheet and seal tightly; flatten with a rolling pin. Place the breast in the basket and cook for 15 minutes at 350 F on AirFry function.

295.   Juicy Balsamic Chicken

Servings: 4
Cooking Time: 25 Minutes
Ingredients:
- 4 chicken breasts, boneless & skinless
- 2 tsp dried oregano
- 2 garlic clove, minced
- 1/2 cup balsamic vinegar
- 2 tbsp soy sauce
- 1/4 cup olive oil
- 1/4 tsp pepper
- 1/4 tsp salt

Directions:
1. Fit the oven with the rack in position
2. Place chicken into the baking dish. Mix together remaining ingredients and pour over chicken and let sit for 10 minutes.
3. Set to bake at 400 F for 30 minutes. After 5 minutes place the baking dish in the preheated oven.
4. Serve and enjoy.
- **Nutrition Info:** Calories 401 Fat 23.5 g Carbohydrates 2 g Sugar 0.3 g Protein 42.9 g Cholesterol 130 mg

296.   Bacon-wrapped Chicken Breasts

Servings:2
Cooking Time: 20 Minutes
Ingredients:
- 2 chicken breasts
- 8 oz onion and chive cream cheese
- 1 tbsp butter
- 6 turkey bacon
- Salt to taste
- 1 tbsp fresh parsley, chopped
- Juice from ½ lemon

Directions:
1. Preheat on AirFry function to 390 F. Stretch out the bacon slightly and lay them in 2 sets; 3 bacon strips together on each side. Place

the chicken breast on each bacon set and use a knife to smear cream cheese on both.
2. Share the butter on top and sprinkle with salt. Wrap the bacon around the chicken and secure the ends into the wrap. Place the wrapped chicken in the basket and press Start.
3. Cook for 14 minutes. Remove the chicken onto a serving platter and top with parsley and lemon juice. Serve with steamed greens.

297.   Veal Patti With Boiled Peas

Servings:x
Cooking Time:x
Ingredients:
- ½ lb. minced veal
- ½ cup breadcrumbs
- A pinch of salt to taste
- ½ cup of boiled peas
- ¼ tsp. ginger finely chopped
- 1 green chili finely chopped
- 1 tsp. lemon juice
- 1 tbsp. fresh coriander leaves. Chop them finely
- ¼ tsp. red chili powder
- ¼ tsp. cumin powder
- ¼ tsp. dried mango powder

Directions:
1. Take a container and into it pour all the masalas, onions, green chilies, peas, coriander leaves, lemon juice, and ginger and 1-2 tbsp. breadcrumbs. Add the minced veal as well. Mix all the ingredients well. Mold the mixture into round patties. Press them gently. Now roll them out carefully.
2. Pre heat the oven at 250 Fahrenheit for 5 minutes. Open the basket of the Fryer and arrange the patties in the basket. Close it carefully. Keep the fryer at 150 degrees for around 10 or 12 minutes. In between the cooking process, turn the patties over to get a uniform cook. Serve hot with mint sauce.

298.   Chicken & Cheese Enchilada

Servings:4
Cooking Time: 35 Minutes
Ingredients:
- 1 lb chicken breasts, chopped
- 2 cups cheddar cheese, grated
- ½ cup salsa
- 1 can green chilies, chopped
- 12 flour tortillas
- 2 cups enchilada sauce

Directions:
1. In a bowl, mix salsa and enchilada sauce. Toss in the chopped chicken to coat. Place the chicken on the tortillas and roll; top with cheese. Place the prepared tortillas in a baking tray and press Start. Cook for 25-30

minutes at 400 F on Bake function. Serve with guacamole and hot dips!

299. Worcestershire Chicken Breasts

Servings: 4
Cooking Time: 20 Minutes
Ingredients:
- ¼ cup flour
- ½ tbsp flour
- 4 chicken breasts, sliced
- 1 tbsp Worcestershire sauce
- 3 tbsp olive oil
- ¼ cup onions, chopped
- 1 ½ cups brown sugar
- ¼ cup yellow mustard
- ¾ cup water
- ½ cup ketchup

Directions:
1. In a bowl, mix flour, salt, and pepper. Cover the chicken slices with flour mixture and drizzle with olive oil. In another bowl, mix brown sugar, water, ketchup, onion, mustard, Worcestershire sauce, and salt. Add in the chicken and let sit for 10 minutes.
2. Preheat on Air Fry function to 360 F. Remove the chicken slices from the marinade and place them in the greased basket. Fit in baking tray and cook for 15 minutes. Serve.

300. Chicken And Sweet Potato Curry

Servings:4
Cooking Time: 20 Minutes
Ingredients:
- 1 pound (454 g) boneless, skinless chicken thighs
- 1 teaspoon kosher salt, divided
- ¼ cup unsalted butter, melted
- 1 tablespoon curry powder
- 2 medium sweet potatoes, peeled and cut in 1-inch cubes
- 12 ounces (340 g) Brussels sprouts, halved

Directions:
1. Sprinkle the chicken thighs with ½ teaspoon of kosher salt. Place them in the single layer in the baking pan.
2. In a small bowl, stir together the butter and curry powder.
3. Place the sweet potatoes and Brussels sprouts in a large bowl. Drizzle half the curry butter over the vegetables and add the remaining kosher salt. Toss to coat. Transfer the vegetables to the baking pan and place in a single layer around the chicken. Brush half of the remaining curry butter over the chicken.

4. Slide the baking pan into Rack Position 2, select Roast, set temperature to 400ºF (205ºC), and set time to 20 minutes.
5. After 10 minutes, remove from the oven and turn over the chicken thighs. Baste them with the remaining curry butter. Return to the oven and continue cooking.
6. Cooking is complete when the sweet potatoes are tender and the chicken is cooked through and reads 165ºF (74ºC) on a meat thermometer.

301. Crispy Honey Garlic Chicken Wings

Servings: 8
Cooking Time: 25 Minutes
Ingredients:
- 1/8 C. water
- ½ tsp. salt
- 4 tbsp. minced garlic
- ¼ C. vegan butter
- ¼ C. raw honey
- ¾ C. almond flour
- 16 chicken wings

Directions:
1. Preparing the Ingredients. Rinse off and dry chicken wings well.
2. Spray air fryer rack/basket with olive oil.
3. Coat chicken wings with almond flour and add coated wings to the air fryer oven.
4. Air Frying. Set temperature to 380°F, and set time to 25 minutes. Cook shaking every 5 minutes.
5. When the timer goes off, cook 5-10 minutes at 400 degrees till skin becomes crispy and dry.
6. As chicken cooks, melt butter in a saucepan and add garlic. Sauté garlic 5 minutes. Add salt and honey, simmering 20 minutes. Make sure to stir every so often, so the sauce does not burn. Add a bit of water after 15 minutes to ensure sauce does not harden.
7. Take out chicken wings from air fryer oven and coat in sauce. Enjoy!
- **Nutrition Info:** CALORIES: 435; FAT: 19G; PROTEIN:31G; SUGAR:6

302. Barbecue Flavored Pork Ribs

Servings: 6
Cooking Time: 15 Minutes
Ingredients:
- ¼ cup honey, divided
- ¾ cup BBQ sauce
- 2 tablespoons tomato ketchup
- 1 tablespoon Worcestershire sauce
- 1 tablespoon soy sauce
- ½ teaspoon garlic powder
- Freshly ground white pepper, to taste
- 1¼ pound pork ribs

Directions:
1. Preparing the Ingredients. In a large bowl, mix together 3 tablespoons of honey and remaining ingredients except pork ribs.
2. Refrigerate to marinate for about 20 minutes.
3. Preheat the air fryer oven to 355 degrees F.
4. Place the ribs in an Air fryer rack/basket.
5. Air Frying. Cook for about 13 minutes.
6. Remove the ribs from the air fryer oven and coat with remaining honey.
7. Serve hot.

303. Lemony Pork Loin Chop Schnitzel

Servings:4
Cooking Time: 15 Minutes
Ingredients:
- 4 thin boneless pork loin chops
- 2 tablespoons lemon juice
- ½ cup flour
- ¼ teaspoon marjoram
- 1 teaspoon salt
- 1 cup panko bread crumbs
- 2 eggs
- Lemon wedges, for serving
- Cooking spray

Directions:
1. On a clean work surface, drizzle the pork chops with lemon juice on both sides.
2. Combine the flour with marjoram and salt on a shallow plate. Pour the bread crumbs on a separate shallow dish. Beat the eggs in a large bowl.
3. Dredge the pork chops in the flour, then dunk in the beaten eggs to coat well. Shake the excess off and roll over the bread crumbs. Arrange the pork chops in the basket and spritz with cooking spray.
4. Put the air fryer basket on the baking pan and slide into Rack Position 2, select Air Fry, set temperature to 400ºF (205ºC) and set time to 15 minutes.
5. After 7 minutes, remove from the oven. Flip the pork. Return to the oven and continue cooking.
6. When cooking is complete, the pork should be crispy and golden.
7. Squeeze the lemon wedges over the fried chops and serve immediately.

304. Chicken Best Homemade Croquette

Servings:x
Cooking Time:x
Ingredients:
- 2 lb. boneless chicken cut into 1½" pieces
- 1st Marinade:

- 3 tbsp. vinegar or lemon juice
- 2 or 3 tsp. paprika
- 1 tsp. black pepper
- 1 tsp. salt
- 3 tsp. ginger-garlic paste
- 2nd Marinade:
- 1 cup yogurt
- 4 tsp. tandoori masala
- 2 tbsp. dry fenugreek leaves
- 1 tsp. black salt
- 1 tsp. chat masala
- 1 tsp. garam masala powder
- 1 tsp. red chili powder
- 1 tsp. salt
- 3 drops of red color

Directions:
1. Make the first marinade and soak the cut chicken in it for four hours. While this is happening, make the second marinade and soak the chicken in it overnight to let the flavors blend.
2. Pre heat the oven at 160 degrees Fahrenheit for 5 minutes. Place the Oregano Fingers in the fry basket and close it. Let them cook at the same temperature for another 15 minutes or so. Toss the Oregano Fingers well so that they are cooked uniformly. Serve them with mint sauce.

305. Spicy Chicken Skewers With Satay Sauce

Servings:4
Cooking Time: 10 Minutes
Ingredients:
- 4 (6-ounce / 170-g) boneless, skinless chicken breasts, sliced into strips
- 1 teaspoon sea salt
- 1 teaspoon paprika
- Cooking spray
- Satay Sauce:
- ¼ cup creamy almond butter
- ½ teaspoon hot sauce
- 1½ tablespoons coconut vinegar
- 2 tablespoons chicken broth
- 1 teaspoon peeled and minced fresh ginger
- 1 clove garlic, minced
- 1 teaspoon sugar
- For Serving:
- ¼ cup chopped cilantro leaves
- Red pepper flakes, to taste
- Thinly sliced red, orange, or / and yellow bell peppers
- Special Equipment:
- 16 wooden or bamboo skewers, soaked in water for 15 minutes

Directions:
1. Spritz the air fryer basket with cooking spray.

2. Run the bamboo skewers through the chicken strips, then arrange the chicken skewers in the basket and sprinkle with salt and paprika.
3. Put the air fryer basket on the baking pan and slide into Rack Position 2, select Air Fry, set temperature to 400ºF (205ºC) and set time to 10 minutes.
4. Flip the chicken skewers halfway during the cooking.
5. When cooking is complete, the chicken should be lightly browned.
6. Meanwhile, combine the ingredients for the sauce in a small bowl. Stir to mix well.
7. Transfer the cooked chicken skewers on a large plate, then top with cilantro, sliced bell peppers, red pepper flakes. Serve with the sauce or just baste the sauce over before serving.

306. Golden Chicken Fries

Servings:4 To 6
Cooking Time: 6 Minutes
Ingredients:
- 1 pound (454 g) chicken tenders, cut into about ½-inch-wide strips
- Salt, to taste
- ¼ cup all-purpose flour
- 2 eggs
- ¾ cup panko bread crumbs
- ¾ cup crushed organic nacho cheese tortilla chips
- Cooking spray
- Seasonings:
- ½ teaspoon garlic powder
- 1 tablespoon chili powder
- ½ teaspoon onion powder
- 1 teaspoon ground cumin

Directions:
1. Stir together all seasonings in a small bowl and set aside.
2. Sprinkle the chicken with salt. Place strips in a large bowl and sprinkle with 1 tablespoon of the seasoning mix. Stir well to distribute seasonings.
3. Add flour to chicken and stir well to coat all sides.
4. Beat eggs in a separate bowl.
5. In a shallow dish, combine the panko, crushed chips, and the remaining 2 teaspoons of seasoning mix.
6. Dip chicken strips in eggs, then roll in crumbs. Mist with oil or cooking spray. Arrange the chicken strips in a single layer in the basket.
7. Put the air fryer basket on the baking pan and slide into Rack Position 2, select Air Fry, set the temperature to 400ºF (205ºC) and set the time to 6 minutes.

8. After 4 minutes, remove from the oven. Flip the strips with tongs. Return to the oven and continue cooking.
9. When cooking is complete, the chicken should be crispy and its juices should be run clear.
10. Allow to cool under room temperature before serving.

307. Baked Pork Ribs

Servings: 8
Cooking Time: 30 Minutes
Ingredients:
- 2 lbs pork ribs, boneless
- 1 tbsp onion powder
- 1 1/2 tbsp garlic powder
- Pepper
- Salt

Directions:
1. Fit the oven with the rack in position
2. Place pork ribs in baking pan and season with onion powder, garlic powder, pepper, and salt.
3. Set to bake at 350 F for 35 minutes. After 5 minutes place the baking pan in the preheated oven.
4. Serve and enjoy.
- **Nutrition Info:** Calories 318 Fat 20.1 g Carbohydrates 1.9 g Sugar 0.7 g Protein 30.4 g Cholesterol 117 mg

308. Mustard & Thyme Chicken

Servings:4
Cooking Time: 20 Minutes
Ingredients:
- 1 tsp garlic powder
- 1 lb chicken breasts, sliced
- 1 tsp dried thyme
- ½ cup dry wine
- ½ cup Dijon mustard
- 1 cup breadcrumbs
- 1 tbsp lemon zest
- 2 tbsp olive oil

Directions:
1. In a bowl, mix breadcrumbs with garlic powder, lemon zest, salt, and pepper. In another bowl, mix mustard, olive oil, and wine. Dip chicken slices in the wine mixture and then in the crumb mixture. Place the chicken in the basket and cook for 15 minutes at 350 F on AirFry function.

309. Goat Cheese Meatballs

Servings: 8
Cooking Time: 12 Minutes
Ingredients:
- 1 lb ground beef
- 1 lb ground pork
- 2 eggs, lightly beaten

- 1/4 cup fresh parsley, chopped
- 1 tbsp garlic, minced
- 1 onion, chopped
- 1 tbsp Worcestershire sauce
- 1/2 cup goat cheese, crumbled
- 1/2 cup breadcrumbs
- Pepper
- Salt

Directions:
1. Fit the oven with the rack in position 2.
2. Line the air fryer basket with parchment paper.
3. Add all ingredients into a large bowl and mix until well combined.
4. Make small balls from meat mixture and place in the air fryer basket then place an air fryer basket in the baking pan.
5. Place a baking pan on the oven rack. Set to air fry at 400 F for 12 minutes.
6. Serve and enjoy.
- **Nutrition Info:** Calories 253 Fat 8.1 g Carbohydrates 7.2 g Sugar 1.6 g Protein 35.6 g Cholesterol 136 mg

310. Cheesy Bacon Chicken

Servings: 4
Cooking Time: 30 Minutes
Ingredients:
- 4 chicken breasts, sliced in half
- 1 cup cheddar cheese, shredded
- 8 bacon slices, cooked & chopped
- 6 oz cream cheese
- Pepper
- Salt

Directions:
1. Fit the oven with the rack in position
2. Place season chicken with pepper and salt and place it into the greased baking dish.
3. Add cream cheese and bacon on top of chicken.
4. Sprinkle shredded cheddar cheese on top of chicken.
5. Set to bake at 400 F for 35 minutes. After 5 minutes place the baking dish in the preheated oven.
6. Serve and enjoy.
- **Nutrition Info:** Calories 745 Fat 50.9 g Carbohydrates 2.1 g Sugar 0.2 g Protein 66.6 g Cholesterol 248 mg

FISH & SEAFOOD RECIPES

311.   Tilapia Meunière With Vegetables

Servings:4
Cooking Time: 20 Minutes
Ingredients:
- 10 ounces (283 g) Yukon Gold potatoes, sliced ¼-inch thick
- 5 tablespoons unsalted butter, melted, divided
- 1 teaspoon kosher salt, divided
- 4 (8-ounce / 227-g) tilapia fillets
- ½ pound (227 g) green beans, trimmed
- Juice of 1 lemon
- 2 tablespoons chopped fresh parsley, for garnish

Directions:
1. In a large bowl, drizzle the potatoes with 2 tablespoons of melted butter and ¼ teaspoon of kosher salt. Transfer the potatoes to the baking pan.
2. Slide the baking pan into Rack Position 2, select Roast, set temperature to 375ºF (190ºC), and set time to 20 minutes.
3. Meanwhile, season both sides of the fillets with ½ teaspoon of kosher salt. Put the green beans in the medium bowl and sprinkle with the remaining ¼ teaspoon of kosher salt and 1 tablespoon of butter, tossing to coat.
4. After 10 minutes, remove from the oven and push the potatoes to one side. Put the fillets in the middle of the pan and add the green beans on the other side. Drizzle the remaining 2 tablespoons of butter over the fillets. Return the pan to the oven and continue cooking, or until the fish flakes easily with a fork and the green beans are crisp-tender.
5. When cooked, remove from the oven. Drizzle the lemon juice over the fillets and sprinkle the parsley on top for garnish. Serve hot.

312.   Prawn French Cuisine Galette

Servings:x
Cooking Time:x
Ingredients:
- 2 tbsp. garam masala
- 1 lb. minced prawn
- 3 tsp ginger finely chopped
- 1-2 tbsp. fresh coriander leaves
- 2 or 3 green chilies finely chopped
- 1 ½ tbsp. lemon juice
- Salt and pepper to taste

Directions:
1. Mix the ingredients in a clean bowl.
2. Mold this mixture into round and flat French Cuisine Galettes.
3. Wet the French Cuisine Galettes slightly with water.
4. Pre heat the oven at 160 degrees Fahrenheit for 5 minutes. Place the French Cuisine Galettes in the fry basket and let them cook for another 25 minutes at the same temperature. Keep rolling them over to get a uniform cook. Serve either with mint sauce or ketchup.

313.   Cheese Carp Fries

Servings:x
Cooking Time:x
Ingredients:
- 1 lb. carp Oregano Fingers
- ingredients for the marinade:
- 1 tbsp. olive oil
- 1 tsp. mixed herbs
- ½ tsp. red chili flakes
- A pinch of salt to taste
- 1 tbsp. lemon juice
- For the garnish:
- 1 cup melted cheddar cheese

Directions:
1. Take all the ingredients mentioned under the heading "For the marinade" and mix them well. Cook the carp Oregano Fingers and soak them in the marinade.
2. Pre heat the oven for around 5 minutes at 300 Fahrenheit. Take out the basket of the fryer and place the carp in them. Close the basket. Now keep the fryer at 220 Fahrenheit for 20 or 25 minutes.
3. In between the process, toss the fries twice or thrice so that they get cooked properly. Towards the end of the cooking process (the last 2 minutes or so), sprinkle the melted cheddar cheese over the fries and serve hot.

314.   Crab Cakes

Servings: 4
Cooking Time: 10 Minutes
Ingredients:
- 8 ounces jumbo lump crabmeat
- 1 tablespoon Old Bay Seasoning
- ⅓ cup bread crumbs
- ¼ cup diced red bell pepper
- ¼ cup diced green bell pepper
- 1 egg
- ¼ cup mayonnaise
- Juice of ½ lemon
- 1 teaspoon flour
- Cooking oil

Directions:

1. Preparing the Ingredients. In a large bowl, combine the crabmeat, Old Bay Seasoning, bread crumbs, red bell pepper, green bell pepper, egg, mayo, and lemon juice. Mix gently to combine.
2. Form the mixture into 4 patties. Sprinkle ¼ teaspoon of flour on top of each patty.
3. Air Frying. Place the crab cakes in the air fryer oven. Spray them with cooking oil. Cook for 10 minutes.
4. Serve.

315.   Seafood Mac N Cheese

Servings: 8
Cooking Time: 30 Minutes
Ingredients:
- Nonstick cooking spray
- 16 oz. macaroni
- 7 tbsp. butter, divided
- ¾ lb. medium shrimp, peel, devein, & cut in ½-inch pieces
- ½ cup Italian panko bread crumbs
- 1 cup onion, chopped fine
- 1 ½ tsp garlic, diced fine
- 1/3 cup flour
- 3 cups milk
- 1/8 tsp nutmeg
- ½ tsp Old Bay seasoning
- 1 tsp salt
- ¾ tsp pepper
- 1 1/3 cup Parmesan cheese, grated
- 1 1/3 cup Swiss cheese, grated
- 1 1/3 cup sharp cheddar cheese, grated
- ½ lb. lump crab meat, cooked

Directions:
1. Place wire rack in position 1 of the oven. Spray a 7x11-inch baking dish with cooking spray.
2. Cook macaroni according to package directions, shortening cooking time by 2 minutes. Drain and rinse with cold water.
3. Melt 1 tablespoon butter in a large skillet over med-high heat. Add shrimp and cook, stirring, until they turn pink. Remove from heat.
4. Melt remaining butter in a large saucepan over medium heat. Once melted, transfer 2 tablespoons to a small bowl and mix in bread crumbs.
5. Add onions and garlic to saucepan and cook, stirring, until they soften.
6. Whisk in flour and cook 1 minute, until smooth.
7. Whisk in milk until there are no lumps. Bring to a boil, reduce heat and simmer until thickened, whisking constantly.
8. Whisk in seasonings. Stir in cheese until melted and smooth. Fold in macaroni and

seafood. Transfer to prepared dish. Sprinkle bread crumb mixture evenly over top.
9. Set oven to bake on 400°F for 25 minutes. After 5 minutes, place dish on the rack and bake 20 minutes, until topping is golden brown and sauce is bubbly. Let cool 5 minutes before serving.
- **Nutrition Info:** Calories 672, Total Fat 26g, Saturated Fat 15g, Total Carbs 68g, Net Carbs 61g, Protein 39g, Sugar 7g, Fiber 7g, Sodium 996mg, Potassium 921mg, Phosphorus 714mg

316.   Air Fryer Spicy Shrimp

Servings: 4
Cooking Time: 6 Minutes
Ingredients:
- 1 lb shrimp, peeled and deveined
- 1/4 tsp chili powder
- 1 tsp dried oregano
- 1 tsp garlic powder
- 1 tsp onion powder
- 2 tsp paprika
- 1/4 tsp cayenne
- 2 tbsp olive oil
- Pepper
- Salt

Directions:
1. Fit the oven with the rack in position 2.
2. In a bowl, toss shrimp with remaining ingredients.
3. Add shrimp to the air fryer basket then place an air fryer basket in the baking pan.
4. Place a baking pan on the oven rack. Set to air fry at 400 F for 6 minutes.
5. Serve and enjoy.
- **Nutrition Info:** Calories 204 Fat 9.2 g Carbohydrates 3.7 g Sugar 0.5 g Protein 26.2 g Cholesterol 239 mg

317.   Baked Buttery Shrimp

Servings: 4
Cooking Time: 15 Minutes
Ingredients:
- 1 lb shrimp, peel & deveined
- 2 tsp garlic powder
- 2 tsp dry mustard
- 2 tsp cumin
- 2 tsp paprika
- 2 tsp black pepper
- 4 tsp cayenne pepper
- 1/2 cup butter, melted
- 2 tsp onion powder
- 1 tsp dried oregano
- 1 tsp dried thyme
- 3 tsp salt

Directions:
1. Fit the oven with the rack in position

2. Add shrimp, butter, and remaining ingredients into the mixing bowl and toss well.
3. Transfer shrimp mixture into the baking pan.
4. Set to bake at 400 F for 20 minutes. After 5 minutes place the baking pan in the preheated oven.
5. Serve and enjoy.
- **Nutrition Info:** Calories 372 Fat 26.2 g Carbohydrates 7.5 g Sugar 1.3 g Protein 27.6 g Cholesterol 300 mg

318. Simple Lemon Salmon

Servings: 2
Cooking Time: 20 Minutes
Ingredients:
- 2 salmon fillets
- Salt to taste
- Zest of a lemon

Directions:
1. Spray the fillets with olive oil and rub them with salt and lemon zest. Line baking paper in a baking dish. Cook the fillets in your for 10 minutes at 360 F on Air Fry, turning once.

319. Healthy Haddock

Servings: 2
Cooking Time: 25 Minutes
Ingredients:
- 1 lb haddock fillets
- 1/4 cup parsley, chopped
- 1 lemon juice
- 1/4 cup brown sugar
- 1/4 cup onion, diced
- 1 tsp ginger, grated
- 3/4 cup soy sauce
- Pepper
- Salt

Directions:
1. Fit the oven with the rack in position
2. Add fish fillets and remaining ingredients into the large bowl and coat well and place in the refrigerator for 1 hour.
3. Place marinated fish fillets into the baking dish.
4. Set to bake at 325 F for 30 minutes. After 5 minutes place the baking dish in the preheated oven.
5. Serve and enjoy.
- **Nutrition Info:** Calories 391 Fat 2.5 g Carbohydrates 28 g Sugar 20.4 g Protein 61.7 g Cholesterol 168 mg

320. Tuna Lettuce Wraps

Servings:4
Cooking Time: 4 To 7 Minutes
Ingredients:

- 1 pound (454 g) fresh tuna steak, cut into 1-inch cubes
- 2 garlic cloves, minced
- 1 tablespoon grated fresh ginger
- ½ teaspoon toasted sesame oil
- 4 low-sodium whole-wheat tortillas
- 2 cups shredded romaine lettuce
- 1 red bell pepper, thinly sliced
- ¼ cup low-fat mayonnaise

Directions:
1. Combine the tuna cubes, garlic, ginger, and sesame oil in a medium bowl and toss until well coated. Allow to sit for 10 minutes.
2. When ready, place the tuna cubes in the air fryer basket.
3. Put the air fryer basket on the baking pan and slide into Rack Position 2, select Air Fry, set temperature to 390ºF (199ºC), and set time to 6 minutes.
4. When cooking is complete, the tuna cubes should be cooked through and golden brown. Remove the tuna cubes from the oven to a plate.
5. Make the wraps: Place the tortillas on a flat work surface and top each tortilla evenly with the cooked tuna, lettuce, bell pepper, and finish with the mayonnaise. Roll them up and serve immediately.

321. Flavorful Baked Halibut

Servings: 4
Cooking Time: 12 Minutes
Ingredients:
- 1 lb halibut fillets
- 1/4 tsp garlic powder
- 1/4 tsp paprika
- 1/4 tsp smoked paprika
- 1/4 tsp pepper
- 1/4 cup olive oil
- 1 lemon juice
- 1/2 tsp salt

Directions:
1. Fit the oven with the rack in position
2. Place fish fillets into the baking dish.
3. In a small bowl, mix lemon juice, oil, paprika, smoked paprika, garlic powder, and salt.
4. Brush lemon juice mixture over fish fillets.
5. Set to bake at 425 F for 17 minutes. After 5 minutes place the baking dish in the preheated oven.
6. Serve and enjoy.
- **Nutrition Info:** Calories 236 Fat 15.3 g Carbohydrates 0.4 g Sugar 0.1 g Protein 24 g Cholesterol 36 mg

322. Cajun Catfish Cakes With Cheese

Servings:4

Cooking Time: 15 Minutes

Ingredients:
- 2 catfish fillets
- 3 ounces (85 g) butter
- 1 cup shredded Parmesan cheese
- 1 cup shredded Swiss cheese
- ½ cup buttermilk
- 1 teaspoon baking powder
- 1 teaspoon baking soda
- 1 teaspoon Cajun seasoning

Directions:
1. Bring a pot of salted water to a boil. Add the catfish fillets to the boiling water and let them boil for 5 minutes until they become opaque.
2. Remove the fillets from the pot to a mixing bowl and flake them into small pieces with a fork.
3. Add the remaining ingredients to the bowl of fish and stir until well incorporated.
4. Divide the fish mixture into 12 equal portions and shape each portion into a patty. Place the patties in the air fryer basket.
5. Put the air fryer basket on the baking pan and slide into Rack Position 2, select Air Fry, set temperature to 380ºF (193ºC), and set time to 15 minutes.
6. Flip the patties halfway through the cooking time.
7. When cooking is complete, the patties should be golden brown and cooked through. Remove from the oven. Let the patties sit for 5 minutes and serve.

323.   Parsley Catfish Fillets

Servings:4
Cooking Time: 25 Minutes

Ingredients:
- 4 catfish fillets, rinsed and dried
- ¼ cup seasoned fish fry
- 1 tbsp olive oil
- 1 tbsp fresh parsley, chopped

Directions:
1. Add seasoned fish fry and fillets in a large Ziploc bag; massage well to coat. Place the fillets in the basket and cook for 14-16 minutes at 360 F on AirFry function. Top with parsley.

324.   Crispy Coated Scallops

Servings: 4
Cooking Time: 10 Minutes

Ingredients:
- Nonstick cooking spray
- 1 lb. sea scallops, patted dry
- 1 teaspoon onion powder
- ½ tsp pepper
- 1 egg
- 1 tbsp. water
- ¼ cup Italian bread crumbs
- Paprika
- 1 tbsp. fresh lemon juice

Directions:
1. Lightly spray fryer basket with cooking spray. Place baking pan in position 2 of the oven.
2. Sprinkle scallops with onion powder and pepper.
3. In a shallow dish, whisk together egg and water.
4. Place bread crumbs in a separate shallow dish.
5. Dip scallops in egg then bread crumbs coating them lightly. Place in fryer basket and lightly spray with cooking spray. Sprinkle with paprika.
6. Place the basket on the baking pan and set oven to air fryer on 400°F. Bake 10-12 minutes until scallops are firm on the inside and golden brown on the outside. Drizzle with lemon juice and serve.
- **Nutrition Info:** Calories 122, Total Fat 2g, Saturated Fat 1g, Total Carbs 10g, Net Carbs 9g, Protein 16g, Sugar 1g, Fiber 1g, Sodium 563mg, Potassium 282mg, Phosphorus 420mg

325.   Sweet Cajun Salmon

Servings: 1
Cooking Time: 10 Minutes

Ingredients:
- 1 salmon fillet
- ¼ tsp brown sugar
- Juice of ½ lemon
- 1 tbsp cajun seasoning
- 2 lemon wedges
- 1 tbsp chopped parsley

Directions:
1. Preheat on Bake function to 350 F. Combine sugar and lemon juice; coat the salmon with this mixture. Coat with the Cajun seasoning as well. Place a parchment paper on a baking tray and cook the fish in your for 10 minutes. Serve with lemon wedges and parsley.

326.   Firecracker Shrimp

Servings: 4
Cooking Time: 8 Minutes

Ingredients:
- For the shrimp
- 1 pound raw shrimp, peeled and deveined
- Salt
- Pepper
- 1 egg
- ½ cup all-purpose flour
- ¾ cup panko bread crumbs

- Cooking oil
- For the firecracker sauce
- ⅓ cup sour cream
- 2 tablespoons Sriracha
- ¼ cup sweet chili sauce

Directions:
1. Preparing the Ingredients. Season the shrimp with salt and pepper to taste. In a small bowl, beat the egg. In another small bowl, place the flour. In a third small bowl, add the panko bread crumbs.
2. Spray the Oven rack/basket with cooking oil. Dip the shrimp in the flour, then the egg, and then the bread crumbs. Place the shrimp in the Oven rack/basket. It is okay to stack them. Spray the shrimp with cooking oil. Place the Rack on the middle-shelf of the air fryer oven.
3. Air Frying. Cook for 4 minutes. Open the air fryer oven and flip the shrimp. I recommend flipping individually instead of shaking to keep the breading intact. Cook for an additional 4 minutes or until crisp.
4. While the shrimp is cooking, make the firecracker sauce: In a small bowl, combine the sour cream, Sriracha, and sweet chili sauce. Mix well. Serve with the shrimp.
- **Nutrition Info:** CALORIES: 266; CARBS:23g; FAT:6G; PROTEIN:27G; FIBER:1G

327.   Saucy Cod With Green Onions

Servings:4
Cooking Time: 20 Minutes
Ingredients:
- 4 cod fillets
- 2 tbsp fresh cilantro, chopped
- Salt to taste
- 4 green onions, chopped
- 5 slices of ginger, chopped
- 5 tbsp soy sauce
- 3 tbsp oil
- 5 rock sugar cubes

Directions:
1. Preheat on AirFry function to 390 F. Season the cod with salt and coriander and drizzle with some olive oil. Place the fish fillet in the basket and press Start. Cook for 15 minutes.
2. Heat the remaining olive oil in a skillet over medium heat and sauté green onions and ginger for 3 minutes. Add in the remaining ingredients and 1 cup of water. Bring to a boil and cook for 5 minutes until the sauce thickens. Pour the sauce over the fish and serve.

328.   Spicy Lemon Garlic Tilapia

Servings: 2
Cooking Time: 15 Minutes

Ingredients:
- 4 tilapia fillets
- 1 lemon, cut into slices
- 1/2 tsp pepper
- 1/2 tsp chili powder
- 1 tsp garlic, minced
- 3 tbsp butter, melted
- 1 tbsp fresh lemon juice
- Salt

Directions:
1. Fit the oven with the rack in position
2. Place fish fillets into the baking dish.
3. Arrange lemon slices on top of fish fillets.
4. Mix together the remaining ingredients and pour over fish fillets.
5. Set to bake at 350 F for 20 minutes. After 5 minutes place the baking dish in the preheated oven.
6. Serve and enjoy.
- **Nutrition Info:** Calories 354 Fat 19.6 g Carbohydrates 4 g Sugar 1 g Protein 42.8 g Cholesterol 156 mg

329.   Tasty Tuna Loaf

Servings: 6
Cooking Time: 40 Minutes
Ingredients:
- Nonstick cooking spray
- 12 oz. can chunk white tuna in water, drain & flake
- ¾ cup bread crumbs
- 1 onion, chopped fine
- 2 eggs, beaten
- ¼ cup milk
- ½ tsp fresh lemon juice
- ½ tsp dill
- 1 tbsp. fresh parsley, chopped
- ½ tsp salt
- ½ tsp pepper

Directions:
1. Place rack in position 1 of the oven. Spray a 9-inch loaf pan with cooking spray.
2. In a large bowl, combine all ingredients until thoroughly mixed. Spread evenly in prepared pan.
3. Set oven to bake on 350°F for 45 minutes. After 5 minutes, place the pan in the oven and cook 40 minutes, or until top is golden brown. Slice and serve.
- **Nutrition Info:** Calories 169, Total Fat 5g, Saturated Fat 1g, Total Carbs 13g, Net Carbs 12g, Protein 18g, Sugar 3g, Fiber 1g, Sodium 540mg, Potassium 247mg, Phosphorus 202mg

330.   Quick Paella

Servings: 4
Cooking Time: 15 Minutes
Ingredients:

- 1 (10-ounce) package frozen cooked rice, thawed
- 1 (6-ounce) jar artichoke hearts, drained and chopped
- ¼ cup vegetable broth
- ½ teaspoon turmeric
- ½ teaspoon dried thyme
- 1 cup frozen cooked small shrimp
- ½ cup frozen baby peas
- 1 tomato, diced

Directions:
1. Preparing the Ingredients. In a 6-by-6-by-2-inch pan, combine the rice, artichoke hearts, vegetable broth, turmeric, and thyme, and stir gently.
2. Air Frying. Place in the air fryer oven and bake for 8 to 9 minutes or until the rice is hot. Remove from the air fryer oven and gently stir in the shrimp, peas, and tomato. Cook for 5 to 8 minutes or until the shrimp and peas are hot and the paella is bubbling.
- **Nutrition Info:** CALORIES: 345; FAT: 1G; PROTEIN:18G; FIBER:4G

331.   Tasty Lemon Pepper Basa

Servings: 4
Cooking Time: 12 Minutes
Ingredients:
- 4 basa fish fillets
- 8 tsp olive oil
- 2 tbsp fresh parsley, chopped
- 1/4 cup green onion, sliced
- 1/2 tsp garlic powder
- 1/4 tsp lemon pepper seasoning
- 4 tbsp fresh lemon juice
- Pepper
- Salt

Directions:
1. Fit the oven with the rack in position
2. Place fish fillets in a baking dish.
3. Pour remaining ingredients over fish fillets.
4. Set to bake at 425 F for 12 minutes. After 5 minutes place the baking dish in the preheated oven.
5. Serve and enjoy.
- **Nutrition Info:** Calories 308 Fat 21.4 g Carbohydrates 5.5 g Sugar 3.4 g Protein 24.1 g Cholesterol 0 mg

332.   Mustard-crusted Sole Fillets

Servings:4
Cooking Time: 10 Minutes
Ingredients:
- 5 teaspoons low-sodium yellow mustard
- 1 tablespoon freshly squeezed lemon juice
- 4 (3.5-ounce / 99-g) sole fillets
- 2 teaspoons olive oil
- ½ teaspoon dried marjoram

- ½ teaspoon dried thyme
- ⅛ teaspoon freshly ground black pepper
- 1 slice low-sodium whole-wheat bread, crumbled

Directions:
1. Whisk together the mustard and lemon juice in a small bowl until thoroughly mixed and smooth. Spread the mixture evenly over the sole fillets, then transfer the fillets to the baking pan.
2. In a separate bowl, combine the olive oil, marjoram, thyme, black pepper, and bread crumbs and stir to mix well. Gently but firmly press the mixture onto the top of fillets, coating them completely.
3. Slide the baking pan into Rack Position 1, select Convection Bake, set temperature to 320ºF (160ºC), and set time to 10 minutes.
4. When cooking is complete, the fish should reach an internal temperature of 145ºF (63ºC) on a meat thermometer. Remove from the oven and serve on a plate.

333.   Flavorful Herb Salmon

Servings: 4
Cooking Time: 15 Minutes
Ingredients:
- 1 lb salmon fillets
- 1/2 tbsp dried rosemary
- 1 tbsp olive oil
- 1/4 tsp dried basil
- 1 tbsp dried chives
- 1/4 tsp dried thyme
- Pepper
- Salt

Directions:
1. Fit the oven with the rack in position 2.
2. Place salmon skin side down in air fryer basket then place an air fryer basket in baking pan.
3. Mix olive oil, thyme, basil, chives, and rosemary in a small bowl.
4. Brush salmon with oil mixture.
5. Place a baking pan on the oven rack. Set to air fry at 400 F for 15 minutes.
6. Serve and enjoy.
- **Nutrition Info:** Calories 182 Fat 10.6 g Carbohydrates 0.4 g Sugar 0 g Protein 22.1 g Cholesterol 50 mg

334.   Goat Cheese Shrimp

Servings:2
Cooking Time: 8 Minutes
Ingredients:
- 1 pound (454 g) shrimp, deveined
- 1½ tablespoons olive oil
- 1½ tablespoons balsamic vinegar
- 1 tablespoon coconut aminos

- ½ tablespoon fresh parsley, roughly chopped
- Sea salt flakes, to taste
- 1 teaspoon Dijon mustard
- ½ teaspoon smoked cayenne pepper
- ½ teaspoon garlic powder
- Salt and ground black peppercorns, to taste
- 1 cup shredded goat cheese

Directions:
1. Except for the cheese, stir together all the ingredients in a large bowl until the shrimp are evenly coated.
2. Place the shrimp in the air fryer basket.
3. Put the air fryer basket on the baking pan and slide into Rack Position 2, select Roast, set temperature to 385ºF (196ºC), and set time to 8 minutes.
4. When cooking is complete, the shrimp should be pink and cooked through. Remove from the oven and serve with the shredded goat cheese sprinkled on top.

335.   Coconut Chili Fish Curry

Servings:4
Cooking Time: 22 Minutes
Ingredients:
- 2 tablespoons sunflower oil, divided
- 1 pound (454 g) fish, chopped
- 1 ripe tomato, puréed
- 2 red chilies, chopped
- 1 shallot, minced
- 1 garlic clove, minced
- 1 cup coconut milk
- 1 tablespoon coriander powder
- 1 teaspoon red curry paste
- ½ teaspoon fenugreek seeds
- Salt and white pepper, to taste

Directions:
1. Coat the air fryer basket with 1 tablespoon of sunflower oil. Place the fish in the basket.
2. Put the air fryer basket on the baking pan and slide into Rack Position 2, select Air Fry, set temperature to 380ºF (193ºC), and set time to 10 minutes.
3. Flip the fish halfway through the cooking time.
4. When cooking is complete, transfer the cooked fish to the baking pan greased with the remaining 1 tablespoon of sunflower oil. Stir in the remaining ingredients.
5. Put the air fryer basket on the baking pan and slide into Rack Position 2, select Air Fry, set temperature to 350ºF (180ºC), and set time to 12 minutes.
6. When cooking is complete, they should be heated through. Cool for 5 to 8 minutes before serving.

336.   Parmesan Salmon & Asparagus

Servings: 4
Cooking Time: 20 Minutes
Ingredients:
- 4 salmon fillets
- 1 cup parmesan cheese, shredded
- 1 tbsp garlic, minced
- 3 tbsp olive oil
- 1 lb asparagus, ends trimmed
- 1/4 tsp pepper
- 1/4 tsp salt

Directions:
1. Fit the oven with the rack in position
2. Place fish fillets and asparagus in a parchment-lined baking pan.
3. Brush fish fillets with olive oil. Season with pepper and salt.
4. Sprinkle with garlic and shredded parmesan cheese on top.
5. Set to bake at 400 F for 25 minutes. After 5 minutes place the baking pan in the preheated oven.
6. Serve and enjoy.
- **Nutrition Info:** Calories 424 Fat 26.5 g Carbohydrates 6 g Sugar 2.2 g Protein 44.4 g Cholesterol 95 mg

337.   Seafood Pizza

Servings:x
Cooking Time:x
Ingredients:
- One pizza base
- Grated pizza cheese (mozzarella cheese preferably) for topping
- Some pizza topping sauce
- Use cooking oil for brushing and topping purposes
- ingredients for topping:
- 2 onions chopped
- 2 cups mixed seafood
- 2 capsicums chopped
- 2 tomatoes that have been deseeded and chopped
- 1 tbsp. (optional) mushrooms/corns
- 2 tsp. pizza seasoning
- Some cottage cheese that has been cut into small cubes (optional)

Directions:
1. Put the pizza base in a pre-heated oven for around 5 minutes. (Pre heated to 340 Fahrenheit). Take out the base. Pour some pizza sauce on top of the base at the center. Using a spoon spread the sauce over the base making sure that you leave some gap around the circumference. Grate some mozzarella cheese and sprinkle it over the sauce layer. Take all the vegetables and the

seafood and mix them in a bowl. Add some oil and seasoning.
2. Also add some salt and pepper according to taste. Mix them properly. Put this topping over the layer of cheese on the pizza. Now sprinkle some more grated cheese and pizza seasoning on top of this layer. Pre heat the oven at 250 Fahrenheit for around 5 minutes.
3. Open the fry basket and place the pizza inside. Close the basket and keep the fryer at 170 degrees for another 10 minutes. If you feel that it is undercooked you may put it at the same temperature for another 2 minutes or so.

338. Delicious Crab Cakes

Servings: 5
Cooking Time: 10 Minutes
Ingredients:
- 18 oz can crab meat, drained
- 2 1/2 tbsp mayonnaise
- 2 eggs, lightly beaten
- 1/4 cup breadcrumbs
- 1 1/2 tsp dried parsley
- 1 tbsp dried celery
- 1 tsp Old bay seasoning
- 1 1/2 tbsp Dijon mustard
- Pepper
- Salt

Directions:
1. Fit the oven with the rack in position 2.
2. Add all ingredients into the mixing bowl and mix until well combined.
3. Make patties from mixture and place in the air fryer basket then place an air fryer basket in the baking pan.
4. Place a baking pan on the oven rack. Set to air fry at 320 F for 10 minutes.
5. Serve and enjoy.
- **Nutrition Info:** Calories 138 Fat 4.7 g Carbohydrates 7.8 g Sugar 2.7 g Protein 16.8 g Cholesterol 127 mg

339. Savory Cod Fish In Soy Sauce

Servings: 4
Cooking Time: 20 Minutes
Ingredients:
- 4 cod fish fillets
- 4 tbsp chopped cilantro
- Salt to taste
- 2 green onions, chopped
- 1 cup water
- 4 slices of ginger
- 4 tbsp light soy sauce
- 3 tbsp oil
- 1 tsp dark soy sauce
- 4 cubes rock sugar

Directions:

1. Sprinkle the cod with salt and cilantro and drizzle with olive oil. Place in the cooking basket and fit in the baking tray; cook for 15 minutes at 360 F on Air Fry function.
2. Place the remaining ingredients in a frying pan over medium heat and cook for 5 minutes until sauce reaches desired consistency. Pour the sauce over the fish and serve.

340. Crispy Paprika Fish Fillets(1)

Servings: 4
Cooking Time: 15 Minutes
Ingredients:
- 1/2 cup seasoned breadcrumbs
- 1 tablespoon balsamic vinegar
- 1/2 teaspoon seasoned salt
- 1 teaspoon paprika
- 1/2 teaspoon ground black pepper
- 1 teaspoon celery seed
- 2 fish fillets, halved
- 1 egg, beaten

Directions:
1. Preparing the Ingredients. Add the breadcrumbs, vinegar, salt, paprika, ground black pepper, and celery seeds to your food processor. Process for about 30 seconds.
2. Coat the fish fillets with the beaten egg; then, coat them with the breadcrumbs mixture.
3. Air Frying. Cook at 350 degrees F for about 15 minutes.

341. Easy Baked Fish Fillet

Servings: 4
Cooking Time: 15 Minutes
Ingredients:
- 1 lb white fish fillets
- 2 tbsp dried parsley
- 1/4 tsp red chili flakes
- 2 tbsp garlic, minced
- 2 tbsp olive oil
- Pepper
- Salt

Directions:
1. Fit the oven with the rack in position
2. Place fish fillets in a baking dish and drizzle with oil.
3. Sprinkle with chili flakes, parsley, and garlic. Season with pepper and salt.
4. Set to bake at 400 F for 20 minutes. After 5 minutes place the baking dish in the preheated oven.
5. Serve and enjoy.
- **Nutrition Info:** Calories 262 Fat 15.6 g Carbohydrates 1.5 g Sugar 0.1 g Protein 28.1 g Cholesterol 87 mg

342. Piri-piri King Prawns

Servings:2
Cooking Time: 8 Minutes
Ingredients:
- 12 king prawns, rinsed
- 1 tablespoon coconut oil
- Salt and ground black pepper, to taste
- 1 teaspoon onion powder
- 1 teaspoon garlic paste
- 1 teaspoon curry powder
- ½ teaspoon piri piri powder
- ½ teaspoon cumin powder

Directions:
1. Combine all the ingredients in a large bowl and toss until the prawns are completely coated. Place the prawns in the air fryer basket.
2. Put the air fryer basket on the baking pan and slide into Rack Position 2, select Air Fry, set temperature to 360ºF (182ºC), and set time to 8 minutes.
3. Flip the prawns halfway through the cooking time.
4. When cooking is complete, the prawns will turn pink. Remove from the oven and serve hot.

343. Crispy Crab Legs

Servings: 4
Cooking Time: 15 Minutes
Ingredients:
- 3 pounds crab legs
- ½ cup butter, melted

Directions:
1. Preheat on Air Fry function to 380 F. Cover the crab legs with salted water and let them stay for a few minutes. Drain, pat them dry, and place the legs in the basket. Fit in the baking tray and brush with some butter; cook for 10 minutes, flipping once. Drizzle with the remaining butter and serve.

344. Shrimp And Cherry Tomato Kebabs

Servings:4
Cooking Time: 5 Minutes
Ingredients:
- 1½ pounds (680 g) jumbo shrimp, cleaned, shelled and deveined
- 1 pound (454 g) cherry tomatoes
- 2 tablespoons butter, melted
- 1 tablespoons Sriracha sauce
- Sea salt and ground black pepper, to taste
- 1 teaspoon dried parsley flakes
- ½ teaspoon dried basil
- ½ teaspoon dried oregano
- ½ teaspoon mustard seeds
- ½ teaspoon marjoram
- Special Equipment:
- 4 to 6 wooden skewers, soaked in water for 30 minutes

Directions:
1. Put all the ingredients in a large bowl and toss to coat well.
2. Make the kebabs: Thread, alternating jumbo shrimp and cherry tomatoes, onto the wooden skewers. Place the kebabs in the air fryer basket.
3. Put the air fryer basket on the baking pan and slide into Rack Position 2, select Air Fry, set temperature to 400ºF (205ºC), and set time to 5 minutes.
4. When cooking is complete, the shrimp should be pink and the cherry tomatoes should be softened. Remove from the oven. Let the shrimp and cherry tomato kebabs cool for 5 minutes and serve hot.

345. Spinach & Tuna Balls With Ricotta

Servings:4
Cooking Time: 20 Minutes
Ingredients:
- 14 oz store-bought crescent dough
- ½ cup spinach, steamed
- 1 cup ricotta cheese, crumbled
- ¼ tsp garlic powder
- 1 tsp fresh oregano, chopped
- ½ cup canned tuna, drained

Directions:
1. Preheat on AirFry function to 350 F. Roll the dough onto a lightly floured flat surface. Combine the ricotta cheese, spinach, tuna, oregano, salt, and garlic powder together in a bowl.
2. Cut the dough into 4 equal pieces. Divide the mixture between the dough pieces. Make sure to place the filling in the center. Fold the dough and secure with a fork. Place onto a lined baking dish and press Start. Cook for 12 minutes until lightly browned. Serve.

346. Carp Best Homemade Croquette

Servings:x
Cooking Time:x
Ingredients:
- 1 lb. Carp filets
- 3 onions chopped
- 5 green chilies-roughly chopped
- 1 ½ tbsp. ginger paste
- 1 ½ tsp garlic paste
- 1 ½ tsp salt
- 3 tsp lemon juice
- 2 tsp garam masala

- 4 tbsp. chopped coriander
- 3 tbsp. cream
- 2 tbsp. coriander powder
- 4 tbsp. fresh mint chopped
- 3 tbsp. chopped capsicum
- 3 eggs
- 2 ½ tbsp. white sesame seeds

Directions:
1. Take all the ingredients mentioned under the first heading and mix them in a bowl. Grind them thoroughly to make a smooth paste. Take the eggs in a different bowl and beat them. Add a pinch of salt and leave them aside. Mold the fish mixture into small balls and flatten them into round and flat Best Homemade Croquettes. Dip these Best Homemade Croquettes in the egg and salt mixture and then in the mixture of breadcrumbs and sesame seeds.
2. Leave these Best Homemade Croquettes in the fridge for an hour or so to set. Pre heat the oven at 160 degrees Fahrenheit for around 5 minutes. Place the Best Homemade Croquettes in the basket and let them cook for another 25 minutes at the same temperature. Turn the Best Homemade Croquettes over in between the cooking process to get a uniform cook. Serve the Best Homemade Croquettes with mint sauce.

347.   Salmon Tandoor

Servings:x
Cooking Time:x
Ingredients:
- 2 lb. boneless salmon filets
- 1st Marinade:
- 3 tbsp. vinegar or lemon juice
- 2 or 3 tsp. paprika
- 1 tsp. black pepper
- 1 tsp. salt
- 3 tsp. ginger-garlic paste
- 2nd Marinade:
- 1 cup yogurt
- 4 tsp. tandoori masala
- 2 tbsp. dry fenugreek leaves
- 1 tsp. black salt
- 1 tsp. chat masala
- 1 tsp. garam masala powder
- 1 tsp. red chili powder
- 1 tsp. salt
- 3 drops of red color

Directions:
1. Make the first marinade and soak the fileted salmon in it for four hours. While this is happening, make the second marinade and soak the salmon in it overnight to let the flavors blend. Pre heat the oven at 160 degrees Fahrenheit for 5 minutes.

2. Place the Oregano Fingers in the fry basket and close it. Let them cook at the same temperature for another 15 minutes or so. Toss the Oregano Fingers well so that they are cooked uniformly. Serve them with mint sauce.

348.   Fish Cakes With Mango Relish

Servings: 4
Cooking Time: 10 Minutes
Ingredients:
- 1 lb White Fish Fillets
- 3 Tbsps Ground Coconut
- 1 Ripened Mango
- ½ Tsps Chili Paste
- Tbsps Fresh Parsley
- 1 Green Onion
- 1 Lime
- 1 Tsp Salt
- 1 Egg

Directions:
1. Preparing the Ingredients. To make the relish, peel and dice the mango into cubes. Combine with a half teaspoon of chili paste, a tablespoon of parsley, and the zest and juice of half a lime.
2. In a food processor, pulse the fish until it forms a smooth texture. Place into a bowl and add the salt, egg, chopped green onion, parsley, two tablespoons of the coconut, and the remainder of the chili paste and lime zest and juice. Combine well
3. Portion the mixture into 10 equal balls and flatten them into small patties. Pour the reserved tablespoon of coconut onto a dish and roll the patties over to coat.
4. Preheat the Air fryer oven to 390 degrees
5. Air Frying. Place the fish cakes into the air fryer oven and cook for 8 minutes. They should be crisp and lightly browned when ready
6. Serve hot with mango relish

349.   Chili-rubbed Jumbo Shrimp

Servings: 2 To 3
Cooking Time: 10 Minutes
Ingredients:
- 1 lb jumbo shrimp
- Salt to taste
- ¼ tsp old bay seasoning
- ⅓ tsp smoked paprika
- ¼ tsp chili powder
- 1 tbsp olive oil

Directions:
1. Preheat on Air Fry function to 390 F. In a bowl, add the shrimp, paprika, olive oil, salt, old bay seasoning, and chili powder; mix well. Place the shrimp in the basket and fit

in the baking tray. Cook for 5 minutes, flipping once. Serve with mayo and rice.

350. Lobster Grandma's Easy To Cook Wontons

Servings:x
Cooking Time:x
Ingredients:
- 1 ½ cup all-purpose flour
- ½ tsp. salt
- 5 tbsp. water
- For filling:
- 2 cups minced lobster
- 2 tbsp. oil
- 2 tsp. ginger-garlic paste
- 2 tsp. soya sauce
- 2 tsp. vinegar

Directions:
1. Squeeze the dough and cover it with plastic wrap and set aside. Next, cook the ingredients for the filling and try to ensure that the lobster is covered well with the sauce.
2. Roll the dough and place the filling in the center. Now, wrap the dough to cover the filling and pinch the edges together.
3. Pre heat the oven at 200° F for 5 minutes. Place the wontons in the fry basket and close it. Let them cook at the same temperature for another 20 minutes. Recommended sides are chili sauce or ketchup.

351. Salmon Beans & Mushrooms

Servings: 6
Cooking Time: 25 Minutes
Ingredients:
- 4 salmon fillets
- 2 tbsp fresh parsley, minced
- 1/4 cup fresh lemon juice
- 1 tsp garlic, minced
- 1 tbsp olive oil
- 1/2 lb mushrooms, sliced
- 1/2 lb green beans, trimmed
- 1/2 cup parmesan cheese, grated
- Pepper
- Salt

Directions:
1. Fit the oven with the rack in position
2. Heat oil in a small saucepan over medium-high heat.
3. Add garlic and sauté for 30 seconds.
4. Remove from heat and stir in lemon juice, parsley, pepper, and salt.
5. Arrange fish fillets, mushrooms, and green beans in baking pan and drizzle with oil mixture.
6. Sprinkle with grated parmesan cheese.

7. Set to bake at 400 F for 30 minutes. After 5 minutes place the baking pan in the preheated oven.
8. Serve and enjoy.
- **Nutrition Info:** Calories 225 Fat 11.5 g Carbohydrates 4.7 g Sugar 1.4 g Protein 27.5 g Cholesterol 58 mg

352. Prawn Grandma's Easy To Cook Wontons

Servings:x
Cooking Time:x
Ingredients:
- 1 ½ cup all-purpose flour
- ½ tsp. salt
- 5 tbsp. water
- 2 cups minced prawn
- 2 tbsp. oil
- 2 tsp. ginger-garlic paste
- 2 tsp. soya sauce
- 2 tsp. vinegar

Directions:
1. Squeeze the dough and cover it with plastic wrap and set aside. Next, cook the ingredients for the filling and try to ensure that the prawn is covered well with the sauce. Roll the dough and place the filling in the center.
2. Now, wrap the dough to cover the filling and pinch the edges together Pre heat the oven at 200° F for 5 minutes. Place the wontons in the fry basket and close it. Let them cook at the same temperature for another 20 minutes. Recommended sides are chili sauce or ketchup.

353. Mediterranean Sole

Servings: 6
Cooking Time: 20 Minutes
Ingredients:
- Nonstick cooking spray
- 2 tbsp. olive oil
- 8 scallions, sliced thin
- 2 cloves garlic, diced fine
- 4 tomatoes, chopped
- ½ cup dry white wine
- 2 tbsp. fresh parsley, chopped fine
- 1 tsp oregano
- 1 tsp pepper
- 2 lbs. sole, cut in 6 pieces
- 4 oz. feta cheese, crumbled

Directions:
1. Place the rack in position 1 of the oven. Spray an 8x11-inch baking dish with cooking spray.
2. Heat the oil in a medium skillet over medium heat. Add scallions and garlic and cook until tender, stirring frequently.

3. Add the tomatoes, wine, parsley, oregano, and pepper. Stir to mix. Simmer for 5 minutes, or until sauce thickens. Remove from heat.
4. Pour half the sauce on the bottom of the prepared dish. Lay fish on top then pour remaining sauce over the top. Sprinkle with feta.
5. Set the oven to bake on 400°F for 25 minutes. After 5 minutes, place the baking dish on the rack and cook 15-18 minutes or until fish flakes easily with a fork. Serve immediately.
- **Nutrition Info:** Calories 220, Total Fat 12g, Saturated Fat 4g, Total Carbs 6g, Net Carbs 4g, Protein 22g, Sugar 4g, Fiber 2g, Sodium 631mg, Potassium 540mg, Phosphorus 478mg

354. Lobster Tails With Lemon-garlic Sauce

Servings:4
Cooking Time: 15 Minutes
Ingredients:
- 1 lb lobster tails
- 1 garlic clove, minced
- 1 tbsp butter
- Salt and black pepper to taste
- ½ tbsp lemon Juice

Directions:
1. Add all the ingredients to a food processor, except for lobster and blend well. Wash lobster and halve using meat knife; clean the skin of the lobster and cover with the marinade.
2. Preheat your to 380 F. Place the lobster in the cooking basket and press Start. Cook for 10 minutes on AirFry function. Serve with fresh herbs.

355. Lemon Pepper Tilapia Fillets

Servings:4
Cooking Time: 15 Minutes
Ingredients:
- 1 lb tilapia fillets
- 1 tbsp Italian seasoning
- 2 tbsp canola oil
- 2 tbsp lemon pepper
- Salt to taste
- 2-3 butter buds

Directions:
1. Preheat your oven to 400 F on Bake function. Drizzle tilapia fillets with canola oil. In a bowl, mix salt, lemon pepper, butter buds, and Italian seasoning; spread on the fish. Place the fillet on a baking tray and press Start. Cook for 10 minutes until tender and crispy. Serve warm.

356. Salmon Fries

Servings:x
Cooking Time:x
Ingredients:
- 1 lb. boneless salmon filets
- 2 cup dry breadcrumbs
- 2 tsp. oregano
- 2 tsp. red chili flakes
- 1 ½ tbsp. ginger-garlic paste
- 4 tbsp. lemon juice
- 2 tsp. salt
- 1 tsp. pepper powder
- 1 tsp. red chili powder
- 6 tbsp. corn flour
- 4 eggs

Directions:
1. Mix all the ingredients for the marinade and put the salmon filets inside and let it rest overnight. Mix the breadcrumbs, oregano and red chili flakes well and place the marinated Oregano Fingers on this mixture. Cover it with plastic wrap and leave it till right before you serve to cook.
2. Pre heat the oven at 160 degrees Fahrenheit for 5 minutes.
3. Place the Oregano Fingers in the fry basket and close it. Let them cook at the same temperature for another 15 minutes or so. Toss the Oregano Fingers well so that they are cooked uniformly.

357. Cheesy Tilapia Fillets

Servings: 4
Cooking Time: 15 Minutes
Ingredients:
- ¾ cup grated Parmesan cheese
- 1 tbsp olive oil
- 2 tsp paprika
- 1 tbsp chopped parsley
- ¼ tsp garlic powder
- 4 tilapia fillets

Directions:
1. Preheat on Air Fry function to 350 F. Mix parsley, Parmesan cheese, garlic, and paprika in a bowl. Brush the olive oil over the fillets and then coat with the Parmesan mixture. Place the tilapia onto a lined baking sheet and cook for 8-10 minutes, turning once. Serve.

358. Greek Cod With Asparagus

Servings: 2
Cooking Time: 20 Minutes
Ingredients:
- 1 lb cod, cut into 4 pieces
- 8 asparagus spears
- 1 leek, sliced
- 1 onion, quartered

- 2 tomatoes, halved
- 1/2 tsp oregano
- 1/2 tsp red chili flakes
- 1/2 cup olives, chopped
- 2 tbsp olive oil
- 1/4 tsp pepper
- 1/4 tsp salt

Directions:
1. Fit the oven with the rack in position
2. Arrange fish pieces, olives, asparagus, leek, onion, and tomatoes in a baking dish.
3. Season with oregano, chili flakes, pepper, and salt and drizzle with olive oil.
4. Set to bake at 400 F for 25 minutes. After 5 minutes place the baking dish in the preheated oven.
5. Serve and enjoy.
- **Nutrition Info:** Calories 489 Fat 20.2 g Carbohydrates 22.5 g Sugar 9.1 g Protein 56.6 g Cholesterol 125 mg

359. Breaded Scallops

Servings:4
Cooking Time: 7 Minutes
Ingredients:
- 1 egg
- 3 tablespoons flour
- 1 cup bread crumbs
- 1 pound (454 g) fresh scallops
- 2 tablespoons olive oil
- Salt and black pepper, to taste

Directions:
1. In a bowl, lightly beat the egg. Place the flour and bread crumbs into separate shallow dishes.
2. Dredge the scallops in the flour and shake off any excess. Dip the flour-coated scallops in the beaten egg and roll in the bread crumbs.
3. Brush the scallops generously with olive oil and season with salt and pepper, to taste. Transfer the scallops to the air fryer basket.
4. Put the air fryer basket on the baking pan and slide into Rack Position 2, select Air Fry, set temperature to 360ºF (182ºC), and set time to 7 minutes.
5. Flip the scallops halfway through the cooking time.
6. When cooking is complete, the scallops should reach an internal temperature of just 145ºF (63ºC) on a meat thermometer. Remove from the oven. Let the scallops cool for 5 minutes and serve.

360. Honey Glazed Salmon

Servings: 4
Cooking Time: 8 Minutes
Ingredients:
- 4 salmon fillets
- 2 tsp soy sauce
- 1 tbsp honey
- Pepper
- Salt

Directions:
1. Fit the oven with the rack in position 2.
2. Brush salmon with soy sauce and season with pepper and salt.
3. Place salmon in the air fryer basket then place an air fryer basket in the baking pan.
4. Place a baking pan on the oven rack. Set to air fry at 375 F for 8 minutes.
5. Brush salmon with honey and serve.
- **Nutrition Info:** Calories 253 Fat 11 g Carbohydrates 4.6 g Sugar 4.4 g Protein 34.7 g Cholesterol 78 mg

361. Prawn Fried Baked Pastry

Servings:x
Cooking Time:x
Ingredients:
- 2 tbsp. unsalted butter
- 1 ½ cup all-purpose flour
- A pinch of salt to taste
- Add as much water as required to make the dough stiff and firm
- 1 lb. prawn
- ¼ cup boiled peas
- 1 tsp. powdered ginger
- 1 or 2 green chilies that are finely chopped or mashed
- ½ tsp. cumin
- 1 tsp. coarsely crushed coriander
- 1 dry red chili broken into pieces
- A small amount of salt (to taste)
- ½ tsp. dried mango powder
- ½ tsp. red chili power.
- 1-2 tbsp. coriander.

Directions:
1. You will first need to make the outer covering. In a large bowl, add the flour, butter and enough water to knead it into dough that is stiff. Transfer this to a container and leave it to rest for five minutes. Place a pan on medium flame and add the oil. Roast the mustard seeds and once roasted, add the coriander seeds and the chopped dry red chilies. Add all the dry ingredients for the filling and mix the ingredients well.
2. Add a little water and continue to stir the ingredients. Make small balls out of the dough and roll them out. Cut the rolled-out dough into halves and apply a little water on the edges to help you fold the halves into a cone. Add the filling to the cone and close up the samosa. Pre-heat the oven for around 5 to 6 minutes at 300 Fahrenheit. Place all the samosas in the fry basket and close the basket properly.

3. Keep the oven at 200 degrees for another 20 to 25 minutes. Around the halfway point, open the basket and turn the samosas over for uniform cooking. After this, fry at 250 degrees for around 10 minutes in order to give them the desired golden-brown color. Serve hot. Recommended sides are tamarind or mint sauce.

362. Old Bay Shrimp

Servings:4
Cooking Time: 10 Minutes
Ingredients:
- 1 lb jumbo shrimp
- Salt to taste
- ¼ tsp old bay seasoning
- ⅓ tsp smoked paprika
- ¼ tsp chili powder
- 1 tbsp olive oil

Directions:
1. Preheat on AirFry function to 390 F. In a bowl, add the shrimp, paprika, oil, salt, old bay seasoning, and chili powder; mix well. Place the shrimp in the oven and cook for 5 minutes.

363. Baked Pesto Salmon

Servings: 4
Cooking Time: 15 Minutes
Ingredients:
- 4 salmon fillets
- 1/3 cup parmesan cheese, grated
- 1/3 cup breadcrumbs
- 6 tbsp pesto

Directions:
1. Fit the oven with the rack in position
2. Place fish fillets into the baking dish.
3. Pour pesto over fish fillets.
4. Mix together breadcrumbs and parmesan cheese and sprinkle over fish.
5. Set to bake at 325 F for 20 minutes. After 5 minutes place the baking dish in the preheated oven.
6. Serve and enjoy.
- **Nutrition Info:** Calories 396 Fat 22.8 g Carbohydrates 8.3 g Sugar 2.1 g Protein 40.4 g Cholesterol 89 mg

364. Fish And Chips

Servings: 4
Cooking Time: 20 Minutes
Ingredients:
- 4 (4-ounce) fish fillets
- Pinch salt
- Freshly ground black pepper
- ½ teaspoon dried thyme
- 1 egg white
- ¾ cup crushed potato chips
- 2 tablespoons olive oil, divided

- 1 russet potatoes, peeled and cut into strips

Directions:
1. Preparing the Ingredients. Pat the fish fillets dry and sprinkle with salt, pepper, and thyme. Set aside.
2. In a shallow bowl, beat the egg white until foamy. In another bowl, combine the potato chips and 1 tablespoon of olive oil and mix until combined.
3. Dip the fish fillets into the egg white, then into the crushed potato chip mixture to coat.
4. Toss the fresh potato strips with the remaining 1 tablespoon olive oil.
5. Air Frying. Use your separator to divide the Oven rack/basket in half, then fry the chips and fish. The chips will take about 20 minutes; the fish will take about 10 to 12 minutes to cook.
- **Nutrition Info:** CALORIES: 374; FAT:16G; PROTEIN:30G; FIBER:4G

365. Lemony Tuna

Servings: 4
Cooking Time: 10 Minutes
Ingredients:
- 2 (6-ounce) cans water packed plain tuna
- 2 teaspoons Dijon mustard
- ½ cup breadcrumbs
- 1 tablespoon fresh lime juice
- 2 tablespoons fresh parsley, chopped
- 1 egg
- Chefman of hot sauce
- 3 tablespoons canola oil
- Salt and freshly ground black pepper, to taste

Directions:
1. Preparing the Ingredients. Drain most of the liquid from the canned tuna.
2. In a bowl, add the fish, mustard, crumbs, citrus juice, parsley, and hot sauce and mix till well combined. Add a little canola oil if it seems too dry. Add egg, salt and stir to combine. Make the patties from tuna mixture. Refrigerate the tuna patties for about 2 hours.
3. Air Frying. Preheat the air fryer oven to 355 degrees F. Cook for about 10-12 minutes.

366. Orange Fish Fillets

Servings: 2
Cooking Time: 25 Minutes
Ingredients:
- 1 lb salmon fillets
- 1 orange juice
- 1 orange zest, grated
- 2 tbsp honey
- 3 tbsp soy sauce

Directions:
1. Fit the oven with the rack in position

2. In a small bowl, whisk together honey, soy sauce, orange juice, and orange zest.
3. Place salmon fillets in a baking dish and pour honey mixture over salmon fillets.
4. Set to bake at 425 F for 30 minutes. After 5 minutes place the baking dish in the preheated oven.
5. Serve and enjoy.
- **Nutrition Info:** Calories 399 Fat 14.1 g Carbohydrates 24.4 g Sugar 21.3 g Protein 45.9 g Cholesterol 100 mg

367. Sweet And Savory Breaded Shrimp

Servings: 2
Cooking Time: 20 Minutes
Ingredients:
- ½ pound of fresh shrimp, peeled from their shells and rinsed
- 2 raw eggs
- ½ cup of breadcrumbs (we like Panko, but any brand or home recipe will do)
- ½ white onion, peeled and rinsed and finely chopped
- 1 teaspoon of ginger-garlic paste
- ½ teaspoon of turmeric powder
- ½ teaspoon of red chili powder
- ½ teaspoon of cumin powder
- ½ teaspoon of black pepper powder
- ½ teaspoon of dry mango powder
- Pinch of salt

Directions:
1. Preparing the Ingredients. Cover the basket of the air fryer oven with a lining of tin foil, leaving the edges uncovered to allow air to circulate through the basket.
2. Preheat the air fryer oven to 350 degrees.
3. In a large mixing bowl, beat the eggs until fluffy and until the yolks and whites are fully combined.
4. Dunk all the shrimp in the egg mixture, fully submerging.
5. In a separate mixing bowl, combine the bread crumbs with all the dry ingredients until evenly blended.
6. One by one, coat the egg-covered shrimp in the mixed dry ingredients so that fully covered, and place on the foil-lined air-fryer basket.
7. Air Frying. Set the air-fryer timer to 20 minutes.
8. Halfway through the cooking time, shake the handle of the air-fryer so that the breaded shrimp jostles inside and fry-coverage is even.
9. After 20 minutes, when the fryer shuts off, the shrimp will be perfectly cooked and their breaded crust golden-brown and delicious! Using tongs, remove from the air fryer oven and set on a serving dish to cool.

368. Herbed Scallops With Vegetables

Servings:4
Cooking Time: 9 Minutes
Ingredients:
- 1 cup frozen peas
- 1 cup green beans
- 1 cup frozen chopped broccoli
- 2 teaspoons olive oil
- ½ teaspoon dried oregano
- ½ teaspoon dried basil
- 12 ounces (340 g) sea scallops, rinsed and patted dry

Directions:
1. Put the peas, green beans, and broccoli in a large bowl. Drizzle with the olive oil and toss to coat well. Transfer the vegetables to the air fryer basket.
2. Put the air fryer basket on the baking pan and slide into Rack Position 2, select Air Fry, set temperature to 400ºF (205ºC), and set time to 5 minutes.
3. When cooking is complete, the vegetables should be fork-tender. Transfer the vegetables to a serving bowl. Scatter with the oregano and basil and set aside.
4. Place the scallops in the basket.
5. Put the air fryer basket on the baking pan and slide into Rack Position 2, select Air Fry, set temperature to 400ºF (205ºC), and set time to 4 minutes.
6. When cooking is complete, the scallops should be firm and just opaque in the center. Remove from the oven to the bowl of vegetables and toss well. Serve warm.

369. Baked Tilapia

Servings: 4
Cooking Time: 10 Minutes
Ingredients:
- 1 1/4 lbs tilapia fillets
- 2 tsp onion powder
- 2 tbsp olive oil
- 1/2 tsp garlic powder
- 1/2 tsp dried thyme
- 1/2 tsp oregano
- 1/2 tsp chili powder
- 2 tbsp sweet paprika
- 1 tsp pepper
- 1/2 tsp salt

Directions:
1. Fit the oven with the rack in position
2. Brush fish fillets with oil and place in baking dish.
3. Mix together spices and sprinkle over the fish fillets.
4. Set to bake at 425 F for 15 minutes. After 5 minutes place the baking dish in the preheated oven.
5. Serve and enjoy.

- **Nutrition Info:** Calories 195 Fat 8.9 g Carbohydrates 3.9 g Sugar 0.9 g Protein 27.2 g Cholesterol 69 mg

370.   Crusty Scallops

Servings:4
Cooking Time: 20 Minutes
Ingredients:
- 12 fresh scallops
- 3 tbsp flour
- Salt and black pepper to taste
- 1 egg, lightly beaten
- 1 cup breadcrumbs

Directions:
1. Coat the scallops with flour. Dip into the egg, then into the breadcrumbs. Arrange them on the frying basket and spray with cooking spray. Cook for 12 minutes at 360 F on AirFry function.

371.   Air-fried Scallops

Servings:2
Cooking Time: 12 Minutes
Ingredients:
- $1/3$ cup shallots, chopped
- 1½ tablespoons olive oil
- 1½ tablespoons coconut aminos
- 1 tablespoon Mediterranean seasoning mix
- ½ tablespoon balsamic vinegar
- ½ teaspoon ginger, grated
- 1 clove garlic, chopped
- 1 pound (454 g) scallops, cleanedCooking spray
- Belgian endive, for garnish

Directions:
1. Place all the ingredients except the scallops and Belgian endive in a small skillet over medium heat and stir to combine. Let this mixture simmer for about 2 minutes.
2. Remove the mixture from the skillet to a large bowl and set aside to cool.
3. Add the scallops, coating them all over, then transfer to the refrigerator to marinate for at least 2 hours.
4. When ready, place the scallops in the air fryer basket in a single layer and spray with cooking spray.
5. Put the air fryer basket on the baking pan and slide into Rack Position 2, select Air Fry, set temperature to 345ºF (174ºC), and set time to 10 minutes.
6. Flip the scallops halfway through the cooking time.
7. When cooking is complete, the scallops should be tender and opaque. Remove from the oven and serve garnished with the Belgian endive.

372.   Air Fryer Salmon

Servings: 2
Cooking Time: 10 Minutes
Ingredients:
- ½ tsp. salt
- ½ tsp. garlic powder
- ½ tsp. smoked paprika
- Salmon

Directions:
1. Preparing the Ingredients. Mix spices and sprinkle onto salmon.
2. Place seasoned salmon into the air fryer oven.
3. Air Frying. Set temperature to 400°F, and set time to 10 minutes.
- **Nutrition Info:** CALORIES: 185; FAT: 11G; PROTEIN:21G; SUGAR:0G

MEATLESS RECIPES

373. Cumin Sweet Potatoes Wedges

Servings:4
Cooking Time: 30 Minutes
Ingredients:
- ½ tsp garlic powder
- ½ tsp cayenne pepper powder
- ¼ tsp ground cumin
- 3 tbsp olive oil
- 3 sweet potatoes, cut into ½-inch thick wedges
- 2 tbsp fresh parsley, chopped
- Sea salt to taste

Directions:
1. In a bowl, mix salt, garlic powder, cayenne pepper powder, and cumin. Whisk in olive oil and coat in the potatoes. Arrange them on the basket, without overcrowding and press Start. Cook for 20-25 minutes at 380 F on AirFry function. Sprinkle with parsley and sea salt and serve.

374. Crispy Potato Lentil Nuggets

Servings: 4
Cooking Time: 10 Minutes
Ingredients:
- Nonstick cooking spray
- 1 cup red lentils
- 1 tbsp. olive oil
- 1 cup onion, grated
- 1 cup carrot, grated
- 1 cup potato, grated
- ½ cup flour
- ½ tsp salt
- ½ tsp garlic powder
- ¾ tsp paprika
- ¼ tsp pepper

Directions:
1. Place baking pan in position 2. Lightly spray fryer basket with cooking spray.
2. Soak lentils in just enough water to cover them for 25 minutes.
3. Heat oil in a large skillet over medium heat. Add onion, carrot, and potato. Cook, stirring frequently until vegetables are tender, 12-15 minutes.
4. Drain the lentils and place them in a food processor. Add flour and spices and pulse to combine, leave some texture to the mixture.
5. Add cooked veggies to the food processor and pulse just until combined. Mixture will be sticky, so oil your hands. Form mixture into nugget shapes and add to the fryer basket in a single layer.
6. Place basket in the oven and set air fry on 350°F for 10 minutes. Turn nuggets over halfway through cooking time. Repeat with remaining mixture. Serve with your favorite dipping sauce.
- **Nutrition Info:** Calories 317, Total Fat 5g, Saturated Fat 1g, Total Carbs 54g, Net Carbs 46g, Protein 14g, Sugar 3g, Fiber 8g, Sodium 317mg, Potassium 625mg, Phosphorus 197mg

375. Cheese And Mushroom Spicy Lemon Kebab

Servings:x
Cooking Time:x
Ingredients:
- 1-2 tbsp. all-purpose flour for coating purposes
- 1-2 tbsp. mint
- 1 cup molten cheese
- 1 onion that has been finely chopped
- ½ cup milk
- 2 cups sliced mushrooms
- 1-2 green chilies chopped finely
- ¼ tsp. red chili powder
- A pinch of salt to taste
- ½ tsp. dried mango powder
- ¼ tsp. black salt

Directions:
1. Take the mushroom slices and add the grated ginger and the cut green chilies. Grind this mixture until it becomes a thick paste.
2. Keep adding water as and when required. Now add the onions, mint, the breadcrumbs and all the various masalas required. Mix this well until you get a soft dough. Now take small balls of this mixture (about the size of a lemon) and mold them into the shape of flat and round kebabs. Here is where the milk comes into play.
3. Pour a very small amount of milk onto each kebab to wet it. Now roll the kebab in the dry breadcrumbs. Pre heat the oven for 5 minutes at 300 Fahrenheit. Take out the basket. Arrange the kebabs in the basket leaving gaps between them so that no two kebabs are touching each other. Keep the fryer at 340 Fahrenheit for around half an hour.
4. Half way through the cooking process, turn the kebabs over so that they can be cooked properly. Recommended sides for this dish are mint sauce, tomato ketchup or yoghurt sauce.

376. Mediterranean Baked Eggs With Spinach

Servings:2
Cooking Time: 10 Minutes

Ingredients:
- 2 tablespoons olive oil
- 4 eggs, whisked
- 5 ounces (142 g) fresh spinach, chopped
- 1 medium-sized tomato, chopped
- 1 teaspoon fresh lemon juice
- ½ teaspoon ground black pepper
- ½ teaspoon coarse salt
- ½ cup roughly chopped fresh basil leaves, for garnish

Directions:
1. Generously grease the baking pan with olive oil.
2. Stir together the remaining ingredients except the basil leaves in the greased baking pan until well incorporated.
3. Slide the baking pan into Rack Position 1, select Convection Bake, set temperature to 280ºF (137ºC), and set time to 10 minutes.
4. When cooking is complete, the eggs should be completely set and the vegetables should be tender. Remove from the oven and serve garnished with the fresh basil leaves.

377.   Parsley Feta Triangles

Servings: 4
Cooking Time: 20 Minutes
Ingredients:
- 4 oz feta cheese
- 2 sheets filo pastry
- 1 egg yolk
- 2 tbsp parsley, finely chopped
- 1 scallion, finely chopped
- 2 tbsp olive oil
- salt and black pepper

Directions:
1. In a bowl, beat the yolk and mix with feta cheese, parsley, scallion, salt, and black pepper. Cut each filo sheet in three parts or strips. Put a teaspoon of the feta mixture on the bottom. Roll the strip in a spinning spiral way until the filling of the inside mixture is wrapped in a triangle.
2. Preheat on Bake function to 360 F. Brush the surface of filo with olive oil. Arrange the triangles on a greased baking tray and cook for 5 minutes. Lower the temperature to 330 F and cook for 3 more minutes or until golden brown. Serve chilled.

378.   Gherkins Flat Cakes

Servings:x
Cooking Time:x
Ingredients:
- 2 or 3 green chilies finely chopped
- 1 ½ tbsp. lemon juice
- Salt and pepper to taste
- 2 tbsp. garam masala
- 2 cups sliced gherkins

- 3 tsp. ginger finely chopped
- 1-2 tbsp. fresh coriander leaves

Directions:
1. Mix the ingredients in a clean bowl and add water to it. Make sure that the paste is not too watery but is enough to apply on the gherkin.
2. Pre heat the oven at 160 degrees Fahrenheit for 5 minutes. Place the French Cuisine Galettes in the fry basket and let them cook for another 25 minutes at the same temperature. Keep rolling them over to get a uniform cook. Serve either with mint sauce or ketchup.

379.   Rosemary Squash With Cheese

Servings: 2
Cooking Time: 20 Minutes
Ingredients:
- 1 pound (454 g) butternut squash, cut into wedges
- 2 tablespoons olive oil
- 1 tablespoon dried rosemary
- Salt, to salt
- 1 cup crumbled goat cheese
- 1 tablespoon maple syrup

Directions:
1. Toss the squash wedges with the olive oil, rosemary, and salt in a large bowl until well coated.
2. Transfer the squash wedges to the air fryer basket, spreading them out in as even a layer as possible.
3. Put the air fryer basket on the baking pan and slide into Rack Position 2, select Air Fry, set temperature to 350ºF (180ºC), and set time to 20 minutes.
4. After 10 minutes, remove from the oven and flip the squash. Return the pan to the oven and continue cooking for 10 minutes.
5. When cooking is complete, the squash should be golden brown. Remove from the oven. Sprinkle the goat cheese on top and serve drizzled with the maple syrup.

380.   Cheesy Ravioli Lunch

Servings:6
Cooking Time: 15 Minutes
Ingredients:
- 1 package cheese ravioli
- 2 cup Italian breadcrumbs
- ¼ cup Parmesan cheese, grated
- 1 cup buttermilk
- 1 tsp olive oil
- ¼ tsp garlic powder

Directions:
1. Preheat on AirFry function to 390 F. In a bowl, combine breadcrumbs, Parmesan cheese, garlic, and olive oil. Dip the ravioli in

the buttermilk and coat with the breadcrumb mixture.

2. Line a baking sheet with parchment paper and arrange the ravioli on it. Press Start and cook for 5 minutes. Serve with marinara jar sauce.

381.   Pizza

Servings:x
Cooking Time:x
Ingredients:
- 2 tomatoes that have been deseeded and chopped
- 1 tbsp. (optional) mushrooms/corns
- 2 tsp. pizza seasoning
- Some cottage cheese that has been cut into small cubes (optional)
- One pizza base
- Grated pizza cheese (mozzarella cheese preferably) for topping
- Use cooking oil for brushing and topping purposes
- ingredients for topping:
- 2 onions chopped
- 2 capsicums chopped

Directions:
1. Put the pizza base in a pre-heated oven for around 5 minutes. (Pre heated to 340 Fahrenheit). Take out the base.
2. Pour some pizza sauce on top of the base at the center. Using a spoon spread the sauce over the base making sure that you leave some gap around the circumference. Grate some mozzarella cheese and sprinkle it over the sauce layer. Take all the vegetables mentioned in the ingredient list above and mix them in a bowl.
3. Add some oil and seasoning. Also add some salt and pepper according to taste. Mix them properly. Put this topping over the layer of cheese on the pizza. Now sprinkle some more grated cheese and pizza seasoning on top of this layer.
4. Pre heat the oven at 250 Fahrenheit for around 5 minutes. Open the fry basket and place the pizza inside. Close the basket and keep the fryer at 170 degrees for another 10 minutes. If you feel that it is undercooked you may put it at the same temperature for another 2 minutes or so.

382.   Onion French Cuisine Galette

Servings:x
Cooking Time:x
Ingredients:
- 2 or 3 green chilies finely chopped
- 1 ½ tbsp. lemon juice
- Salt and pepper to taste
- 2 tbsp. garam masala

- 2 medium onions (Cut long)
- 1 ½ cup coarsely crushed peanuts
- 3 tsp. ginger finely chopped
- 1-2 tbsp. fresh coriander leaves

Directions:
1. Mix the ingredients in a clean bowl.
2. Mold this mixture into round and flat French Cuisine Galettes.
3. Wet the French Cuisine Galettes slightly with water. Coat each French Cuisine Galette with the crushed peanuts.
4. Pre heat the oven at 160 degrees Fahrenheit for 5 minutes. Place the French Cuisine Galettes in the fry basket and let them cook for another 25 minutes at the same temperature. Keep rolling them over to get a uniform cook. Serve either with mint sauce or ketchup.

383.   Dal Mint Spicy Lemon Kebab

Servings:x
Cooking Time:x
Ingredients:
- 2 tsp. coriander powder
- 1 ½ tbsp. chopped coriander
- ½ tsp. dried mango powder
- 1 cup dry breadcrumbs
- ¼ tsp. black salt
- 1-2 tbsp. all-purpose flour for coating purposes
- 1-2 tbsp. mint (finely chopped)
- 1 cup chickpeas
- Half inch ginger grated or one and a half tsp. of ginger-garlic paste
- 1-2 green chilies chopped finely
- ¼ tsp. red chili powder
- A pinch of salt to taste
- ½ tsp. roasted cumin powder
- 1 onion that has been finely chopped
- ½ cup milk

Directions:
1. Take an open vessel. Boil the chickpeas in the vessel until their texture becomes soft. Make sure that they do not become soggy. Now take this chickpea into another container. Add the grated ginger and the cut green chilies.
2. Grind this mixture until it becomes a thick paste. Keep adding water as and when required. Now add the onions, mint, the breadcrumbs and all the various masalas required. Mix this well until you get a soft dough. Now take small balls of this mixture (about the size of a lemon) and mold them into the shape of flat and round kebabs.
3. Here is where the milk comes into play. Pour a very small amount of milk onto each kebab to wet it. Now roll the kebab in the dry breadcrumbs. Pre heat the oven for 5

minutes at 300 Fahrenheit. Take out the basket.

4. Arrange the kebabs in the basket leaving gaps between them so that no two kebabs are touching each other. Keep the fryer at 340 Fahrenheit for around half an hour. Half way through the cooking process, turn the kebabs over so that they can be cooked properly. Recommended sides for this dish are mint sauce, tomato ketchup or yoghurt sauce.

384. Cauliflower Momo's Recipe

Servings:x
Cooking Time:x
Ingredients:
- 2 tsp. ginger-garlic paste
- 2 tsp. soya sauce
- 2 tsp. vinegar
- 1 ½ cup all-purpose flour
- ½ tsp. salt
- 5 tbsp. water
- 2 cups grated cauliflower
- 2 tbsp. oil

Directions:
1. Squeeze the dough and cover it with plastic wrap and set aside. Next, cook the ingredients for the filling and try to ensure that the cauliflower is covered well with the sauce.
2. Roll the dough and cut it into a square. Place the filling in the center. Now, wrap the dough to cover the filling and pinch the edges together.
3. Pre heat the oven at 200° F for 5 minutes. Place the gnocchi's in the fry basket and close it. Let them cook at the same temperature for another 20 minutes. Recommended sides are chili sauce or ketchup

385. Cumin And Cayenne Spicy Sweet Potatoes

Servings: 4
Cooking Time: 30 Minutes
Ingredients:
- ½ tsp garlic powder
- ½ tsp cayenne pepper
- ¼ tsp cumin
- 3 tbsp olive oil
- 3 sweet potatoes, cut into ½-inch thick wedges
- 2 tbsp chopped fresh parsley
- Sea salt to taste

Directions:
1. In a bowl, mix olive oil, salt, garlic powder, chili powder, and cumin. Add in potatoes and toss to coat. Arrange them on the basket and fit in the baking tray.

2. Cook in your for 20 minutes at 380 F on Air Fry function. Toss every 5 minutes. Sprinkle with parsley and serve.

386. Gorgonzola Cheese & Pumpkin Salad

Servings:2
Cooking Time: 30 Minutes + Chilling Time
Ingredients:
- ½ lb pumpkin
- 2 oz gorgonzola cheese, crumbled
- 2 tbsp pine nuts, toasted
- 1 tbsp olive oil
- ½ cup baby spinach
- 1 spring onion, sliced
- 2 radishes, thinly sliced
- 1 tsp apple cider vinegar

Directions:
1. Preheat on Bake function to 360 F. Peel the pumpkin and chop it into small pieces. Place in a greased baking dish and bake for 20 minutes. Let cool.
2. Add baby spinach, radishes, and spring onion in a serving bowl and toss with olive oil and vinegar. Top with the pumpkin and gorgonzola cheese and sprinkle with the pine nuts to serve.

387. Cottage Cheese Fried Baked Pastry

Servings:x
Cooking Time:x
Ingredients:
- 1 or 2 green chilies that are finely chopped or mashed
- ½ tsp. cumin
- 1 tsp. coarsely crushed coriander
- 1 dry red chili broken into pieces
- A small amount of salt (to taste)
- ½ tsp. dried mango powder
- ½ tsp. red chili power
- 1-2 tbsp. coriander
- 2 tbsp. unsalted butter
- 1 ½ cup all-purpose flour
- A pinch of salt to taste
- Water
- 2 cups mashed cottage cheese
- ¼ cup boiled peas
- 1 tsp. powdered ginger

Directions:
1. Mix the dough for the outer covering and make it stiff and smooth. Leave it to rest in a container while making the filling.
2. Cook the ingredients in a pan and stir them well to make a thick paste. Roll the paste out.
3. Roll the dough into balls and flatten them. Cut them in halves and add the filling. Use

water to help you fold the edges to create the shape of a cone.

4. Pre-heat the oven for around 5 to 6 minutes at 300 Fahrenheit. Place all the samosas in the fry basket and close the basket properly. Keep the oven at 200 degrees for another 20 to 25 minutes. Around the halfway point, open the basket and turn the samosas over for uniform cooking. After this, fry at 250 degrees for around 10 minutes in order to give them the desired golden-brown color. Serve hot. Recommended sides are tamarind or mint sauce.

388. Cottage Cheese Homemade Fried Sticks

Servings:x
Cooking Time:x
Ingredients:
- One or two poppadums'
- 4 or 5 tbsp. corn flour
- 1 cup of water
- 2 cups cottage cheese
- 1 big lemon-juiced
- 1 tbsp. ginger-garlic paste
- For seasoning, use salt and red chili powder in small amounts
- ½ tsp. carom

Directions:
1. Take the cottage cheese. Cut it into long pieces. Now, make a mixture of lemon juice, red chili powder, salt, ginger garlic paste and carom to use as a marinade. Let the cottage cheese pieces marinate in the mixture for some time and then roll them in dry corn flour. Leave them aside for around 20 minutes.
2. Take the poppadum into a pan and roast them. Once they are cooked, crush them into very small pieces. Now take another container and pour around 100 ml of water into it. Dissolve 2 tbsp. of corn flour in this water. Dip the cottage cheese pieces in this solution of corn flour and roll them on to the pieces of crushed poppadum so that the poppadum sticks to the cottage cheese
3. . Pre heat the oven for 10 minutes at 290 Fahrenheit. Then open the basket of the fryer and place the cottage cheese pieces inside it. Close the basket properly. Let the fryer stay at 160 degrees for another 20 minutes. Halfway through, open the basket and toss the cottage cheese around a bit to allow for uniform cooking. Once they are done, you can serve it either with ketchup or mint sauce. Another recommended side is mint sauce.

389. Simple Ricotta & Spinach Balls

Servings: 4
Cooking Time: 20 Minutes
Ingredients:
- 14 oz store-bought crescent dough
- 1 cup steamed spinach
- 1 cup crumbled ricotta cheese
- ¼ tsp garlic powder
- 1 tsp chopped oregano
- ¼ tsp salt

Directions:
1. Preheat on Air Fry function to 350 F. Roll the dough onto a lightly floured flat surface. Combine the ricotta cheese, spinach, oregano, salt, and garlic powder together in a bowl. Cut the dough into 4 equal pieces.
2. Divide the spinach/feta mixture between the dough pieces. Make sure to place the filling in the center. Fold the dough and secure with a fork. Place onto a lined baking dish and then in your oven. Cook for 12 minutes until lightly browned. Serve.

390. Butter Burgers

Servings: 4
Cooking Time: 30 Minutes
Ingredients:
- Nonstick cooking spray
- ½ cup black beans, rinsed & drained
- 12 oz. mushrooms, sliced
- 1 ½ cup brown rice, cooked
- ½ cup oats
- 1 tsp salt
- ½ tsp pepper
- 1 tsp garlic powder
- 1 tsp onion powder
- ¼ tsp red pepper flakes
- ¼ cup Vegan butter
- 2 cups onions, sliced

Directions:
1. Place baking pan in position 2 in the oven. Lightly spray fryer basket with cooking spray.
2. Pat the beans with paper towel to get them as dry as possible.
3. Heat a medium skillet over med-high heat. Add mushrooms and cook, stirring frequently, until almost no moisture remains.
4. Add mushrooms, beans, rice, oats, and seasonings to a food processor. Pulse to chop and combine ingredients. Do not over blend. Let mixture rest 20 minutes.
5. Melt butter in a large skillet over medium heat. Add onions and cook until browned and tender.
6. Form mushroom mixture into 4 patties and place in the fryer basket. Place in oven and

set to air fry on 350°F for 10 minutes. Cook burgers 8-10 minutes, until nicely browned, turning over halfway through cooking time.
7. Serve on toasted buns topped with cooked onions.
- **Nutrition Info:** Calories 351, Total Fat 15g, Saturated Fat 8g, Total Carbs 44g, Net Carbs 37g, Protein 10g, Sugar 4g, Fiber 7g, Sodium 704mg, Potassium 604mg, Phosphorus 286mg

391.   Baked Turnip And Zucchini

Servings:4
Cooking Time: 18 Minutes
Ingredients:
- 3 turnips, sliced
- 1 large zucchini, sliced
- 1 large red onion, cut into rings
- 2 cloves garlic, crushed
- 1 tablespoon olive oil
- Salt and black pepper, to taste

Directions:
1. Put the turnips, zucchini, red onion, and garlic in the baking pan. Drizzle the olive oil over the top and sprinkle with the salt and pepper.
2. Slide the baking pan into Rack Position 1, select Convection Bake, set temperature to 330ºF (166ºC), and set time to 18 minutes.
3. When cooking is complete, the vegetables should be tender. Remove from the oven and serve on a plate.

392.   Potato Fried Baked Pastry

Servings:x
Cooking Time:x
Ingredients:
- 1 tsp. powdered ginger
- 1 or 2 green chilies that are finely chopped or mashed
- ½ tsp. cumin
- 1 tsp. coarsely crushed coriander
- 1 dry red chili broken into pieces
- A small amount of salt (to taste)
- 2 tbsp. unsalted butter
- 1 ½ cup all-purpose flour
- A pinch of salt to taste
- Add as much water as required to make the dough stiff and firm
- 2-3 big potatoes boiled and mashed
- ¼ cup boiled peas
- ½ tsp. dried mango powder
- ½ tsp. red chili power.
- 1-2 tbsp. coriander.

Directions:
1. Mix the dough for the outer covering and make it stiff and smooth. Leave it to rest in a container while making the filling. Cook the

ingredients in a pan and stir them well to make a thick paste. Roll the paste out.
2. Roll the dough into balls and flatten them. Cut them in halves and add the filling. Use water to help you fold the edges to create the shape of a cone. Pre-heat the oven for around 5 to 6 minutes at 300 Fahrenheit.
3. Place all the samosas in the fry basket and close the basket properly. Keep the oven at 200 degrees for another 20 to 25 minutes. Around the halfway point, open the basket and turn the samosas over for uniform cooking. After this, fry at 250 degrees for around 10 minutes in order to give them the desired golden-brown color. Serve hot. Recommended sides are tamarind or mint sauce.

393.   Cornflakes French Toast

Servings:x
Cooking Time:x
Ingredients:
- 1 tsp. sugar for every 2 slices
- Crushed cornflakes
- Bread slices (brown or white)
- 1 egg white for every 2 slices

Directions:
1. Put two slices together and cut them along the diagonal.
2. In a bowl, whisk the egg whites and add some sugar.
3. Dip the bread triangles into this mixture and then coat them with the crushed cornflakes.
4. Pre heat the oven at 180° C for 4 minutes. Place the coated bread triangles in the fry basket and close it. Let them cook at the same temperature for another 20 minutes at least. Halfway through the process, turn the triangles over so that you get a uniform cook. Serve these slices with chocolate sauce.

394.   Okra Spicy Lemon Kebab

Servings:x
Cooking Time:x
Ingredients:
- 3 tsp. lemon juice
- 2 tsp. garam masala
- 4 tbsp. chopped coriander
- 3 tbsp. cream
- 3 tbsp. chopped capsicum
- 3 eggs
- 2 cups sliced okra
- 3 onions chopped
- 5 green chilies-roughly chopped
- 1 ½ tbsp. ginger paste
- 1 ½ tsp. garlic paste
- 1 ½ tsp. salt

- 2 ½ tbsp. white sesame seeds

Directions:
1. Grind the ingredients except for the egg and form a smooth paste. Coat the okra in the paste. Now, beat the eggs and add a little salt to it.
2. Dip the coated vegetables in the egg mixture and then transfer to the sesame seeds and coat the okra well. Place the vegetables on a stick.
3. Pre heat the oven at 160 degrees Fahrenheit for around 5 minutes. Place the sticks in the basket and let them cook for another 25 minutes at the same temperature. Turn the sticks over in between the cooking process to get a uniform cook.

395. Roasted Vegetable Mélange With Herbs

Servings:4
Cooking Time: 16 Minutes
Ingredients:
- 1 (8-ounce / 227-g) package sliced mushrooms
- 1 yellow summer squash, sliced
- 1 red bell pepper, sliced
- 3 cloves garlic, sliced
- 1 tablespoon olive oil
- ½ teaspoon dried basil
- ½ teaspoon dried thyme
- ½ teaspoon dried tarragon

Directions:
1. Toss the mushrooms, squash, and bell pepper with the garlic and olive oil in a large bowl until well coated. Mix in the basil, thyme, and tarragon and toss again.
2. Spread the vegetables evenly in the air fryer basket.
3. Put the air fryer basket on the baking pan and slide into Rack Position 2, select Roast, set temperature to 350ºF (180ºC), and set time to 16 minutes.
4. When cooking is complete, the vegetables should be fork-tender. Remove from the oven and cool for 5 minutes before serving.

396. Cauliflower French Cuisine Galette

Servings:x
Cooking Time:x
Ingredients:
- 3 tsp. ginger finely chopped
- 1-2 tbsp. fresh coriander leaves
- 2 or 3 green chilies finely chopped
- 1 ½ tbsp. lemon juice
- Salt and pepper to taste
- 2 tbsp. garam masala

- 2 cups cauliflower
- 1 ½ cup coarsely crushed peanuts

Directions:
1. Mix the ingredients in a clean bowl.
2. Mold this mixture into round and flat French Cuisine Galettes.
3. Wet the French Cuisine Galettes slightly with water. Coat each French Cuisine Galette with the crushed peanuts.
4. Pre heat the oven at 160 degrees Fahrenheit for 5 minutes. Place the French Cuisine Galettes in the fry basket and let them cook for another 25 minutes at the same temperature. Keep rolling them over to get a uniform cook. Serve either with mint sauce or ketchup.

397. Parmesan Breaded Zucchini Chips

Servings: 5
Cooking Time: 20 Minutes
Ingredients:
- For the zucchini chips:
- 2 medium zucchini
- 2 eggs
- ⅓ cup bread crumbs
- ⅓ cup grated Parmesan cheese
- Salt
- Pepper
- Cooking oil
- For the lemon aioli:
- ½ cup mayonnaise
- ½ tablespoon olive oil
- Juice of ½ lemon
- 1 teaspoon minced garlic
- Salt
- Pepper

Directions:
1. Preparing the Ingredients. To make the zucchini chips:
2. Slice the zucchini into thin chips (about ⅛ inch thick) using a knife or mandoline.
3. In a small bowl, beat the eggs. In another small bowl, combine the bread crumbs, Parmesan cheese, and salt and pepper to taste.
4. Spray the Oven rack/basket with cooking oil.
5. Dip the zucchini slices one at a time in the eggs and then the bread crumb mixture. You can also sprinkle the bread crumbs onto the zucchini slices with a spoon.
6. Place the zucchini chips in the Oven rack/basket, but do not stack. Place the Rack on the middle-shelf of the air fryer oven.
7. Air Frying. Cook in batches. Spray the chips with cooking oil from a distance (otherwise,

the breading may fly off). Cook for 10 minutes.

8. Remove the cooked zucchini chips from the air fryer oven, then repeat step 5 with the remaining zucchini.
9. To make the lemon aioli:
10. While the zucchini is cooking, combine the mayonnaise, olive oil, lemon juice, and garlic in a small bowl, adding salt and pepper to taste. Mix well until fully combined.
11. Cool the zucchini and serve alongside the aioli.
- **Nutrition Info:** CALORIES: 192; FAT: 13G; PROTEIN: 6

398. Stuffed Portobello Mushrooms With Vegetables

Servings:4
Cooking Time: 8 Minutes
Ingredients:
- 4 portobello mushrooms, stem removed
- 1 tablespoon olive oil
- 1 tomato, diced
- ½ green bell pepper, diced
- ½ small red onion, diced
- ½ teaspoon garlic powder
- Salt and black pepper, to taste
- ½ cup grated Mozzarella cheese

Directions:
1. Using a spoon to scoop out the gills of the mushrooms and discard them. Brush the mushrooms with the olive oil.
2. In a mixing bowl, stir together the remaining ingredients except the Mozzarella cheese. Using a spoon to stuff each mushroom with the filling and scatter the Mozzarella cheese on top.
3. Arrange the mushrooms in the air fryer basket.
4. Put the air fryer basket on the baking pan and slide into Rack Position 2, select Roast, set temperature to 330ºF (166ºC) and set time to 8 minutes.
5. When cooking is complete, the cheese should be melted.
6. Serve warm.

399. Baked Macaroni Pasta

Servings:x
Cooking Time:x
Ingredients:
- ½ tsp. basil
- 2 tbsp. olive oil
- 2 tbsp. all-purpose flour
- 2 cups of milk
- 1 tsp. dried oregano
- 1 cup pasta
- 7 cups of boiling water
- 1 ½ tbsp. olive oil
- A pinch of salt
- For tossing pasta:
- 1 ½ tbsp. olive oil
- ½ cup carrot small pieces
- Salt and pepper to taste
- ½ tsp. oregano
- ½ tsp. dried basil
- ½ tsp. dried parsley
- Salt and pepper to taste

Directions:
1. Boil the pasta and sieve it when done. You will need to toss the pasta in the ingredients mentioned above and set aside.
2. For the sauce, add the ingredients to a pan and bring the ingredients to a boil. Stir the sauce and continue to simmer to make a thicker sauce. Add the pasta to the sauce and transfer this into a glass bowl garnished with cheese.
3. Pre heat the oven at 160 degrees for 5 minutes. Place the bowl in the basket and close it. Let it continue to cook at the same temperature for 10 minutes more. Keep stirring the pasta in between.

400. Cottage Cheese Club Sandwich

Servings:x
Cooking Time:x
Ingredients:
- ¼ tbsp. Worcestershire sauce
- ½ tsp. olive oil
- ½ flake garlic crushed
- ¼ cup chopped onion
- ¼ tbsp. red chili sauce
- 2 slices of white bread
- 1 tbsp. softened butter
- 1 cup sliced cottage cheese
- 1 small capsicum

Directions:
1. Take the slices of bread and remove the edges. Now cut the slices horizontally.
2. Cook the ingredients for the sauce and wait till it thickens. Now, add the cottage cheese to the sauce and stir till it obtains the flavors. Roast the capsicum and peel the skin off. Cut the capsicum into slices. Mix the ingredients together and apply it to the bread slices.
3. Pre-heat the oven for 5 minutes at 300 Fahrenheit. Open the basket of the Fryer and place the prepared Classic Sandwiches in it such that no two Classic Sandwiches are touching each other. Now keep the fryer at 250 degrees for around 15 minutes. Turn the Classic Sandwiches in between the cooking process to cook both slices. Serve the Classic Sandwiches with tomato ketchup or mint sauce.

401. Chickpea Fritters

Servings: 4
Cooking Time: 10 Minutes
Ingredients:
- Nonstick cooking spray
- 1 cup chickpeas, cooked
- 1 onion, chopped
- ¼ tsp salt
- ¼ tsp pepper
- ¼ tsp turmeric
- ¼ tsp coriander

Directions:
1. Place the baking pan in position 2. Lightly spray the fryer basket with cooking spray.
2. Add the onion to a food processor and pulse until finely diced.
3. Add remaining ingredients and pulse until combined but not pureed.
4. Form the mixture into 8 patties and place them in the fryer basket, these may need to be cooked in two batches.
5. Place the basket in the oven and set to air fry on 350°F for 10 minutes. Cook fritters until golden brown and crispy, turning over halfway through cooking time. Serve with your favorite dipping sauce.
- **Nutrition Info:** Calories 101, Total Fat 1g, Saturated Fat 0g, Total Carbs 14g, Net Carbs 10g, Protein 4g, Sugar 3g, Fiber 4g, Sodium 149mg, Potassium 159mg, Phosphorus 77mg

402. Black Gram French Cuisine Galette

Servings:x
Cooking Time:x
Ingredients:
- 2 or 3 green chilies finely chopped
- 1 ½ tbsp. lemon juice
- Salt and pepper to taste
- 2 cup black gram
- 2 medium potatoes boiled and mashed
- 1 ½ cup coarsely crushed peanuts
- 3 tsp. ginger finely chopped
- 1-2 tbsp. fresh coriander leaves

Directions:
1. Mix the ingredients in a clean bowl.
2. Mold this mixture into round and flat French Cuisine Galettes.
3. Wet the French Cuisine Galettes slightly with water.
4. Pre heat the oven at 160 degrees Fahrenheit for 5 minutes. Place the French Cuisine Galettes in the fry basket and let them cook for another 25 minutes at the same temperature. Keep rolling them over to get a uniform cook. Serve either with mint sauce or ketchup.

403. Potato Club Barbeque Sandwich

Servings:x
Cooking Time:x
Ingredients:
- ½ flake garlic crushed
- ¼ cup chopped onion
- ¼ tbsp. red chili sauce
- 2 slices of white bread
- 1 tbsp. softened butter
- 1 cup boiled potato
- 1 small capsicum
- ¼ tbsp. Worcestershire sauce
- ½ tsp. olive oil

Directions:
1. Take the slices of bread and remove the edges. Now cut the slices horizontally.
2. Cook the ingredients for the sauce and wait till it thickens. Now, add the potato to the sauce and stir till it obtains the flavors. Roast the capsicum and peel the skin off. Cut the capsicum into slices. Mix the ingredients together and apply it to the bread slices.
3. Pre-heat the oven for 5 minutes at 300 Fahrenheit. Open the basket of the Fryer and place the prepared Classic Sandwiches in it such that no two Classic Sandwiches are touching each other. Now keep the fryer at 250 degrees for around 15 minutes. Turn the Classic Sandwiches in between the cooking process to cook both slices. Serve the Classic Sandwiches with tomato ketchup or mint sauce.

404. Potato Wedges

Servings:x
Cooking Time:x
Ingredients:
- 1 tsp. mixed herbs
- ½ tsp. red chili flakes
- A pinch of salt to taste
- 1 tbsp. lemon juice
- 2 medium sized potatoes (Cut into wedges)
- ingredients for the marinade:
- 1 tbsp. olive oil

Directions:
1. Boil the potatoes and blanch them. Mix the ingredients for the marinade and add the potato Oregano Fingers to it making sure that they are coated well.
2. Pre heat the oven for around 5 minutes at 300 Fahrenheit. Take out the basket of the fryer and place the potato Oregano Fingers in them. Close the basket.
3. Now keep the fryer at 200 Fahrenheit for 20 or 25 minutes. In between the process, toss

the fries twice or thrice so that they get cooked properly.

405. Cauliflower Bites

Servings: 4
Cooking Time: 18 Minutes
Ingredients:
- 1 Head Cauliflower, cut into small florets
- Tsps Garlic Powder
- Pinch of Salt and Pepper
- 1 Tbsp Butter, melted
- 1/2 Cup Chili Sauce
- Olive Oil

Directions:
1. Preparing the Ingredients. Place cauliflower into a bowl and pour oil over florets to lightly cover.
2. Season florets with salt, pepper, and the garlic powder and toss well.
3. Air Frying. Place florets into the air fryer oven at 350 degrees for 14 minutes.
4. Remove cauliflower from the Air fryer oven.
5. Combine the melted butter with the chili sauce
6. Pour over the florets so that they are well coated.
7. Return to the air fryer oven and cook for additional 3 to 4 minutes
8. Serve as a side or with ranch or cheese dip as a snack.

406. Cheese French Fries

Servings:x
Cooking Time:x
Ingredients:
- 2 medium sized potatoes peeled and cut into thick pieces lengthwise
- 1 tsp. mixed herbs
- ½ tsp. red chili flakes
- A pinch of salt to taste
- 1 tbsp. lemon juice
- 1 cup melted cheddar cheese (You could put this into a piping bag and
- 1 tbsp. olive oil
- create a pattern of it on the fries.)

Directions:
1. Take all the ingredients mentioned under the heading "For the marinade" and mix them well. Now pour into a container 3 cups of water.
2. Add a pinch of salt into this water. Bring it to the boil. Now blanch the pieces of potato for around 5 minutes. Drain the water using a sieve. Dry the potato pieces on a towel and then place them on another dry towel. Coat these potato Oregano Fingers with the marinade made in the previous step. Pre heat the oven for around 5 minutes at 300 Fahrenheit. Take out the basket of the fryer

and place the potato Oregano Fingers in them.
3. Close the basket. Now keep the fryer at 220 Fahrenheit for 20 or 25 minutes. In between the process, toss the fries twice or thrice so that they get cooked properly. Towards the end of the cooking process (the last 2 minutes or so), sprinkle the cut coriander leaves on the fries. Add the melted cheddar cheese over the fries and serve hot.

407. Roasted Brussels Sprouts With Parmesan

Servings:4
Cooking Time: 20 Minutes
Ingredients:
- 1 pound (454 g) fresh Brussels sprouts, trimmed
- 1 tablespoon olive oil
- ½ teaspoon salt
- ⅛ teaspoon pepper
- ¼ cup grated Parmesan cheese

Directions:
1. In a large bowl, combine the Brussels sprouts with olive oil, salt, and pepper and toss until evenly coated.
2. Spread the Brussels sprouts evenly in the air fryer basket.
3. Put the air fryer basket on the baking pan and slide into Rack Position 2, select Air Fry, set temperature to 330ºF (166ºC), and set time to 20 minutes.
4. Stir the Brussels sprouts twice during cooking.
5. When cooking is complete, the Brussels sprouts should be golden brown and crisp. Sprinkle the grated Parmesan cheese on top and serve warm.

408. Potato Flat Cakes

Servings:x
Cooking Time:x
Ingredients:
- 2 or 3 green chilies finely chopped
- 1 ½ tbsp. lemon juice
- Salt and pepper to taste
- 2 tbsp. garam masala
- 2 cups sliced potato
- 3 tsp. ginger finely chopped
- 1-2 tbsp. fresh coriander leaves

Directions:
1. Mix the ingredients in a clean bowl and add water to it. Make sure that the paste is not too watery but is enough to apply on the potato slices.
2. Pre heat the oven at 160 degrees Fahrenheit for 5 minutes. Place the French Cuisine Galettes in the fry basket and let

them cook for another 25 minutes at the same temperature. Keep rolling them over to get a uniform cook. Serve either with mint sauce or ketchup.

409. Apricot Spicy Lemon Kebab

Servings:x
Cooking Time:x
Ingredients:
- 3 tsp. lemon juice
- 2 tsp. garam masala
- 3 eggs
- 2 ½ tbsp. white sesame seeds
- 2 cups fresh apricots
- 3 onions chopped
- 5 green chilies-roughly chopped
- 1 ½ tbsp. ginger paste
- 1 ½ tsp. garlic paste
- 1 ½ tsp. salt

Directions:
1. Grind the ingredients except for the egg and form a smooth paste. Coat the apricots in the paste. Now, beat the eggs and add a little salt to it.
2. Dip the coated apricots in the egg mixture and then transfer to the sesame seeds and coat the apricots well. Place the vegetables on a stick.
3. Pre heat the oven at 160 degrees Fahrenheit for around 5 minutes. Place the sticks in the basket and let them cook for another 25 minutes at the same temperature. Turn the sticks over in between the cooking process to get a uniform cook.

410. Stuffed Capsicum Baskets

Servings:x
Cooking Time:x
Ingredients:
- 1 green chili finely chopped
- 2 or 3 large potatoes boiled and mashed
- 1 ½ tbsp. chopped coriander leaves
- 1 tsp. fenugreek
- 1 tsp. dried mango powder
- 3-4 long capsicum
- ½ tsp. salt
- ½ tsp. pepper powder
- For filling:
- 1 medium onion finely chopped
- 1 tsp. cumin powder
- Salt and pepper to taste
- 3 tbsp. grated cheese
- 1 tsp. red chili flakes
- ½ tsp. oregano
- ½ tsp. basil
- ½ tsp. parsley

Directions:

1. Take all the ingredients under the heading "Filling" and mix them together in a bowl.
2. Remove the stem of the capsicum. Cut off the caps. Remove the seeds as well. Sprinkle some salt and pepper on the inside of the capsicums. Leave them aside for some time.
3. Now fill the hollowed-out capsicums with the filling prepared but leave a small space at the top. Sprinkle grated cheese and also add the seasoning.
4. Pre heat the oven at 140 degrees Fahrenheit for 5 minutes. Put the capsicums in the fry basket and close it. Let them cook at the same temperature for another 20 minutes. Turn them over in between to prevent over cooking.

411. Caramelized Eggplant With Yogurt Sauce

Servings:2
Cooking Time: 15 Minutes
Ingredients:
- 1 medium eggplant, quartered and cut crosswise into ½-inch-thick slices
- 2 tablespoons vegetable oil
- Kosher salt and freshly ground black pepper, to taste
- ½ cup plain yogurt (not Greek)
- 2 tablespoons harissa paste
- 1 garlic clove, grated
- 2 teaspoons honey

Directions:
1. Toss the eggplant slices with the vegetable oil, salt, and pepper in a large bowl until well coated.
2. Lay the eggplant slices in the air fryer basket.
3. Put the air fryer basket on the baking pan and slide into Rack Position 2, select Air Fry, set temperature to 400ºF (205ºC), and set time to 15 minutes.
4. Stir the slices two to three times during cooking.
5. Meanwhile, make the yogurt sauce by whisking together the yogurt, harissa paste, and garlic in a small bowl.
6. When cooking is complete, the eggplant slices should be golden brown. Spread the yogurt sauce on a platter, and pile the eggplant slices over the top. Serve drizzled with the honey.

412. Rosemary Beets With Balsamic Glaze

Servings:2
Cooking Time: 10 Minutes
Ingredients:
- Beet:
- 2 beets, cubed

- 2 tablespoons olive oil
- 2 springs rosemary, chopped
- Salt and black pepper, to taste
- Balsamic Glaze:
- $^1/_3$ cup balsamic vinegar
- 1 tablespoon honey

Directions:
1. Combine the beets, olive oil, rosemary, salt, and pepper in a mixing bowl and toss until the beets are completely coated.
2. Place the beets in the air fryer basket.
3. Put the air fryer basket on the baking pan and slide into Rack Position 2, select Air Fry, set temperature to 400ºF (205ºC) and set time to 10 minutes.
4. Stir the vegetables halfway through.
5. When cooking is complete, the beets should be crisp and browned at the edges.
6. Meanwhile, make the balsamic glaze: Place the balsamic vinegar and honey in a small saucepan and bring to a boil over medium heat. When the sauce boils, reduce the heat to medium-low heat and simmer until the liquid is reduced by half.
7. When ready, remove the beets from the oven to a platter. Pour the balsamic glaze over the top and serve immediately.

413.   Yummy Chili Bean Burritos

Servings: 3
Cooking Time: 30 Minutes
Ingredients:
- 6 tortillas
- 1 cup grated cheddar cheese
- 1 can (8 oz) beans
- 1 tsp Italian seasoning

Directions:
1. Preheat on Bake function to 350 F. Season the beans with the seasoning and divide them between the tortillas. Top with cheddar cheese. Roll the burritos and arrange them on a lined baking dish. Cook for 5 minutes. Serve.

414.   Snake Gourd French Cuisine Galette

Servings:x
Cooking Time:x
Ingredients:
- 1-2 tbsp. fresh coriander leaves
- 2 or 3 green chilies finely chopped
- 1 ½ tbsp. lemon juice
- Salt and pepper to taste
- 2 tbsp. garam masala
- 1 cup sliced snake gourd
- 1 ½ cup coarsely crushed peanuts
- 3 tsp. ginger finely chopped

Directions:

1. Mix the ingredients in a clean bowl.
2. Mold this mixture into round and flat French Cuisine Galettes.
3. Wet the French Cuisine Galettes slightly with water. Coat each French Cuisine Galette with the crushed peanuts.
4. Pre heat the oven at 160 degrees Fahrenheit for 5 minutes. Place the French Cuisine Galettes in the fry basket and let them cook for another 25 minutes at the same temperature. Keep rolling them over to get a uniform cook. Serve either with mint sauce or ketchup.

415.   Spicy Kung Pao Tofu

Servings:4
Cooking Time: 10 Minutes
Ingredients:
- $^1/_3$ cup Asian-Style sauce
- 1 teaspoon cornstarch
- ½ teaspoon red pepper flakes, or more to taste
- 1 pound (454 g) firm or extra-firm tofu, cut into 1-inch cubes
- 1 small carrot, peeled and cut into ¼-inch-thick coins
- 1 small green bell pepper, cut into bite-size pieces
- 3 scallions, sliced, whites and green parts separated
- 3 tablespoons roasted unsalted peanuts

Directions:
1. In a large bowl, whisk together the sauce, cornstarch, and red pepper flakes. Fold in the tofu, carrot, pepper, and the white parts of the scallions and toss to coat. Spread the mixture evenly in the baking pan.
2. Slide the baking pan into Rack Position 2, select Roast, set temperature to 375ºF (190ºC), and set time to 10 minutes.
3. Stir the ingredients once halfway through the cooking time.
4. When done, remove from the oven. Serve sprinkled with the peanuts and scallion greens.

416.   Jalapeño Cheese Balls

Servings: 12
Cooking Time: 8 Minutes
Ingredients:
- 4 ounces cream cheese
- ⅓ cup shredded mozzarella cheese
- ⅓ cup shredded Cheddar cheese
- 2 jalapeños, finely chopped
- ½ cup bread crumbs
- 2 eggs
- ½ cup all-purpose flour
- Salt
- Pepper

- Cooking oil

Directions:
1. Preparing the Ingredients. In a medium bowl, combine the cream cheese, mozzarella, Cheddar, and jalapeños. Mix well.
2. Form the cheese mixture into balls about an inch thick. Using a small ice cream scoop works well.
3. Arrange the cheese balls on a sheet pan and place in the freezer for 15 minutes. This will help the cheese balls maintain their shape while frying.
4. Spray the Oven rack/basket with cooking oil. Place the bread crumbs in a small bowl. In another small bowl, beat the eggs. In a third small bowl, combine the flour with salt and pepper to taste, and mix well. Remove the cheese balls from the freezer. Dip the cheese balls in the flour, then the eggs, and then the bread crumbs.
5. Air Frying. Place the cheese balls in the Oven rack/basket. Spray with cooking oil. Place the Rack on the middle-shelf of the air fryer oven. Cook for 8 minutes.
6. Open the air fryer oven and flip the cheese balls. I recommend flipping them instead of shaking, so the balls maintain their form. Cook an additional 4 minutes. Cool before serving.
- **Nutrition Info:** CALORIES: 96; FAT: 6G; PROTEIN:4G; SUGAR:

417. Grandma´s Ratatouille

Servings:2
Cooking Time: 30 Minutes
Ingredients:
- 1 tbsp olive oil
- 3 Roma tomatoes, thinly sliced
- 2 garlic cloves, minced
- 1 zucchini, thinly sliced
- 2 yellow bell peppers, sliced
- 1 tbsp vinegar
- 2 tbsp herbs de Provence
- Salt and black pepper to taste

Directions:
1. Preheat on AirFry function to 390 F. Place all ingredients in a bowl. Season with salt and pepper and stir to coat. Arrange the vegetable on a baking dish and place in the oven. Cook for 15 minutes, shaking occasionally. Let sit for 5 more minutes after the timer goes off.

418. Yam French Cuisine Galette

Servings:x
Cooking Time:x
Ingredients:
- 1 ½ tbsp. lemon juice

- Salt and pepper to taste
- 2 cups minced yam
- 3 tsp. ginger finely chopped
- 1-2 tbsp. fresh coriander leaves
- 2 or 3 green chilies finely chopped

Directions:
1. Mix the ingredients in a clean bowl.
2. Mold this mixture into round and flat French Cuisine Galettes.
3. Wet the French Cuisine Galettes slightly with water.
4. Pre heat the oven at 160 degrees Fahrenheit for 5 minutes. Place the French Cuisine Galettes in the fry basket and let them cook for another 25 minutes at the same temperature. Keep rolling them over to get a uniform cook. Serve either with mint sauce or ketchup.

419. Cheese With Spinach Enchiladas

Servings: 4
Cooking Time: 20 Minutes
Ingredients:
- 8 corn tortillas, warm
- 2 cups mozzarella cheese, shredded
- 1 cup ricotta cheese
- 1 cup spinach, torn
- 1 garlic clove, minced
- ½ cup sliced onions
- ½ cup sour cream
- 1 tbsp butter
- 1 can enchilada sauce

Directions:
1. Warm olive oil In a saucepan over medium heat and sauté garlic and onion for 3 minutes until soft. Stir in the spinach and cook for 5 more minutes until wilted. Remove from the heat and stir in the ricotta cheese, sour cream, and half of the mozzarella cheese.
2. Spoon ¼ cup of the spinach mixture in the middle of each tortilla. Roll up and place seam side down in a baking dish. Pour the enchilada sauce over the tortillas and sprinkle with the remaining cheese. Cook in your for 15 minutes at 380 F on Air Fry function.

420. Pineapple Spicy Lemon Kebab

Servings:x
Cooking Time:x
Ingredients:
- 4 tbsp. chopped coriander
- 3 tbsp. cream
- 3 tbsp. chopped capsicum
- 3 eggs
- 2 ½ tbsp. white sesame seeds

- 2 cups cubed pineapples
- 3 onions chopped
- 5 green chilies-roughly chopped
- 1 ½ tbsp. ginger paste
- 1 ½ tsp. garlic paste
- 1 ½ tsp. salt
- 3 tsp. lemon juice
- 2 tsp. garam masala

Directions:
1. Grind the ingredients except for the egg and form a smooth paste. Coat the pineapples in the paste. Now, beat the eggs and add a little salt to it.
2. Dip the coated vegetables in the egg mixture and then transfer to the sesame seeds and coat the pineapples well. Place the vegetables on a stick.
3. Pre heat the oven at 160 degrees Fahrenheit for around 5 minutes. Place the sticks in the basket and let them cook for another 25 minutes at the same temperature. Turn the sticks over in between the cooking process to get a uniform cook.

421. Vegetable Fried Mix Chips

Servings: 4
Cooking Time: 45 Minutes
Ingredients:
- 1 large eggplant
- 4 potatoes
- 3 zucchinis
- ½ cup cornstarch
- ½ cup olive oil
- Salt to season

Directions:
1. Preheat on Air Fry function to 390 F. Cut the eggplant and zucchini in long 3-inch strips. Peel and cut the potatoes into 3-inch strips; set aside.
2. In a bowl, stir in cornstarch, ½ cup of water, salt, pepper, oil, eggplant, zucchini, and potatoes. Place one-third of the veggie strips in the basket and fit in the baking tray; cook for 12 minutes, shaking once.
3. Once ready, transfer them to a serving platter. Repeat the cooking process for the remaining veggie strips. Serve warm.

422. Spaghetti Squash Lasagna

Servings: 4
Cooking Time: 15 Minutes
Ingredients:
- 3 lb. spaghetti squash, halved lengthwise & seeded
- 4 tbsp. water, divided
- 1 tbsp. extra-virgin olive oil
- 1 bunch broccolini, chopped
- 4 cloves garlic, chopped fine

- ¼ tsp crushed red pepper flakes
- 1 cup mozzarella cheese, grated &divided
- ¼ cup parmesan cheese, grated & divided
- ¾ tsp Italian seasoning
- ½ tsp salt
- ¼ tsp ground pepper

Directions:
1. Place squash, cut side down, in a microwave safe dish. Add 2 tablespoons water and microwave on high until tender, about 10 minutes.
2. Heat oil in a large skillet over medium heat. Add broccoli, garlic, and red pepper. Cook, stirring frequently, 2 minutes.
3. Add remaining water and cook until broccolini is tender, about 3-5 minutes. Transfer to a large bowl.
4. With a fork, scrape the squash from the shells into the bowl with the broccolini. Place the shells in an 8x11-inch baking pan.
5. Add ¾ cup mozzarella, 2 tablespoons parmesan, and seasonings to the squash mixture and stir to combine. Spoon evenly into the shells and top with remaining cheese.
6. Place rack in position 1 and set oven to bake on 450°F for 15 minutes. After 5 minutes, place the squash in the oven and cook 10 minutes.
7. Set the oven to broil on high and move the pan to position 2. Broil until cheese starts to brown, about 2 minutes. Serve immediately.
- **Nutrition Info:** Calories 328, Total Fat 6g, Saturated Fat 2g, Total Carbs 48g, Net Carbs 39g, Protein 18g, Sugar 3g, Fiber 9g, Sodium 674mg, Potassium 1714mg, Phosphorus 452mg

423. Cashew Cauliflower With Yogurt Sauce

Servings:2
Cooking Time: 12 Minutes
Ingredients:
- 4 cups cauliflower florets (about half a large head)
- 1 tablespoon olive oil
- 1 teaspoon curry powder
- Salt, to taste
- ½ cup toasted, chopped cashews, for garnish
- Yogurt Sauce:
- ¼ cup plain yogurt
- 2 tablespoons sour cream
- 1 teaspoon honey
- 1 teaspoon lemon juice
- Pinch cayenne pepper
- Salt, to taste
- 1 tablespoon chopped fresh cilantro, plus leaves for garnish

Directions:

1. In a large mixing bowl, toss the cauliflower florets with the olive oil, curry powder, and salt.
2. Place the cauliflower florets in the air fryer basket.
3. Put the air fryer basket on the baking pan and slide into Rack Position 2, select Air Fry, set temperature to 400ºF (205ºC) and set time to 12 minutes.
4. Stir the cauliflower florets twice during cooking.
5. When cooking is complete, the cauliflower should be golden brown.
6. Meanwhile, mix all the ingredients for the yogurt sauce in a small bowl and whisk to combine.
7. Remove the cauliflower from the oven and drizzle with the yogurt sauce. Scatter the toasted cashews and cilantro on top and serve immediately.

424. Broccoli Momo's Recipe

Servings:x
Cooking Time:x
Ingredients:

- 2 tbsp. oil
- 2 tsp. ginger-garlic paste
- 2 tsp. soya sauce
- 2 tsp. vinegar
- 1 ½ cup all-purpose flour
- ½ tsp. salt
- 5 tbsp. water
- 2 cups grated broccoli

Directions:

1. Squeeze the dough and cover it with plastic wrap and set aside. Next, cook the ingredients for the filling and try to ensure that the broccoli is covered well with the sauce.
2. Roll the dough and cut it into a square. Place the filling in the center. Now, wrap the dough to cover the filling and pinch the edges together.
3. Pre heat the oven at 200° F for 5 minutes. Place the gnocchi's in the fry basket and close it. Let them cook at the same temperature for another 20 minutes. Recommended sides are chili sauce or ketchup.

425. Tofu & Pea Cauli Rice

Servings:4
Cooking Time: 30 Minutes
Ingredients:

- Tofu:
- ½ block tofu
- ½ cup onions, chopped
- 2 tbsp soy sauce

- 1 tsp turmeric
- 1 cup carrots, chopped
- Cauliflower:
- 3 cups cauliflower rice
- 2 tbsp soy sauce
- ½ cup broccoli, chopped
- 2 garlic cloves, minced
- 1 ½ tsp toasted sesame oil
- 1 tbsp fresh ginger, minced
- ½ cup frozen peas
- 1 tbsp rice vinegar

Directions:

1. Preheat on AirFry function to 370 F. Crumble the tofu and combine it with all tofu ingredients. Place in a baking dish and cook for 10 minutes.
2. Meanwhile, place all cauliflower ingredients in a large bowl; mix to combine. Add the cauliflower mixture to the tofu and stir to combine. Press Start and cook for 12 minutes. Serve.

426. Jalapeño & Tomato Gratin

Servings: 4
Cooking Time: 35 Minutes
Ingredients:

- 1 (16 oz) can jalapeño peppers
- 1 cup cheddar cheese, shredded
- 1 cup Monterey Jack cheese, shredded
- 2 tbsp all-purpose flour
- 2 large eggs, beaten
- ½ cup milk
- 1 can tomato sauce

Directions:

1. Preheat on Air Fry function to 380 F. Arrange the jalapeño peppers on the greased Air Fryer baking pan and top with half of the cheese.
2. In a medium bowl, combine the eggs, milk, and flour and pour the mixture over the chilies. Cook in your for 20 minutes. Take out the chilies and pour the tomato sauce over them. Return and cook for 15 more minutes. Sprinkle with the remaining cheese and serve.

427. Crispy Veggies With Halloumi

Servings:2
Cooking Time: 14 Minutes
Ingredients:

- 2 zucchinis, cut into even chunks
- 1 large eggplant, peeled, cut into chunks
- 1 large carrot, cut into chunks
- 6 ounces (170 g) halloumi cheese, cubed
- 2 teaspoons olive oil
- Salt and black pepper, to taste
- 1 teaspoon dried mixed herbs

Directions:

1. Combine the zucchinis, eggplant, carrot, cheese, olive oil, salt, and pepper in a large bowl and toss to coat well.
2. Spread the mixture evenly in the air fryer basket.
3. Put the air fryer basket on the baking pan and slide into Rack Position 2, select Air Fry, set temperature to 340ºF (171ºC), and set time to 14 minutes.
4. Stir the mixture once during cooking.
5. When cooking is complete, they should be crispy and golden. Remove from the oven and serve topped with mixed herbs.

428.   Roasted Vegetables Salad

Servings: 5
Cooking Time: 85 Minutes
Ingredients:
- 3 eggplants
- 1 tbsp of olive oil
- 3 medium zucchini
- 1 tbsp of olive oil
- 4 large tomatoes, cut them in eighths
- 4 cups of one shaped pasta
- 2 peppers of any color
- 1 cup of sliced tomatoes cut into small cubes
- 2 teaspoon of salt substitute
- 8 tbsp of grated parmesan cheese
- ½ cup of Italian dressing
- Leaves of fresh basil

Directions:
1. Preparing the Ingredients. Wash your eggplant and slice it off then discard the green end. Make sure not to peel.
2. Slice your eggplant into1/2 inch of thick rounds. 1/2 inch)
3. Pour 1tbsp of olive oil on the eggplant round.
4. Air Frying. Put the eggplants in the basket of the air fryer oven and then toss it in the air fryer oven. Cook the eggplants for 40 minutes. Set the heat to 360 ° F
5. Meanwhile, wash your zucchini and slice it then discard the green end. But do not peel it.
6. Slice the Zucchini into thick rounds of ½ inch each. Toss your ingredients
7. Add 1 tbsp of olive oil.
8. Air Frying. Cook the zucchini for 25 minutes on a heat of 360° F and when the time is off set it aside.
9. Wash and cut the tomatoes.
10. Air Frying. Arrange your tomatoes in the basket of the air fryer oven. Set the timer to 30 minutes. Set the heat to 350° F
11. When the time is off, cook your pasta according to the pasta guiding directions, empty it into a colander. Run the cold water

on it and wash it and drain the pasta and put it aside.
12. Meanwhile, wash and chop your peppers and place it in a bow
13. Wash and thinly slice your cherry tomatoes and add it to the bowl. Add your roasted veggies.
14. Add the pasta, a pinch of salt, the topping dressing, add the basil and the parm and toss everything together. (It is better to mix with your hands). Set the ingredients together in the refrigerator, and let it chill
15. Serve your salad and enjoy it!

429.   Roasted Fall Veggies

Servings: 6
Cooking Time: 30 Minutes
Ingredients:
- 2 cups sweet potatoes, cubed
- 2 cups Brussel sprouts, halved
- 3 cups button mushrooms, halved
- ½ red onion, chopped
- 3 cloves garlic, chopped fine
- 4 sage leaves, chopped
- 2 sprigs rosemary, chopped
- 2 sprigs thyme, chopped
- 1 tsp garlic powder
- 1 tsp onion powder
- ½ tsp salt
- ¼ tsp pepper
- 3 tbsp. balsamic vinegar
- Nonstick cooking spray

Directions:
1. Chop vegetables so that they are as close to equal in size as possible. Roughly chop the herbs.
2. In a large bowl, toss vegetables, herbs, and spices to mix. Drizzle vinegar overall and toss to coat.
3. Spray the baking pan with cooking spray. Set oven to bake on 350°F for 35 minutes.
4. Transfer the vegetable mixture to the baking pan and after 5 minutes, place in the oven in position 1. Bake vegetables 25-30 minutes or until vegetables are tender. Turn them over halfway through cooking. Serve immediately.
- **Nutrition Info:** Calories 76, Total Fat 0g, Saturated Fat 0g, Total Carbs 16g, Net Carbs 13g, Protein 3g, Sugar 5g, Fiber 3g, Sodium 231mg, Potassium 455mg, Phosphorus 92mg

430.   Beetroot Chips

Servings: 3
Cooking Time: 25 Minutes
Ingredients:
- 1lb golden beetroots, sliced
- 2 tbsp olive oil

- 1 tbsp yeast flakes
- 1 tsp vegan seasoning
- Salt to taste

Directions:
1. In a bowl, add the olive oil, beetroots, vegan seasoning, and yeast and mix well. Dump the coated chips in the basket.
2. Fit in the baking tray and cook in your for 15 minutes at 370 F on Air Fry function, shaking once halfway through. Serve.

431. Pumpkin French Cuisine Galette

Servings:x
Cooking Time:x
Ingredients:
- 2 or 3 green chilies finely chopped
- 1 ½ tbsp. lemon juice
- Salt and pepper to taste
- 2 tbsp. garam masala
- 1 cup sliced pumpkin
- 3 tsp. ginger finely chopped
- 1-2 tbsp. fresh coriander leaves

Directions:
1. Mix the ingredients in a clean bowl.
2. Mold this mixture into round and flat French Cuisine Galettes.
3. Wet the French Cuisine Galettes slightly with water.
4. Pre heat the oven at 160 degrees Fahrenheit for 5 minutes. Place the French Cuisine Galettes in the fry basket and let them cook for another 25 minutes at the same temperature. Keep rolling them over to get a uniform cook. Serve either with mint sauce or ketchup.

432. Vegan Beetroot Chips

Servings:2
Cooking Time: 9 Minutes
Ingredients:
- 4 cups golden beetroot slices
- 2 tbsp olive oil
- 1 tbsp yeast flakes
- 1 tsp vegan seasoning
- Salt to taste

Directions:
1. In a bowl, add the oil, beetroot slices, vegan seasoning, and yeast and mix well. Dump the coated chips in the basket. Set the heat to 370 F and press Start. Cook on AirFry function for14-16 minutes, shaking once halfway through. Serve.

433. Asian Tofu "meatballs"

Servings: 4
Cooking Time: 10 Minutes
Ingredients:

- 3 dried shitake mushrooms
- Nonstick cooking spray
- 14 oz. firm tofu, drained & pressed
- ¼ cup carrots, cooked
- ¼ cup bamboo shoots, sliced thin
- ½ cup Panko bread crumbs
- 2 tbsp. corn starch
- 3 ½ tablespoon soy sauce, divided
- 1 tsp garlic powder
- ¼ tsp salt
- 1/8 tsp pepper
- 1 tbsp. olive oil
- 2 tbsp. garlic, diced fine
- 2 tbsp. ketchup
- 2 tsp sugar

Directions:
1. Place the shitake mushrooms in a bowl and add just enough water to cover. Let soak 20 minutes until soft. Drain well and chop.
2. Place the baking pan in position Lightly spray the fryer basket with cooking spray.
3. Place mushrooms, tofu, carrots, bamboo shoots, bread crumbs, corn starch, 1 ½ tablespoons soy sauce, and seasonings in a food processor. Pulse until thoroughly combined. Form mixture into 1-inch balls.
4. Place balls in fryer basket, these may need to be cooked in batches, and place in oven. Set to air fry on 380°F for 10 minutes. Turn the balls around halfway through cooking time.
5. Heat oil in a saucepan over medium heat. Add garlic and cook 1 minute.
6. Stir in remaining soy sauce, ketchup, and sugar. Bring to a simmer and cook until sauce thickens, 3-5 minutes.
7. When the meatballs are done, add them to sauce and stir to coat. Serve immediately.
- **Nutrition Info:** Calories 305, Total Fat 13g, Saturated Fat 2g, Total Carbs 28g, Net Carbs 24g, Protein 20g, Sugar 5g, Fiber 4g, Sodium 789mg, Potassium 470mg, Phosphorus 260mg

434. Zucchini Fried Baked Pastry

Servings:x
Cooking Time:x
Ingredients:
- 1 or 2 green chilies that are finely chopped or mashed
- ½ tsp. cumin
- 1 tsp. coarsely crushed coriander
- 1 dry red chili broken into pieces
- A small amount of salt (to taste)
- ½ tsp. dried mango powder
- ½ tsp. red chili power.
- 2 tbsp. unsalted butter
- 1 ½ cup all-purpose flour
- A pinch of salt to taste

- Add as much water as required to make the dough stiff and firm
- 3 medium zucchinis (mashed)
- ¼ cup boiled peas
- 1 tsp. powdered ginger
- 1-2 tbsp. coriander.

Directions:
1. Mix the dough for the outer covering and make it stiff and smooth. Leave it to rest in a container while making the filling.
2. Cook the ingredients in a pan and stir them well to make a thick paste. Roll the paste out.
3. Roll the dough into balls and flatten them. Cut them in halves and add the
4. filling. Use water to help you fold the edges to create the shape of a cone.
5. Pre-heat the oven for around 5 to 6 minutes at 300 Fahrenheit. Place all the samosas in the fry basket and close the basket properly. Keep the oven at 200 degrees for another 20 to 25 minutes. Around the halfway point, open the basket and turn the samosas over for uniform cooking. After this, fry at 250 degrees for around 10 minutes in order to give them the desired golden-brown color. Serve hot. Recommended sides are tamarind or mint sauce.

SNACKS AND DESSERTS RECIPES

435.   Air Fryer Cinnamon Rolls

Servings: 8
Cooking Time: 5 Minutes
Ingredients:
- 1 ½ tbsp. cinnamon
- ¾ C. brown sugar
- ¼ C. melted coconut oil
- 1 pound frozen bread dough, thawed
- Glaze:
- ½ tsp. vanilla
- 1 ¼ C. powdered erythritol
- 2 tbsp. softened ghee
- 3   ounces softened cream cheese

Directions:
1. Preparing the Ingredients. Lay out bread dough and roll out into a rectangle. Brush melted ghee over dough and leave a 1-inch border along edges.
2. Mix cinnamon and sweetener together and then sprinkle over the dough.
3. Roll dough tightly and slice into 8 pieces. Let sit 1-2 hours to rise.
4. To make the glaze, simply mix ingredients together till smooth.
5. Air Frying. Once rolls rise, place into the air fryer oven and cook 5 minutes at 350 degrees.
6. Serve rolls drizzled in cream cheese glaze. Enjoy!
- **Nutrition Info:** CALORIES: 390; FAT:8G; PROTEIN:1G; SUGAR:7G

436.   Roasted Grapes With Yogurt

Servings:6
Cooking Time: 10 Minutes
Ingredients:
- 2 cups seedless red grapes, rinsed and patted dry
- 1 tablespoon apple cider vinegar
- 1 tablespoon honey
- 1 cup low-fat Greek yogurt
- 2 tablespoons 2 percent milk
- 2 tablespoons minced fresh basil

Directions:
1. Spread the red grapes in the baking pan and drizzle with the cider vinegar and honey. Lightly toss to coat.
2. Slide the baking pan into Rack Position 2, select Roast, set temperature to 380ºF (193ºC) and set time to 10 minutes.
3. When cooking is complete, the grapes will be wilted but still soft. Remove from the oven.
4. In a medium bowl, whisk together the yogurt and milk. Gently fold in the grapes and basil.
5. Serve immediately.

437.   Jalapeno Pops

Servings:x
Cooking Time:x
Ingredients:
- 1 cup flour
- ½ teaspoon salt
- 1 egg, beaten
- cup ginger ale
- 3 tablespoons cornstarch
- 24 small jalapeno peppers
- 2 cups grated Swiss cheese
- 1 (8-ounce) package cream cheese, softened

Directions:
1. Cut slit in side of peppers and gently remove seeds and membranes. Combine Swiss cheese and cream cheese in medium bowl and blend well. Stuff peppers with cheese mixture and press gently to seal.
2. In a small bowl, combine flour, salt, egg, and ginger ale and mix until a thick batter form. Put cornstarch in another small bowl. Dip each stuffed pepper in cornstarch and shake off excess. Dip each pepper in batter and hold over bowl a few seconds for excess batter to drip off. Flash freeze peppers in single layer on baking sheet. When frozen solid, pack in rigid containers, with waxed paper separating layers. Label peppers and freeze.
3. To reheat: Preheat oven to 400ºF. Place frozen peppers on baking sheet and bake at 400ºF for 20 to 30 minutes or until brown, crisp, and thoroughly heated.

438.   Tasty Cauliflower Tots

Servings: 16
Cooking Time: 18 Minutes
Ingredients:
- 2 cups cauliflower, steamed and shredded
- 1 tbsp butter
- 1/2 cup parmesan cheese, shredded
- 1/4 tsp onion powder
- 1 large egg
- Pepper
- Salt

Directions:
1. Fit the oven with the rack in position
2. Add all ingredients to the bowl and mix well to combine.
3. Using a tablespoon make small tots from cauliflower mixture and arrange in baking pan.
4. Set to bake at 425 F for 23 minutes. After 5 minutes place the baking pan in the preheated oven.
5. Serve and enjoy.

- **Nutrition Info:** Calories 23 Fat 1.6 g Carbohydrates 0.8 g Sugar 0.3 g Protein 1.6 g Cholesterol 16 mg

439. Handmade Donuts

Servings:4
Cooking Time: 25 Minutes
Ingredients:
- 8 oz self-rising flour
- 1 tsp baking powder
- ½ cup milk
- 2 ½ tbsp butter
- 1 egg
- 2 oz brown sugar

Directions:
1. Preheat on Bake function to 350 F. In a bowl, beat the butter with sugar until smooth. Whisk in egg and milk. In another bowl, combine the flour with the baking powder.
2. Fold the flour into the butter mixture. Form donut shapes and cut off the center with cookie cutters. Arrange on a lined baking sheet and cook for 15 minutes. Serve with whipped cream.

440. Tangy Fried Pickle Spears

Servings:6
Cooking Time: 15 Minutes
Ingredients:
- 2 jars sweet and sour pickle spears, patted dry
- 2 medium-sized eggs
- $^1/_3$ cup milk
- 1 teaspoon garlic powder
- 1 teaspoon sea salt
- ½ teaspoon shallot powder
- $^1/_3$ teaspoon chili powder
- $^1/_3$ cup all-purpose flour
- Cooking spray

Directions:
1. Spritz the air fryer basket with cooking spray.
2. In a bowl, beat together the eggs with milk. In another bowl, combine garlic powder, sea salt, shallot powder, chili powder and all-purpose flour until well blended.
3. One by one, roll the pickle spears in the powder mixture, then dredge them in the egg mixture. Dip them in the powder mixture a second time for additional coating.
4. Place the coated pickles in the basket.
5. Put the air fryer basket on the baking pan and slide into Rack Position 2, select Air Fry, set temperature to 385ºF (196ºC), and set time to 15 minutes.
6. Stir the pickles halfway through the cooking time.

7. When cooking is complete, they should be golden and crispy. Transfer to a plate and let cool for 5 minutes before serving.

441. Strawberry Muffins

Servings: 12
Cooking Time: 20 Minutes
Ingredients:
- 4 eggs
- 1/4 cup water
- 1/2 cup butter, melted
- 2 tsp baking powder
- 2 cups almond flour
- 2/3 cup strawberries, chopped
- 2 tsp vanilla
- 1/4 cup erythritol
- Pinch of salt

Directions:
1. Fit the oven with the rack in position
2. Line 12-cups muffin tin with cupcake liners and set aside.
3. In a medium bowl, mix together almond flour, baking powder, and salt.
4. In a separate bowl, whisk eggs, sweetener, vanilla, water, and butter.
5. Add almond flour mixture into the egg mixture and mix until well combined.
6. Add strawberries and stir well.
7. Pour batter into the prepared muffin tin.
8. Set to bake at 350 F for 25 minutes. After 5 minutes place muffin tin in the preheated oven.
9. Serve and enjoy.
- **Nutrition Info:** Calories 201 Fat 18.5 g Carbohydrates 5.2 g Sugar 1.3 g Protein 6 g Cholesterol 75 mg

442. Chocolate Sponge Cake

Servings:x
Cooking Time:x
Ingredients:
- 3 tbsp. powdered sugar
- ½ cup soda
- 1 tsp. vanilla essence
- Parchment or butter paper to line the tin
- ½ cup condensed milk
- 1 cup all-purpose flour
- ½ cup cocoa powder
- ½ tsp. baking soda
- ½ tsp. baking powder
- ½ cup oil

Directions:
1. Mix the ingredients together to create a batter that is smooth and thick.
2. Grease a cake tin with butter and line it with the parchment or butter paper.
3. Transfer the batter into the tin.
4. Preheat the fryer to 300 Fahrenheit for five minutes. You will need to place the tin in

the basket and cover it. Cook the cake for fifteen minutes and check whether or not the cake is cooked using a toothpick. Remove the tin and cut the cake into slices and serve.

443. Cheesy Roasted Jalapeño Poppers

Servings:8
Cooking Time: 15 Minutes
Ingredients:
- 6 ounces (170 g) cream cheese, at room temperature
- 4 ounces (113 g) shredded Cheddar cheese
- 1 teaspoon chili powder
- 12 large jalapeño peppers, deseeded and sliced in half lengthwise
- 2 slices cooked bacon, chopped
- ¼ cup panko bread crumbs
- 1 tablespoon butter, melted

Directions:
1. In a medium bowl, whisk together the cream cheese, Cheddar cheese and chili powder. Spoon the cheese mixture into the jalapeño halves and arrange them in the baking pan.
2. In a small bowl, stir together the bacon, bread crumbs and butter. Sprinkle the mixture over the jalapeño halves.
3. Slide the baking pan into Rack Position 2, select Roast, set temperature to 375ºF (190ºC) and set time to 15 minutes.
4. When cooking is complete, remove from the oven. Let the poppers cool for 5 minutes before serving.

444. Cream Caramel

Servings:x
Cooking Time:x
Ingredients:
- 3 tbsp. unsalted butter
- 4 tbsp. caramel
- 2 cups milk
- 2 cups custard powder
- 3 tbsp. powdered sugar

Directions:
1. Boil the milk and the sugar in a pan and add the custard powder and stir till you get a thick mixture.
2. Preheat the fryer to 300 Fahrenheit for five minutes. Place the dish in the basket and reduce the temperature to 250 Fahrenheit. Cook for ten minutes and set aside to cool.
3. Spread the caramel over the dish and serve warm.

445. Chocolate Chip Pan Cookie

Servings: 4
Cooking Time: 15 Minutes

Ingredients:
- ½ cup blanched finely ground almond flour.
- 1 large egg.
- ¼ cup powdered erythritol
- 2 tbsp. unsalted butter; softened.
- 2 tbsp. low-carb, sugar-free chocolate chips
- ½ tsp. unflavored gelatin
- ½ tsp. baking powder.
- ½ tsp. vanilla extract.

Directions:
1. Take a large bowl, mix almond flour and erythritol. Stir in butter, egg and gelatin until combined.
2. Stir in baking powder and vanilla and then fold in chocolate chips
3. Pour batter into 6-inch round baking pan. Place pan into the air fryer basket.
4. Adjust the temperature to 300 Degrees F and set the timer for 7 minutes
5. When fully cooked, the top will be golden brown and a toothpick inserted in center will come out clean. Let cool at least 10 minutes.
- **Nutrition Info:** Calories: 188; Protein: 5.6g; Fiber: 2.0g; Fat: 15.7g; Carbs: 16.8g

446. Cheese Artichoke Spinach Dip

Servings: 10
Cooking Time: 17 Minutes
Ingredients:
- 1/2 cup mozzarella cheese, shredded
- 3 cups spinach, chopped
- 2 garlic cloves, minced
- 1/3 cup sour cream
- 1/3 can artichoke hearts, drained and chopped
- 1/2 cup mayonnaise
- 7 oz brie cheese
- 1/3 tsp dried basil
- 1/3 tsp pepper
- 1 tsp sea salt

Directions:
1. Fit the oven with the rack in position 2.
2. Add all ingredients except mozzarella cheese into the air fryer baking dish and mix until well combined.
3. Spread mozzarella cheese on top.
4. Set to bake at 325 F for 22 minutes. After 5 minutes place the baking dish in the preheated oven.
5. Serve and enjoy.
- **Nutrition Info:** Calories 138 Fat 11.3 g Carbohydrates 4.3 g Sugar 0.9 g Protein 5.3 g Cholesterol 27 mg

447. Churros With Chocolate Dipping Sauce

Servings: 4

Cooking Time: 10 Minutes
Ingredients:
- 1 ½ cup water, divided
- ¼ cup + 1 tsp butter, unsalted
- ¼ cup + 1 tsp sugar
- 1 cup flour
- 2 eggs
- 1/8 tsp salt
- 1 cup dark chocolate (60-70% cocoa solids), chopped

Directions:
1. Lightly spray baking pan with cooking spray.
2. In a saucepan, combine 1 cup water, ¼ cup butter, and 1 teaspoon sugar. Cook over medium heat until butter has melted, stirring frequently.
3. Add the flour and stir quickly to form a loose paste. Reduce heat to low and cook, stirring, until mixture starts to come away from sides of pan and firm up. Remove from heat and let cool 10 minutes.
4. Beat in eggs and salt until combined, mixture should be smooth and glossy. Transfer to a pastry bag fitted with a star shaped nozzle.
5. Pipe mixture into any shape desired on the baking pan. Place the pan in position 2 and set oven to air fry on 390°F for 6 minutes. Cook until crisp and golden brown. Repeat with remaining batter.
6. Place the chocolate, remaining water, and sugar in a double boiler. Let sit until chocolate and sugar melts completely, stirring occasionally.
7. When the mixture is melted and smooth, stir in butter and continue cooking until melted and combined. Serve immediately with churros.
- **Nutrition Info:** Calories 638, Total Fat 36g, Saturated Fat 20g, Total Carbs 66g, Net Carbs 61g, Protein 10g, Sugar 33g, Fiber 5g, Sodium 211mg, Potassium 393mg, Phosphorus 234mg

448.   Quick Coffee Cake

Servings: 2
Cooking Time: 30 Minutes
Ingredients:
- ¼ cup butter
- ½ tsp instant coffee
- 1 tbsp black coffee, brewed
- 1 egg
- ¼ cup sugar
- ¼ cup flour
- 1 tsp cocoa powder
- Powdered sugar, for icing

Directions:
1. Preheat on Bake function to 330 F. Beat the sugar and egg together in a bowl. Beat in

cocoa, instant and black coffees; stir in flour. Transfer the batter to a greased cake pan. Cook for 15 minutes. Dust with powdered sugar and serve.

449.   Choco Cookies

Servings: 8
Cooking Time: 8 Minutes
Ingredients:
- 3 egg whites
- 3/4 cup cocoa powder, unsweetened
- 1 3/4 cup confectioner sugar
- 1 1/2 tsp vanilla

Directions:
1. Fit the oven with the rack in position
2. In a mixing bowl, whip egg whites until fluffy soft peaks. Slowly add in cocoa, sugar, and vanilla.
3. Drop teaspoonful onto parchment-lined baking pan into 32 small cookies.
4. Set to bake at 350 F for 8 minutes. After 5 minutes place the baking pan in the preheated oven.
5. Serve and enjoy.
- **Nutrition Info:** Calories 132 Fat 1.1 g Carbohydrates 31 g Sugar 0.3 g Protein 2 g Cholesterol 0 mg

450.   Apple Pastries

Servings: 6
Cooking Time: 10 Minutes
Ingredients:
- ½ of large apple, peeled, cored and chopped
- 1 teaspoon fresh orange zest, grated finely
- ½ tablespoon white sugar
- ½ teaspoon ground cinnamon
- 7.05 oz. prepared frozen puff pastry

Directions:
1. In a bowl, mix together all ingredients except puff pastry.
2. Cut the pastry in 16 squares.
3. Place about a teaspoon of the apple mixture in the center of each square.
4. Fold each square into a triangle and press the edges slightly with wet fingers.
5. Then with a fork, press the edges firmly.
6. Press "Power Button" of Air Fry Oven and turn the dial to select the "Air Fry" mode.
7. Press the Time button and again turn the dial to set the cooking time to 10 minutes.
8. Now push the Temp button and rotate the dial to set the temperature at 390 degrees F.
9. Press "Start/Pause" button to start.
10. When the unit beeps to show that it is preheated, open the lid.
11. Arrange the pastries in greased "Air Fry Basket" and insert in the oven.
12. Serve warm.

- **Nutrition Info:** Calories 198 Total Fat 12.7 g Saturated Fat 3.2 g Cholesterol 0 mg Sodium 83 mg Total Carbs 18.8 g Fiber 1.1 g Sugar 3.2 g Protein 2.5 g

451. Coconut Butter Apple Bars

Servings: 8
Cooking Time: 45 Minutes
Ingredients:
- 1 tbsp ground flax seed
- 1/4 cup coconut butter, softened
- 1 cup pecans
- 1 cup of water
- 1/4 cup dried apples
- 1 1/2 tsp baking powder
- 1 1/2 tsp cinnamon
- 1 tsp vanilla
- 2 tbsp swerve

Directions:
1. Fit the oven with the rack in position
2. Add all ingredients into the blender and blend until smooth.
3. Pour blended mixture into the greased baking dish.
4. Set to bake at 350 F for 50 minutes. After 5 minutes place the baking dish in the preheated oven.
5. Slice and serve.
- **Nutrition Info:** Calories 161 Fat 15 g Carbohydrates 6 g Sugar 2 g Protein 2 g Cholesterol 0 mg

452. Cheesy Meatballs

Servings: 16 Meatballs
Cooking Time: 15 Minutes
Ingredients:
- 1 lb. 80/20 ground beef.
- 3 oz. low-moisture, whole-milk mozzarella, cubed
- 1 large egg.
- ½ cup low-carb, no-sugar-added pasta sauce.
- ¼ cup grated Parmesan cheese.
- ¼ cup blanched finely ground almond flour.
- ¼ tsp. onion powder.
- 1 tsp. dried parsley.
- ½ tsp. garlic powder.

Directions:
1. Take a large bowl, add ground beef, almond flour, parsley, garlic powder, onion powder and egg. Fold ingredients together until fully combined
2. Form the mixture into 2-inch balls and use your thumb or a spoon to create an indent in the center of each meatball. Place a cube of cheese in the center and form the ball around it.
3. Place the meatballs into the air fryer, working in batches if necessary. Adjust the temperature to 350 Degrees F and set the timer for 15 minutes
4. Meatballs will be slightly crispy on the outside and fully cooked when at least 180 Degrees F internally.
5. When they are finished cooking, toss the meatballs in the sauce and sprinkle with grated Parmesan for serving.
- **Nutrition Info:** Calories: 447; Protein: 26g; Fiber: 8g; Fat: 27g; Carbs: 4g

453. Strawberry Tart

Servings:x
Cooking Time:x
Ingredients:
- 2 cups sliced strawberries
- 1 cup fresh cream
- 3 tbsp. butter
- 1 ½ cup plain flour
- 3 tbsp. unsalted butter
- 2 tbsp. powdered sugar
- 2 cups cold water

Directions:
1. In a large bowl, mix the flour, cocoa powder, butter and sugar with your Oregano Fingers. The mixture should resemble breadcrumbs. Squeeze the dough using the cold milk and wrap it and leave it to cool for ten minutes. Roll the dough out into the pie and prick the sides of the pie.
2. Mix the ingredients for the filling in a bowl. Make sure that it is a little
3. thick. Preheat the fryer to 300 Fahrenheit for five minutes. You will need to place the tin in the basket and cover it. When the pastry has turned golden brown, you will need to remove the tin and let it cool. Cut into slices and serve with a dollop of cream.

454. Air Fried Lemon-pepper Wings

Servings:10
Cooking Time: 24 Minutes
Ingredients:
- 2 pounds (907 g) chicken wings
- 4½ teaspoons salt-free lemon pepper seasoning
- 1½ teaspoons baking powder
- 1½ teaspoons kosher salt

Directions:
1. In a large bowl, toss together all the ingredients until well coated. Place the wings in the air fryer basket, making sure they don't crowd each other too much.
2. Put the air fryer basket on the baking pan and slide into Rack Position 2, select Air Fry, set temperature to 375ºF (190ºC) and set time to 24 minutes.

3. After 12 minutes, remove from the oven. Use tongs to turn the wings over. Return to the oven to continue cooking.
4. When cooking is complete, the wings should be dark golden brown and a bit charred in places. Remove from the oven and let rest for 5 minutes before serving.

455. Baked Sardines With Tomato Sauce

Servings:4
Cooking Time: 20 Minutes
Ingredients:
- 2 pounds (907 g) fresh sardines
- 3 tablespoons olive oil, divided
- 4 Roma tomatoes, peeled and chopped
- 1 small onion, sliced thinly
- Zest of 1 orange
- Sea salt and freshly ground pepper, to taste
- 2 tablespoons whole-wheat bread crumbs
- ½ cup white wine

Directions:
1. Grease the baking pan with a little olive oil. Set aside.
2. Rinse the sardines under running water. Slit the belly, remove the spine and butterfly the fish. Set aside.
3. Heat the remaining olive oil in a large skillet. Add the tomatoes, onion, orange zest, salt and pepper to the skillet and simmer for 20 minutes, or until the mixture thickens and softens.
4. Place half the sauce in the bottom of the greased pan. Arrange the sardines on top and spread the remaining half the sauce over the fish. Sprinkle with the bread crumbs and drizzle with the white wine.
5. Slide the baking pan into Rack Position 1, select Convection Bake, set temperature to 425ºF (220ºC) and set time to 20 minutes.
6. When cooking is complete, remove the pan from the oven. Serve immediately.

456. Berry Crumble With Lemon

Servings:6
Cooking Time: 30 Minutes
Ingredients:
- 12 oz fresh strawberries
- 7 oz fresh raspberries
- 5 oz fresh blueberries
- 5 tbsp cold butter
- 2 tbsp lemon juice
- 1 cup flour
- ½ cup sugar
- 1 tbsp water
- A pinch of salt

Directions:

1. Preheat on Bake function to 360 F. Gently mash the berries, but make sure there are chunks left. Mix with the lemon juice and 2 tbsp of sugar. Place the berry mixture at the bottom of a greased cake pan. Combine the flour with salt and sugar in a bowl. Mix well.
2. Add the water and rub the butter with your fingers until the mixture becomes crumbled. Pour the batter over the berries. Press Start and cook for 20 minutes. Serve chilled.

457. Air Fryer Mixed Nuts

Servings: 2
Cooking Time: 4 Minutes
Ingredients:
- 2 cup mixed nuts
- 1 tbsp olive oil
- 1 tsp ground cumin
- 1 tsp pepper
- 1/4 tsp cayenne
- 1 tsp salt

Directions:
1. Fit the oven with the rack in position 2.
2. In a bowl, add all ingredients and toss well.
3. Add the nuts mixture to the air fryer basket then place an air fryer basket in the baking pan.
4. Place a baking pan on the oven rack. Set to air fry at 350 F for 4 minutes.
5. Serve and enjoy.
- **Nutrition Info:** Calories 953 Fat 88.2 g Carbohydrates 33.3 g Sugar 6.4 g Protein 22.7 g Cholesterol 0 mg

458. Peanut Butter Fudge Cake

Servings: 10
Cooking Time: 15 Minutes
Ingredients:
- 1 cup peanut butter
- 1 ¼ cups monk fruit
- 3 eggs
- 1 cup almond flour
- 1 teaspoon baking powder
- 1/4 teaspoon kosher salt
- 1 cup unsweetened bakers' chocolate, broken into chunks

Directions:
1. Start by preheating your Air Fryer to 350 degrees F. Now, spritz the sides and bottom of a baking pan with cooking spray.
2. In a mixing dish, thoroughly combine the peanut butter with the monk fruit until creamy. Next, fold in the egg and beat until fluffy.
3. After that, stir in the almond flour, baking powder, salt, and bakers'chocolate. Mix until everything is well combined.

4. Bake in the preheated Air Fryer for 20 to 22 minutes. Transfer to a wire rack to cool before slicing and serving.
- **Nutrition Info:** 207 Calories; 11g Fat; 4g Carbs; 4g Protein; 1g Sugars; 4g Fiber

459. Plum Cream(2)

Servings: 4
Cooking Time: 15 Minutes
Ingredients:
- 1 lb. plums, pitted and chopped.
- 1 ½ cups heavy cream
- ¼ cup swerve
- 1 tbsp. lemon juice

Directions:
1. Take a bowl and mix all the ingredients and whisk really well.
2. Divide this into 4 ramekins, put them in the air fryer and cook at 340°F for 20 minutes. Serve cold
- **Nutrition Info:** Calories: 171; Fat: 4g; Fiber: 2g; Carbs: 4g; Protein: 4g

460. Olive Tarts With Mushrooms

Servings:x
Cooking Time:x
Ingredients:
- ½ cup sliced black olives
- ½ cup sliced green olives
- ½ teaspoon dried thyme leaves
- 2 sheets frozen puff pastry, thawed
- 1 cup shredded Gouda cheese
- 1 onion, chopped
- 2 cloves garlic, minced
- ½ cup chopped mushrooms
- 1 tablespoon olive oil

Directions:
1. Preheat oven to 400ºF. In heavy skillet, sauté onion, garlic, and mushrooms in olive oil until tender. Remove from heat and add olives and thyme.
2. Gently roll puff pastry dough with rolling pin until ¼-inch thick. Using a 3-inch cookie cutter, cut 24 circles from pastry. Line muffin cups with dough.
3. Place a spoonful of filling in each pastry-lined cup. Bake at 400ºF for 10 to 12 minutes or until crust is golden brown and filling is set.
4. Remove from muffin cups and cool on wire rack. Flash freeze; when frozen solid, pack tarts into zipper-lock bags. Attach zipper-lock bag filled with shredded cheese; label and freeze.
5. To thaw and reheat: Thaw tarts in single layer overnight in refrigerator. Top each tart with cheese and bake at 400ºF for 5 to 6 minutes or until hot and cheese is melted.

461. Coconut Chip Mixed Berry Crisp

Servings:6
Cooking Time: 20 Minutes
Ingredients:
- 1 tablespoon butter, melted
- 12 ounces (340 g) mixed berries
- $^1/_3$ cup granulated Swerve
- 1 teaspoon pure vanilla extract
- ½ teaspoon ground cinnamon
- ¼ teaspoon ground cloves
- ¼ teaspoon grated nutmeg
- ½ cup coconut chips, for garnish

Directions:
1. Coat the baking pan with melted butter.
2. Put the remaining ingredients except the coconut chips in the prepared baking pan.
3. Slide the baking pan into Rack Position 1, select Convection Bake, set temperature to 330ºF (166ºC), and set time to 20 minutes.
4. When cooking is complete, remove from the oven. Serve garnished with the coconut chips.

462. Fried Pickles

Servings: 6
Cooking Time: 3 Minutes
Ingredients:
- Cold dill pickle slices, 36.
- Chopped fresh dill, 2 tbsps.
- Salt, 1 tsp.
- Divided cornstarch, 1 cup
- Ranch dressing
- Cayenne, ¼ tsp.
- Black pepper, 2 tsps.
- Almond meal, ½ cup
- Large egg, 1.
- Almond milk, ¾ cup
- Paprika, 2 tsps.
- Canola oil

Directions:
1. Whisk together cayenne, milk, and egg.
2. Spread half-cup cornstarch in a shallow dish.
3. Mix the remaining ½-cup cornstarch with almond meal, salt, pepper, dill, and paprika.
4. Dredge the pickle slices first through the cornstarch then dip them in an egg wash.
5. Coat them with almond meal mixture and shake off the excess.
6. Place them in the fryer basket and spray them with oil.
7. Return the basket to the fryer and air fry the pickles for 3 minutes at 3700 F working in batches as to not crowd the basket.
8. Serve warm.
- **Nutrition Info:** Calories: 138 Fat: 12.2 g Carbs: 5.8 g Protein: 4 g

463. Shrimp Toasts With Sesame Seeds

Servings:4 To 6
Cooking Time: 8 Minutes
Ingredients:
- ½ pound (227 g) raw shrimp, peeled and deveined
- 1 egg, beaten
- 2 scallions, chopped, plus more for garnish
- 2 tablespoons chopped fresh cilantro
- 2 teaspoons grated fresh ginger
- 1 to 2 teaspoons sriracha sauce
- 1 teaspoon soy sauce
- ½ teaspoon toasted sesame oil
- 6 slices thinly sliced white sandwich bread
- ½ cup sesame seeds
- Cooking spray
- Thai chili sauce, for serving

Directions:
1. In a food processor, add the shrimp, egg, scallions, cilantro, ginger, sriracha sauce, soy sauce and sesame oil, and pulse until chopped finely. You'll need to stop the food processor occasionally to scrape down the sides. Transfer the shrimp mixture to a bowl.
2. On a clean work surface, cut the crusts off the sandwich bread. Using a brush, generously brush one side of each slice of bread with shrimp mixture.
3. Place the sesame seeds on a plate. Press bread slices, shrimp-side down, into sesame seeds to coat evenly. Cut each slice diagonally into quarters.
4. Spritz the air fryer basket with cooking spray. Spread the coated slices in a single layer in the basket.
5. Put the air fryer basket on the baking pan and slide into Rack Position 2, select Air Fry, set temperature to 400ºF (205ºC), and set time to 8 minutes.
6. Flip the bread slices halfway through.
7. When cooking is complete, they should be golden and crispy. Remove from the oven to a plate and let cool for 5 minutes. Top with the chopped scallions and serve warm with Thai chili sauce.

464. Roasted Veggie Bowl

Servings: 2
Cooking Time: 35 Minutes
Ingredients:
- ¼ medium white onion; peeled.and sliced ¼-inch thick
- ½ medium green bell pepper; seeded and sliced ¼-inch thick
- 1 cup broccoli florets
- 1 cup quartered Brussels sprouts
- ½ cup cauliflower florets
- 1 tbsp. coconut oil
- ½ tsp. garlic powder.
- ½ tsp. cumin
- 2 tsp. chili powder

Directions:
1. Toss all ingredients together in a large bowl until vegetables are fully coated with oil and seasoning. Pour vegetables into the air fryer basket.
2. Adjust the temperature to 360 Degrees F and set the timer for 15 minutes. Shake two- or three-times during cooking. Serve warm.
- **Nutrition Info:** Calories: 121; Protein: 4.3g; Fiber: 5.2g; Fat: 7.1g; Carbs: 13.1g

465. Fried Peaches

Servings: 4
Cooking Time: 15 Minutes
Ingredients:
- 4 ripe peaches (1/2 a peach = 1 serving)
- 1 1/2 cups flour
- Salt
- 2 egg yolks
- 3/4 cups cold water
- 1 1/2 tablespoons olive oil
- 2 tablespoons brandy
- 4 egg whites
- Cinnamon/sugar mix

Directions:
1. Preparing the Ingredients. Mix flour, egg yolks, and salt in a mixing bowl. Slowly mix in water, then add brandy. Set the mixture aside for 2 hours and go do something for 1 hour 45 minutes.
2. Boil a large pot of water and cut an X at the bottom of each peach. While the water boils, fill another large bowl with water and ice. Boil each peach for about a minute, then plunge it in the ice bath. Now the peels should basically fall off the peach. Beat the egg whites and mix into the batter mix. Dip each peach in the mix to coat.
3. Air Frying. Cook at 360 degrees for 10 Minutes.
4. Prepare a plate with cinnamon/sugar mix, roll peaches in the mix and serve.
- **Nutrition Info:** CALORIES: 306; FAT:.3G; PROTEIN:10G; FIBER:2.7G

466. Garlic Cauliflower Florets

Servings: 4
Cooking Time: 20 Minutes
Ingredients:
- 5 cups cauliflower florets
- 6 garlic cloves, chopped
- 4 tablespoons olive oil
- 1/2 tsp cumin powder

- 1/2 tsp salt

Directions:
1. Fit the oven with the rack in position 2.
2. Add all ingredients into the large bowl and toss well.
3. Add cauliflower florets in air fryer basket then place air fryer basket in baking pan.
4. Place a baking pan on the oven rack. Set to air fry at 400 F for 20 minutes.
5. Serve and enjoy.
- **Nutrition Info:** Calories 159 Fat 14.2 g Carbohydrates 8.2 g Sugar 3.1 g Protein 2.8 g Cholesterol 0 mg

467. Bacon Cheese Jalapeno Poppers

Servings: 5
Cooking Time: 5 Minutes
Ingredients:
- 10 fresh jalapeno peppers, cut in half and remove seeds
- 1/4 cup cheddar cheese, shredded
- 5 oz cream cheese, softened
- ¼ tsp paprika
- 2 bacon slices, cooked and crumbled

Directions:
1. Fit the oven with the rack in position 2.
2. In a bowl, mix bacon, cream cheese, paprika and cheddar cheese.
3. Stuff cheese mixture into each jalapeno.
4. Place stuffed jalapeno halved in air fryer basket then place air fryer basket in baking pan.
5. Place a baking pan on the oven rack. Set to air fry at 370 F for 5 minutes.
6. Serve and enjoy.
- **Nutrition Info:** Calories 176 Fat 15.7 g Carbohydrates 3.2 g Sugar 1 g Protein 6.2 g Cholesterol 47 mg

468. Crunchy Chickpeas

Servings:4
Cooking Time: 18 Minutes
Ingredients:
- ½ teaspoon chili powder
- ½ teaspoon ground cumin
- ¼ teaspoon cayenne pepper
- ¼ teaspoon salt
- 1 (19-ounce / 539-g) can chickpeas, drained and rinsed
- Cooking spray

Directions:
1. Lina the air fryer basket with parchment paper and lightly spritz with cooking spray.
2. Mix the chili powder, cumin, cayenne pepper, and salt in a small bowl.
3. Place the chickpeas in a medium bowl and lightly mist with cooking spray.

4. Add the spice mixture to the chickpeas and toss until evenly coated. Transfer the chickpeas to the parchment.
5. Put the air fryer basket on the baking pan and slide into Rack Position 2, select Air Fry, set temperature to 390ºF (199ºC), and set time to 18 minutes.
6. Stir the chickpeas twice during cooking.
7. When cooking is complete, the chickpeas should be crunchy. Remove from the oven and let the chickpeas cool for 5 minutes before serving.

469. Raspberry-coco Desert

Servings: 12
Cooking Time: 20 Minutes
Ingredients:
- Vanilla bean, 1 tsp.
- Pulsed raspberries, 1 cup
- Coconut milk, 1 cup
- Desiccated coconut, 3 cup
- Coconut oil, ¼ cup
- Erythritol powder, 1/3 cup

Directions:
1. Preheat the air fryer for 5 minutes.
2. Combine all ingredients in a mixing bowl.
3. Pour into a greased baking dish.
4. Bake in the air fryer for 20 minutes at 375 ºF.
- **Nutrition Info:** Calories: 132 Carbs: 9.7g Fat: 9.7g Protein: 1.5g

470. Perfect Ranch Potatoes

Servings: 2
Cooking Time: 20 Minutes
Ingredients:
- 1/2 lb baby potatoes, wash and cut in half
- 1/4 tsp parsley
- 1/2 tbsp olive oil
- 1/4 tsp dill
- 1/4 tsp paprika
- 1/4 tsp onion powder
- 1/4 tsp garlic powder
- 1/4 tsp chives
- Salt

Directions:
1. Fit the oven with the rack in position 2.
2. Add all ingredients into the bowl and toss well.
3. Spread potatoes in the air fryer basket then place an air fryer basket in the baking pan.
4. Place a baking pan on the oven rack. Set to air fry at 400 F for 20 minutes.
5. Serve and enjoy.
- **Nutrition Info:** Calories 99 Fat 3.7 g Carbohydrates 14.8 g Sugar 0.2 g Protein 3.1 g Cholesterol 0 mg

471. Cheesy Zucchini Tots

Servings: 8
Cooking Time: 6 Minutes
Ingredients:
- 2 medium zucchini (about 12 ounces / 340 g), shredded
- 1 large egg, whisked
- ½ cup grated pecorino romano cheese
- ½ cup panko bread crumbs
- ¼ teaspoon black pepper
- 1 clove garlic, minced
- Cooking spray

Directions:
1. Using your hands, squeeze out as much liquid from the zucchini as possible. In a large bowl, mix the zucchini with the remaining ingredients except the oil until well incorporated.
2. Make the zucchini tots: Use a spoon or cookie scoop to place tablespoonfuls of the zucchini mixture onto a lightly floured cutting board and form into 1-inch logs.
3. Spritz the air fryer basket with cooking spray. Place the zucchini tots in the pan.
4. Put the air fryer basket on the baking pan and slide into Rack Position 2, select Air Fry, set temperature to 375ºF (190ºC), and set time to 6 minutes.
5. When cooking is complete, the tots should be golden brown. Remove from the oven to a serving plate and serve warm.

472. Blackberry Chocolate Cake

Servings: 8
Cooking Time: 22 Minutes
Ingredients:
- ½ cup butter, at room temperature
- 2 ounces (57 g) Swerve
- 4 eggs
- 1 cup almond flour
- 1 teaspoon baking soda
- $^1/_3$ teaspoon baking powder
- ½ cup cocoa powder
- 1 teaspoon orange zest
- $^1/_3$ cup fresh blackberries

Directions:
1. With an electric mixer or hand mixer, beat the butter and Swerve until creamy.
2. One at a time, mix in the eggs and beat again until fluffy.
3. Add the almond flour, baking soda, baking powder, cocoa powder, orange zest and mix well. Add the butter mixture to the almond flour mixture and stir until well blended. Fold in the blackberries.
4. Scrape the batter into the baking pan.
5. Slide the baking pan into Rack Position 1, select Convection Bake, set temperature to 335ºF (168ºC), and set time to 22 minutes.
6. When cooking is complete, a toothpick inserted into the center of the cake should come out clean.
7. Allow the cake cool on a wire rack to room temperature. Serve immediately.

473. Marshmallow Pastries

Servings: 4
Cooking Time: 5 Minutes
Ingredients:
- 4 phyllo pastry sheets, thawed
- 2 oz. butter, melted
- ¼ cup chunky peanut butter
- 4 teaspoons marshmallow fluff
- Pinch of salt

Directions:
1. Brush 1 sheet of phyllo with butter.
2. Place a second sheet of phyllo on top of first one and brush it with butter.
3. Repeat until all 4 sheets are used.
4. Cut the phyllo layers in 4 (3x12-inch) strips.
5. Place 1 tablespoon of peanut butter and 1 teaspoon of marshmallow fluff on the underside of a strip of phyllo.
6. Carefully, fold the tip of sheet over the filling to make a triangle.
7. Fold repeatedly in a zigzag manner until the filling is fully covered.
8. Press "Power Button" of Air Fry Oven and turn the dial to select the "Air Fry" mode.
9. Press the Time button and again turn the dial to set the cooking time to 5 minutes.
10. Now push the Temp button and rotate the dial to set the temperature at 360 degrees F.
11. Press "Start/Pause" button to start.
12. When the unit beeps to show that it is preheated, open the lid.
13. Arrange the pastries in greased "Air Fry Basket" and insert in the oven.
14. Sprinkle with a pinch of salt and serve warm.
- **Nutrition Info:** Calories 248 Total Fat 20.5 g Saturated Fat 9.2 g Cholesterol 30 mg Sodium 268 mg Total Carbs 12.7 g Fiber 1.3 g Sugar 2.6 g Protein 5.2 g

474. Italian Pork Skewers

Servings: x
Cooking Time: x
Ingredients:
- ¼ cup finely minced onion
- 1 teaspoon dried Italian seasoning
- ½ teaspoon salt
- teaspoon pepper
- 2 pounds pork tenderloin
- ¼ cup balsamic vinegar

- ¼ cup olive oil

Directions:
1. Trim excess fat from tenderloin. Cut pork, on a slant, into ¼-inch-thick slices, each about 4 inches long. In large bowl, combine remaining ingredients and mix well with wire whisk. Add tenderloin slices and mix gently to coat. Cover and refrigerate for 2 to 3 hours. Meanwhile, soak 8-inch wooden skewers in cold water.
2. Remove pork from marinade and thread onto soaked skewers. Flash freeze on baking sheet in single layer. When frozen solid, pack skewers in rigid containers, with layers separated by waxed paper. Label skewers and freeze.
3. To thaw and reheat: Thaw overnight in refrigerator. Cook skewers 4 to 6 inches from medium coals on grill, or broil 4 to 6 inches from heat source, for about 4 to 6 minutes or until cooked (160ºF on an instant-read thermometer), turning once.

475. Chocolate Chip Waffles

Servings:x
Cooking Time:x
Ingredients:
- Salt and Pepper to taste
- 3 tbsp. Butter
- 1 cup chocolate chips
- 3 cups cocoa powder
- 3 eggs
- 2 tsp. dried basil
- 2 tsp. dried parsley

Directions:
1. Preheat the air fryer to 250 Fahrenheit.
2. In a small bowl, mix the ingredients, except for the chocolate chips, together. Ensure that the mixture is smooth and well balanced. Take a waffle mold and grease it with butter. Add the batter to the mold and place it in the air fryer basket. Cook till both the sides have browned. Garnish with chips and serve.

476. Tasty Pumpkin Cookies

Servings: 27
Cooking Time: 25 Minutes
Ingredients:
- 1 egg
- 2 cups almond flour
- 1/2 tsp baking powder
- 1 tsp vanilla
- 1/2 cup butter
- 1 tsp liquid stevia
- 1/2 tsp pumpkin pie spice
- 1/2 cup pumpkin puree

Directions:
1. Fit the oven with the rack in position

2. In a large bowl, add all ingredients and mix until well combined.
3. Make cookies from mixture and place onto a parchment-lined baking pan.
4. Set to bake at 300 F for 30 minutes. After 5 minutes place the baking dish in the preheated oven.
5. Serve and enjoy.
- **Nutrition Info:** Calories 46 Fat 4.6 g Carbohydrates 0.9 g Sugar 0.3 g Protein 0.7 g Cholesterol 15 mg

477. Keto Mixed Berry Crumble Pots

Servings: 6
Cooking Time: 15 Minutes
Ingredients:
- 2 ounces unsweetened mixed berries
- 1/2 cup granulated swerve
- 2 tablespoons golden flaxseed meal
- 1/4 teaspoon ground star anise
- 1/2 teaspoon ground cinnamon
- 1 teaspoon xanthan gum
- 2/3 cup almond flour
- 1 cup powdered swerve
- 1/2 teaspoon baking powder
- 1/3 cup unsweetened coconut, finely shredded
- 1/2 stick butter, cut into small pieces

Dirctions:
1. Toss the mixed berries with the granulated swerve, golden flaxseed meal, star anise, cinnamon, and xanthan gum. Divide between six custard cups coated with cooking spray.
2. In a mixing dish, thoroughly combine the remaining ingredients. Sprinkle over the berry mixture.
3. Bake in the preheated Air Fryer at 330 degrees F for 35 minutes. Work in batches if needed.
- **Nutrition Info:** 155 Calories; 13g Fat; 1g Carbs; 1g Protein; 8g Sugars; 6g Fiber

478. Chocolate Cheesecake

Servings:6
Cooking Time: 18 Minutes
Ingredients:
- Crust:
- ½ cup butter, melted
- ½ cup coconut flour
- 2 tablespoons stevia
- Cooking spray
- Topping:
- 4 ounces (113 g) unsweetened baker's chocolate
- 1 cup mascarpone cheese, at room temperature

- 1 teaspoon vanilla extract
- 2 drops peppermint extract

Directions:
1. Lightly coat the baking pan with cooking spray.
2. In a mixing bowl, whisk together the butter, flour, and stevia until well combined. Transfer the mixture to the prepared baking pan.
3. Slide the baking pan into Rack Position 1, select Convection Bake, set temperature to 350ºF (180ºC), and set time to 18 minutes.
4. When done, a toothpick inserted in the center should come out clean.
5. Remove the crust from the oven to a wire rack to cool.
6. Once cooled completely, place it in the freezer for 20 minutes.
7. When ready, combine all the ingredients for the topping in a small bowl and stir to incorporate.
8. Spread this topping over the crust and let it sit for another 15 minutes in the freezer.
9. Serve chilled.

479. Yogurt Pumpkin Bread

Servings: 4
Cooking Time: 15 Minutes
Ingredients:
- 2 large eggs
- 8 tablespoons pumpkin puree
- 6 tablespoons banana flour
- 4 tablespoons honey
- 4 tablespoons plain Greek yogurt
- 2 tablespoons vanilla essence
- Pinch of ground nutmeg 6 tablespoons oats

Directions:
1. In a bowl, add in all the ingredients except oats and with a hand mixer, mix until smooth.
2. Add the oats and with a fork, mix well.
3. Grease and flour a loaf pan.
4. Place the mixture into the prepared loaf pan.
5. Press "Power Button" of Air Fry Oven and turn the dial to select the "Air Crisp" mode.
6. Press the Time button and again turn the dial to set the cooking time to 15 minutes.
7. Now push the Temp button and rotate the dial to set the temperature at 360 degrees F.
8. Press "Start/Pause" button to start.
9. When the unit beeps to show that it is preheated, open the lid.
10. Arrange the pan in "Air Fry Basket" and insert in the oven.
11. Carefully, invert the bread onto wire rack to cool completely before slicing.
12. Cut the bread into desired-sized slices and serve.

- **Nutrition Info:** Calories 232 Total Fat 8.33 g Saturated Fat 1.5 g Cholesterol 94 mg Sodium 53 mg Total Carbs 29.3 g Fiber 2.8 g Sugar 20.5 g Protein 7.7 g

480. Buttermilk Biscuits

Servings:x
Cooking Time:x
Ingredients:
- 4 tsp baking powder
- ¼ tsp baking soda
- ¼ tsp salt
- 4 Tbsp softened butter
- 1 cup all-purpose flour
- 1 cup whole wheat flour
- 2 Tbsp sugar
- 1¼ cups cold buttermilk

Directions:
1. Preheat oven to 400°F.
2. In a bowl, combine flours, sugar, baking powder, baking soda and salt.
3. Add softened butter and use your Oregano Fingers to work the butter into the flour until the mixture resembles coarse crumbs.
4. Stir in the buttermilk, forming a soft dough.
5. Turn the dough onto a floured surface and pat into a ¾ inch thick circle.
6. With a 2-inch biscuit cutter, cut out biscuits, gathering dough as needed to shape more biscuits.
7. Arrange biscuits in oven and bake until golden brown, about 12 minutes.

481. Healthy Lemon Tofu

Servings: 4
Cooking Time: 15 Minutes
Ingredients:
- 1 lb tofu, drained and pressed
- 1 tbsp tamari
- 1 tbsp arrowroot powder
- For sauce:
- 2 tsp arrowroot powder
- 1/3 cup lemon juice
- 1 tsp lemon zest
- 2 tbsp erythritol
- 1/2 cup water

Directions:
1. Fit the oven with the rack in position 2.
2. Cut tofu into cubes. Add tofu and tamari into the zip-lock bag and shake well.
3. Add 1 tbsp arrowroot into the bag and shake well to coat the tofu. Set aside for 15 minutes.
4. Meanwhile, in a bowl, mix together all sauce ingredients and set aside.
5. Add tofu to the air fryer basket then place an air fryer basket in the baking pan.
6. Place a baking pan on the oven rack. Set to air fry at 390 F for 15 minutes.

7. Serve and enjoy.
- **Nutrition Info:** Calories 102 Fat 4.9 g Carbohydrates 6 g Sugar 1.2 g Protein 9.9 g Cholesterol 0 mg

482. Walnut Brownies

Servings: 4
Cooking Time: 22 Minutes
Ingredients:
- ½ cup chocolate, roughly chopped
- 1/3 cup butter
- 5 tablespoons sugar
- 1 egg, beaten
- 1 teaspoon vanilla extract
- Pinch of salt
- 5 tablespoons self-rising flour
- ¼ cup walnuts, chopped

Directions:
1. In a microwave-safe bowl, add the chocolate and butter. Microwave on high heat for about 2 minutes, stirring after every 30 seconds.
2. Remove from microwave and set aside to cool.
3. In another bowl, add the sugar, egg, vanilla extract, and salt and whisk until creamy and light.
4. Add the chocolate mixture and whisk until well combined.
5. Add the flour, and walnuts and mix until well combined.
6. Line a baking pan with a greased parchment paper.
7. Place mixture evenly into the prepared pan and with the back of spatula, smooth the top surface.
8. Press "Power Button" of Air Fry Oven and turn the dial to select the "Air Fry" mode.
9. Press the Time button and again turn the dial to set the cooking time to 20 minutes.
10. Now push the Temp button and rotate the dial to set the temperature at 355 degrees F.
11. Press "Start/Pause" button to start.
12. When the unit beeps to show that it is preheated, open the lid.
13. Arrange the pan in "Air Fry Basket" and insert in the oven.
14. Place the baking pan onto a wire rack to cool completely.
15. Cut into 4 equal-sized squares and serve.
- **Nutrition Info:** Calories 407 Total Fat 27.4g Saturated Fat 14.7 g Cholesterol 86 mg Sodium 180 mg Total Carbs 35.9 g Fiber 1.5 g Sugar 26.2 g Protein 6 g

483. Cherry Apple Risotto

Servings: 4
Cooking Time: 12 Minutes
Ingredients:
- 1 tablespoon of butter
- ¼ cup of brown sugar
- ½ cup of apple juice
- 1½ cups of milk
- ¾ cup of Arborio rice, boiled
- 1 apple, diced
- 2 pinches salt
- ¾ teaspoon of cinnamon powder
- ¼ cup of dried cherries
- 1½ tablespoons of almonds, roasted and sliced
- ¼ cup of whipped cream

Directions:
1. Set the Instant Vortex on Air fryer to 375 degrees F for 12 minutes. Combine rice with butter, sugar, apple juice, milk, apple, salt, and cinnamon in a bowl. Pour the rice mixture into the cooking tray. Insert the cooking tray in the Vortex when it displays "Add Food". Toss the food when it displays "Turn Food". Remove from the oven when cooking time is complete. Top with the dried cherries, almonds, and whipped cream to serve.
- **Nutrition Info:** Calories: 317 Cal Total Fat: 8.5 g Saturated Fat: 0 g Cholesterol: 0 mg Sodium: 0 mg Total Carbs: 54.8 g Fiber: 0 g Sugar: 0 g Protein: 6.2 g

484. Chocolate Pecan Pie

Servings:8
Cooking Time: 25 Minutes
Ingredients:
- 1 (9-inch) unbaked pie crust
- Filling:
- 2 large eggs
- $1/_3$ cup butter, melted
- 1 cup sugar
- ½ cup all-purpose flour
- 1 cup milk chocolate chips
- 1½ cups coarsely chopped pecans
- 2 tablespoons bourbon

Directions:
1. Whisk the eggs and melted butter in a large bowl until creamy.
2. Add the sugar and flour and stir to incorporate. Mix in the milk chocolate chips, pecans, and bourbon and stir until well combined.
3. Use a fork to prick holes in the bottom and sides of the pie crust. Pour the prepared filling into the pie crust. Place the pie crust in the baking pan.
4. Slide the baking pan into Rack Position 1, select Convection Bake, set temperature to 350ºF (180ºC), and set time to 25 minutes.
5. When cooking is complete, a toothpick inserted in the center should come out clean.

6. Allow the pie cool for 10 minutes in the pan before serving.

485. Crustless Pizza

Servings: 1
Cooking Time: 15 Minutes
Ingredients:
- 2 slices sugar-free bacon; cooked and crumbled
- 7 slices pepperoni
- ½ cup shredded mozzarella cheese
- ¼ cup cooked ground sausage
- 2 tbsp. low-carb, sugar-free pizza sauce, for dipping
- 1 tbsp. grated Parmesan cheese

Directions:
1. Cover the bottom of a 6-inch cake pan with mozzarella. Place pepperoni, sausage and bacon on top of cheese and sprinkle with Parmesan
2. Place pan into the air fryer basket. Adjust the temperature to 400 Degrees F and set the timer for 5 minutes.
3. Remove when cheese is bubbling and golden. Serve warm with pizza sauce for dipping.
- **Nutrition Info:** Calories: 466; Protein: 21g; Fiber: 5g; Fat: 30g; Carbs: 2g

486. Raspberry Cream Rol-ups

Servings: 4
Cooking Time: 25 Minutes
Ingredients:
- 1 cup of fresh raspberries rinsed and patted dry
- ½ cup of cream cheese softened to room temperature
- ¼ cup of brown sugar
- ¼ cup of sweetened condensed milk
- 1 egg
- 1 teaspoon of corn starch
- 6 spring roll wrappers (any brand will do, we like Blue Dragon or Tasty Joy, both available through Target or Walmart, or any large grocery chain)
- ¼ cup of water

Directions:
1. Preparing the Ingredients. Cover the basket of the air fryer oven with a lining of tin foil, leaving the edges uncovered to allow air to circulate through the basket. Preheat the air fryer oven to 350 degrees.
2. In a mixing bowl, combine the cream cheese, brown sugar, condensed milk, cornstarch, and egg. Beat or whip thoroughly, until all ingredients are completely mixed and fluffy, thick and stiff.
3. Spoon even amounts of the creamy filling into each spring roll wrapper, then top each dollop of filling with several raspberries.

4. Roll up the wraps around the creamy raspberry filling, and seal the seams with a few dabs of water.
5. Place each roll on the foil-lined Oven rack/basket, seams facing down. Place the Rack on the middle-shelf of the air fryer oven.
6. Air Frying. Set the air fryer oven timer to 10 minutes. During cooking, shake the handle of the fryer basket to ensure a nice even surface crisp.
7. After 10 minutes, when the air fryer oven shuts off, the spring rolls should be golden brown and perfect on the outside, while the raspberries and cream filling will have cooked together in a glorious fusion. Remove with tongs and serve hot or cold.

487. Cheesy Crab Toasts

Servings: 15 To 18 Toasts
Cooking Time: 5 Minutes
Ingredients:
- 1 (6-ounce / 170-g) can flaked crab meat, well drained
- 3 tablespoons light mayonnaise
- ¼ cup shredded Parmesan cheese
- ¼ cup shredded Cheddar cheese
- 1 teaspoon Worcestershire sauce
- ½ teaspoon lemon juice
- 1 loaf artisan bread, French bread, or baguette, cut into ⅜-inch-thick slices

Directions:
1. In a large bowl, stir together all the ingredients except the bread slices.
2. On a clean work surface, lay the bread slices. Spread ½ tablespoon of crab mixture onto each slice of bread.
3. Arrange the bread slices in the baking pan in a single layer.
4. Slide the baking pan into Rack Position 1, select Convection Bake, set temperature to 360ºF (182ºC), and set time to 5 minutes.
5. When cooking is complete, the tops should be lightly browned. Remove from the oven and serve warm.

488. Coffee Flavored Doughnuts

Servings: 6
Cooking Time: 6 Minutes
Ingredients:
- Coconut sugar, ¼ cup
- White all-purpose flour, 1 cup
- Baking powder, 1 tsp.
- Salt, ½ tsp.
- Sunflower oil, 1 tbsp.
- Coffee, ¼ cup
- Aquafaba, 2 tbsps.

Directions:
1. Combine the sugar, flour, baking powder, salt in a mixing bowl.
2. In another bowl, combine the aquafaba, sunflower oil, and coffee.

3. Mix to form a dough.
4. Let the dough rest inside the fridge.
5. Preheat the air fryer to 4000 F.
6. Knead the dough and create doughnuts.
7. Arrange inside the air fryer in single layer and cook for 6 minutes.
8. Do not shake so that the donut maintains its shape.
- **Nutrition Info:** Calories: 113 Protein: 2.16g Fat: 2.54g Carbs: 20.45g

489. Apple-peach Crisp With Oatmeal

Servings:4
Cooking Time: 10 To 12 Minutes
Ingredients:
- 2 peaches, peeled, pitted, and chopped
- 1 apple, peeled and chopped
- 2 tablespoons honey
- 3 tablespoons packed brown sugar
- 2 tablespoons unsalted butter, at room temperature
- ½ cup quick-cooking oatmeal
- $1/3$ cup whole-wheat pastry flour
- ½ teaspoon ground cinnamon

Directions:
1. Place the peaches, apple, and honey in the baking pan and toss until thoroughly combined.
2. Mix together the brown sugar, butter, oatmeal, pastry flour, and cinnamon in a medium bowl and stir until crumbly. Sprinkle this mixture generously on top of the peaches and apples.
3. Slide the baking pan into Rack Position 1, select Convection Bake, set temperature to 380ºF (193ºC), and set the time to 10 minutes.
4. Bake until the fruit is bubbling and the topping is golden brown.
5. Once cooking is complete, remove from the oven and allow to cool for 5 minutes before serving.

490. Cheese-stuffed Mushrooms With Pimientos

Servings:12
Cooking Time: 18 Minutes
Ingredients:
- 24 medium raw white button mushrooms, rinsed and drained
- 4 ounces (113 g) shredded extra-sharp Cheddar cheese
- 2 ounces (57 g) cream cheese, at room temperature
- 1 ounce (28 g) chopped jarred pimientos
- 2 tablespoons grated onion
- ⅛ teaspoon smoked paprika
- ⅛ teaspoon hot sauce
- 2 tablespoons butter, melted, divided
- $1/3$ cup panko bread crumbs

- 2 tablespoons grated Parmesan cheese

Directions:
1. Gently pull out the stems of the mushrooms and discard. Set aside.
2. In a medium bowl, stir together the Cheddar cheese, cream cheese, pimientos, onion, paprika and hot sauce.
3. Brush the baking pan with 1 tablespoon of the melted butter. Arrange the mushrooms evenly on the pan, hollow-side up.
4. Place the cheese mixture into a large heavy plastic bag and cut off the end. Fill the mushrooms with the cheese mixture.
5. In a small bowl, whisk together the remaining 1 tablespoon of the melted butter, bread crumbs and Parmesan cheese. Sprinkle the panko mixture over each mushroom.
6. Slide the baking pan into Rack Position 2, select Roast, set temperature to 350ºF (180ºC) and set time to 18 minutes.
7. When cooking is complete, let the stuffed mushrooms rest for 2 minutes before serving.

491. Delicious Banana Pastry With Berries

Servings:2
Cooking Time: 15 Minutes
Ingredients:
- 3 bananas, sliced
- 3 tbsp honey
- 2 puff pastry sheets, cut into thin strips
- Fresh berries to serve

Directions:
1. Preheat on AirFry function to 340 F. Place the banana slices into the cooking basket. Cover with the pastry strips and top with honey. Press Start and cook for 10-12 minutes on Bake function. Serve with fresh berries.

492. Healthy Broccoli Tots

Servings: 4
Cooking Time: 12 Minutes
Ingredients:
- 1 lb broccoli, cooked & chopped
- 1/2 tsp garlic powder
- 1/2 cup almond flour
- 1/4 cup ground flaxseed
- 1 tsp salt

Directions:
1. Fit the oven with the rack in position 2.
2. Add broccoli into the food processor and process until it looks like rice.
3. Transfer broccoli to a large mixing bowl.
4. Add remaining ingredients into the bowl and mix until well combined.
5. Make tots from broccoli mixture and place in the air fryer basket then place an air fryer basket in the baking pan.

6. Place a baking pan on the oven rack. Set to air fry at 375 F for 12 minutes.
7. Serve and enjoy.
- **Nutrition Info:** Calories 97 Fat 4.3 g Carbohydrates 10.5 g Sugar 2.3 g Protein 5.3 g Cholesterol 0 mg

493. Vanilla Brownie Squares

Servings: 2
Cooking Time: 25 Minutes
Ingredients:
- 1 whole egg, beaten
- ¼ cup chocolate chips
- 2 tbsp white sugar
- ⅓ cup flour
- 2 tbsp safflower oil
- 1 tsp vanilla
- ¼ cup cocoa powder

Directions:
1. Preheat on Bake function to 360 F. In a bowl, mix the egg, sugar, olive oil, and vanilla. In another bowl, mix cocoa powder and flour. Add the flour mixture to the vanilla mixture and stir until fully incorporated.
2. Pour the mixture into a greased baking pan and sprinkle chocolate chips on top. Cook for 20 minutes. Chill and cut into squares to serve.

494. Plum Cake

Servings: 8
Cooking Time: 30 Minutes
Ingredients:
- ½ cup butter, soft
- 3 eggs
- ½ cup swerve
- ¼ teaspoon almond extract
- 1 tablespoon vanilla extract
- 1 and ½ cups almond flour
- ½ cup coconut flour
- 2 teaspoons baking powder
- ¾ cup almond milk
- 4 plums, pitted and chopped

Directions:
1. In a bowl, mix all the ingredients and whisk well.
2. Pour this into a cake pan that fits the air fryer after you've lined it with parchment paper, put the pan in the machine and cook at 370 degrees F for 30 minutes.
3. Cool the cake down, slice and serve.
- **Nutrition Info:** calories 183, fat 4, fiber 3, carbs 4, protein 7

495. Cheese And Leeks Dip

Servings: 6
Cooking Time: 15 Minutes
Ingredients:
- 2 spring onions; minced
- 4 leeks; sliced
- ¼ cup coconut cream
- 3 tbsp. coconut milk
- 2 tbsp. butter; melted
- Salt and white pepper to the taste

Directions:
1. In a pan that fits your air fryer, mix all the ingredients and whisk them well.
2. Introduce the pan in the fryer and cook at 390°F for 12 minutes. Divide into bowls and serve
- **Nutrition Info:** Calories: 204; Fat: 12g; Fiber: 2g; Carbs: 4g; Protein: 14g

496. Oats Muffins

Servings:x
Cooking Time:x
Ingredients:
- 1 cup sugar
- 3 tsp. vinegar
- 1 cup oats
- ½ tsp. vanilla essence
- Muffin cups or butter paper cups.
- 2 cups All-purpose flour
- 1 ½ cup milk
- ½ tsp. baking powder
- ½ tsp. baking soda
- 2 tbsp. butter

Directions:
1. Mix the ingredients together and use your Oregano Fingers to get a crumbly mixture. You will need to divide the milk into two parts and add one part to the baking soda and the other to the vinegar. Now, mix both the milk mixtures together and wait till the milk begins to foam. Add this to the crumbly mixture and begin to whisk the ingredients very fast. Once you have obtained a smooth batter, you will need to transfer the mixture into a muffin cup and set aside.
2. Preheat the fryer to 300 Fahrenheit for five minutes. You will need to place the muffin cups in the basket and cover it. Cook the muffins for fifteen minutes and check whether or not the muffins are cooked using a toothpick. Remove the cups and serve hot.

497. Chocolate Buttermilk Cake

Servings:8
Cooking Time: 20 Minutes
Ingredients:

- 1 cup all-purpose flour
- $2/3$ cup granulated white sugar
- ¼ cup unsweetened cocoa powder
- ¾ teaspoon baking soda
- ¼ teaspoon salt
- $2/3$ cup buttermilk
- 2 tablespoons plus 2 teaspoons vegetable oil
- 1 teaspoon vanilla extract
- Cooking spray

Directions:

1. Spritz the baking pan with cooking spray.
2. Combine the flour, cocoa powder, baking soda, sugar, and salt in a large bowl. Stir to mix well.
3. Mix in the buttermilk, vanilla, and vegetable oil. Keep stirring until it forms a grainy and thick dough.
4. Scrape the chocolate batter from the bowl and transfer to the pan, level the batter in an even layer with a spatula.
5. Slide the baking pan into Rack Position 1, select Convection Bake, set temperature to 325°F (163°C) and set time to 20 minutes.
6. After 15 minutes, remove the pan from the oven. Check the doneness. Return the pan to the oven and continue cooking.
7. When done, a toothpick inserted in the center should come out clean.
8. Invert the cake on a cooling rack and allow to cool for 15 minutes before slicing to serve.

498. Salty Tortilla Chips

Servings:4
Cooking Time: 10 Minutes
Ingredients:

- 4 six-inch corn tortillas, cut in half and slice into thirds
- 1 tablespoon canola oil
- ¼ teaspoon kosher salt
- Cooking spray

Directions:

1. Spritz the air fryer basket with cooking spray.
2. On a clean work surface, brush the tortilla chips with canola oil, then transfer the chips to the basket.
3. Put the air fryer basket on the baking pan and slide into Rack Position 2, select Air Fry, set temperature to 360°F (182°C) and set time to 10 minutes.

4. Flip the chips and sprinkle with salt halfway through the cooking time.
5. When cooked, the chips will be crunchy and lightly browned. Transfer the chips to a plate lined with paper towels. Serve immediately.

499. Apple Fritters With Sugary Glaze

Servings: 15 Fritters
Cooking Time: 8 Minutes
Ingredients:

- Apple Fritters:
- 2 firm apples, peeled, cored, and diced
- ½ teaspoon cinnamon
- Juice of 1 lemon
- 1 cup all-purpose flour
- 1½ teaspoons baking powder
- ½ teaspoon kosher salt
- 2 eggs
- ¼ cup milk
- 2 tablespoons unsalted butter, melted
- 2 tablespoons granulated sugar
- Cooking spray
- Glaze:
- ½ teaspoon vanilla extract
- 1¼ cups powdered sugar, sifted
- ¼ cup water

Directions:

1. Line the air fryer basket with parchment paper.
2. Combine the apples with cinnamon and lemon juice in a small bowl. Toss to coat well.
3. Combine the flour, baking powder, and salt in a large bowl. Stir to mix well.
4. Whisk the egg, milk, butter, and sugar in a medium bowl. Stir to mix well.
5. Make a well in the center of the flour mixture, then pour the egg mixture into the well and stir to mix well. Mix in the apple until a dough forms.
6. Use an ice cream scoop to scoop 15 balls from the dough onto the pan. Spritz with cooking spray.
7. Put the air fryer basket on the baking pan and slide into Rack Position 2, select Air Fry, set temperature to 360°F (182°C) and set time to 8 minutes.
8. Flip the apple fritters halfway through the cooking time.
9. Meanwhile, combine the ingredients for the glaze in a separate small bowl. Stir to mix well.
10. When cooking is complete, the apple fritters will be golden brown. Serve the fritters with the glaze on top or use the glaze for dipping.

500. Southwest Corn And Bell Pepper Roast

Servings:4
Cooking Time: 10 Minutes
Ingredients:
- Corn:
- 1½ cups thawed frozen corn kernels
- 1 cup mixed diced bell peppers
- 1 jalapeño, diced
- 1 cup diced yellow onion
- ½ teaspoon ancho chile powder
- 1 tablespoon fresh lemon juice
- 1 teaspoon ground cumin
- ½ teaspoon kosher salt
- Cooking spray
- For Serving:
- ¼ cup feta cheese
- ¼ cup chopped fresh cilantro
- 1 tablespoon fresh lemon juice

Directions:
1. Spritz the air fryer basket with cooking spray.
2. Combine the ingredients for the corn in a large bowl. Stir to mix well.
3. Pour the mixture into the basket.
4. Put the air fryer basket on the baking pan and slide into Rack Position 2, select Air Fry, set temperature to 375ºF (190ºC) and set time to 10 minutes.
5. Stir the mixture halfway through the cooking time.
6. When done, the corn and bell peppers should be soft.
7. Transfer them onto a large plate, then spread with feta cheese and cilantro. Drizzle with lemon juice and serve.

501. Riced Cauliflower Casserole

Servings:4
Cooking Time: 12 Minutes
Ingredients:
- 1 head cauliflower, cut into florets
- 1 cup okra, chopped
- 1 yellow bell pepper, chopped
- 2 eggs, beaten
- ½ cup chopped onion
- 1 tablespoon soy sauce
- 2 tablespoons olive oil
- Salt and ground black pepper,
- to taste Spritz the baking pan with cooking spray.

Directions:
1. Put the cauliflower in a food processor and pulse to rice the cauliflower.
2. Pour the cauliflower rice in the baking pan and add the remaining ingredients. Stir to mix well.

3. Slide the baking pan into Rack Position 1, select Convection Bake, set temperature to 380ºF (193ºC) and set time to 12 minutes.
4. When cooking is complete, the eggs should be set.
5. Remove from the oven and serve immediately.

502. Ritzy Chicken And Vegetable Casserole

Servings:4
Cooking Time: 15 Minutes
Ingredients:
- 4 boneless and skinless chicken breasts, cut into cubes
- 2 carrots, sliced
- 1 yellow bell pepper, cut into strips
- 1 red bell pepper, cut into strips
- 15 ounces (425 g) broccoli florets
- 1 cup snow peas
- 1 scallion, sliced
- Cooking spray
- Sauce:
- 1 teaspoon Sriracha
- 3 tablespoons soy sauce
- 2 tablespoons oyster sauce
- 1 tablespoon rice wine vinegar
- 1 teaspoon cornstarch
- 1 tablespoon grated ginger
- 2 garlic cloves, minced
- 1 teaspoon sesame oil
- 1 tablespoon brown sugar

Directions:
1. Spritz the baking pan with cooking spray.
2. Combine the chicken, carrot, and bell peppers in a large bowl. Stir to mix well.
3. Combine the ingredients for the sauce in a separate bowl. Stir to mix well.
4. Pour the chicken mixture into the baking pan, then pour the sauce over. Stir to coat well.
5. Slide the baking pan into Rack Position 1, select Convection Bake, set temperature to 370ºF (188ºC) and set time to 13 minutes.
6. Add the broccoli and snow peas to the pan halfway through.
7. When cooking is complete, the vegetables should be tender.
8. Remove from the oven and sprinkle with sliced scallion before serving.

503. Simple Butter Cake

Servings:8
Cooking Time: 20 Minutes
Ingredients:
- 1 cup all-purpose flour
- 1¼ teaspoons baking powder
- ¼ teaspoon salt

- ½ cup plus 1½ tablespoons granulated white sugar
- 9½ tablespoons butter, at room temperature
- 2 large eggs
- 1 large egg yolk
- 2½ tablespoons milk
- 1 teaspoon vanilla extract
- Cooking spray

Directions:
1. Spritz the baking pan with cooking spray.
2. Combine the flour, baking powder, and salt in a large bowl. Stir to mix well.
3. Whip the sugar and butter in a separate bowl with a hand mixer on medium speed for 3 minutes.
4. Whip the eggs, egg yolk, milk, and vanilla extract into the sugar and butter mix with a hand mixer.
5. Pour in the flour mixture and whip with hand mixer until sanity and smooth.
6. Scrape the batter into the baking pan and level the batter with a spatula.
7. Slide the baking pan into Rack Position 1, select Convection Bake, set temperature to 325ºF (163ºC) and set time to 20 minutes.
8. After 15 minutes, remove the pan from the oven. Check the doneness. Return the pan to the oven and continue cooking.
9. When done, a toothpick inserted in the center should come out clean.
10. Invert the cake on a cooling rack and allow to cool for 15 minutes before slicing to serve.

504.   Simple Air Fried Okra Chips

Servings:6
Cooking Time: 16 Minutes
Ingredients:
- 2 pounds (907 g) fresh okra pods, cut into 1-inch pieces
- 2 tablespoons canola oil
- 1 teaspoon coarse sea salt

Directions:
1. Stir the oil and salt in a bowl to mix well. Add the okra and toss to coat well. Place the okra in the air fryer basket.
2. Put the air fryer basket on the baking pan and slide into Rack Position 2, select Air Fry, set temperature to 400ºF (205ºC) and set time to 16 minutes.
3. Flip the okra at least three times during cooking.
4. When cooked, the okra should be lightly browned. Remove from the oven and serve immediately.

505.   Kale Chips With Soy Sauce

Servings:2

Cooking Time: 5 Minutes
Ingredients:
- 4 medium kale leaves, about 1 ounce (28 g) each, stems removed, tear the leaves in thirds
- 2 teaspoons soy sauce
- 2 teaspoons olive oil

Directions:
1. Toss the kale leaves with soy sauce and olive oil in a large bowl to coat well. Place the leaves in the baking pan.
2. Put the air fryer basket on the baking pan and slide into Rack Position 2, select Air Fry, set temperature to 400ºF (205ºC) and set time to 5 minutes.
3. Flip the leaves with tongs gently halfway through.
4. When cooked, the kale leaves should be crispy. Remove from the oven and serve immediately.

506.   Spinach And Chickpea Casserole

Servings:4
Cooking Time: 21 To 22 Minutes
Ingredients:
- 2 tablespoons olive oil
- 2 garlic cloves, minced
- 1 tablespoon ginger, minced
- 1 onion, chopped
- 1 chili pepper, minced
- Salt and ground black pepper, to taste
- 1 pound (454 g) spinach
- 1 can coconut milk
- ½ cup dried tomatoes, chopped
- 1 (14-ounce / 397-g) can chickpeas, drained

Directions:
1. Heat the olive oil in a saucepan over medium heat. Sauté the garlic and ginger in the olive oil for 1 minute, or until fragrant.
2. Add the onion, chili pepper, salt and pepper to the saucepan. Sauté for 3 minutes.
3. Mix in the spinach and sauté for 3 to 4 minutes or until the vegetables become soft. Remove from heat.
4. Pour the vegetable mixture into the baking pan. Stir in coconut milk, dried tomatoes and chickpeas until well blended.
5. Slide the baking pan into Rack Position 1, select Convection Bake, set temperature to 370ºF (188ºC) and set time to 15 minutes.
6. When cooking is complete, transfer the casserole to a serving dish. Let cool for 5 minutes before serving.

507.   Caesar Salad Dressing

Servings: About $^2/_3$ Cup
Cooking Time: 0 Minutes
Ingredients:

- ½ cup extra-virgin olive oil
- 2 tablespoons freshly squeezed lemon juice
- 1 teaspoon anchovy paste
- ¼ teaspoon kosher salt or ⅛ teaspoon fine salt
- ¼ teaspoon minced or pressed garlic
- 1 egg, beaten
- Add all the ingredients to a tall, narrow container.

Directions:
1. Purée the mixture with an immersion blender until smooth.
2. Use immediately.

508. Baked Cherry Tomatoes With Basil

Servings:2
Cooking Time: 5 Minutes
Ingredients:
- 2 cups cherry tomatoes
- 1 clove garlic, thinly sliced
- 1 teaspoon olive oil
- ⅛ teaspoon kosher salt
- 1 tablespoon freshly chopped basil, for topping
- Cooking spray

Directions:
1. Spritz the baking pan with cooking spray and set aside.
2. In a large bowl, toss together the cherry tomatoes, sliced garlic, olive oil, and kosher salt. Spread the mixture in an even layer in the prepared pan.
3. Slide the baking pan into Rack Position 1, select Convection Bake, set temperature to 360ºF (182ºC) and set time to 5 minutes.
4. When cooking is complete, the tomatoes should be the soft and wilted.
5. Transfer to a bowl and rest for 5 minutes. Top with the chopped basil and serve warm.

509. Crunchy And Beery Onion Rings

Servings:2 To 4
Cooking Time: 16 Minutes
Ingredients:
- $^2/_3$ cup all-purpose flour
- 1 teaspoon paprika
- ½ teaspoon baking soda
- 1 teaspoon salt
- ½ teaspoon freshly ground black pepper
- 1 egg, beaten
- ¾ cup beer
- 1½ cups bread crumbs
- 1 tablespoons olive oil
- 1 large Vidalia onion, peeled and sliced into ½-inch rings
- Cooking spray

Directions:
1. Spritz the air fryer basket with cooking spray.
2. Combine the flour, paprika, baking soda, salt, and ground black pepper in a bowl. Stir to mix well.
3. Combine the egg and beer in a separate bowl. Stir to mix well.
4. Make a well in the center of the flour mixture, then pour the egg mixture in the well. Stir to mix everything well.
5. Pour the bread crumbs and olive oil in a shallow plate. Stir to mix well.
6. Dredge the onion rings gently into the flour and egg mixture, then shake the excess off and put into the plate of bread crumbs. Flip to coat the both sides well. Arrange the onion rings in the basket.
7. Put the air fryer basket on the baking pan and slide into Rack Position 2, select Air Fry, set temperature to 360ºF (182ºC) and set time to 16 minutes.
8. Flip the rings and put the bottom rings to the top halfway through.
9. When cooked, the rings will be golden brown and crunchy. Remove from the oven and serve immediately.

510. Hillbilly Broccoli Cheese Casserole

Servings:6
Cooking Time: 30 Minutes
Ingredients:
- 4 cups broccoli florets
- ¼ cup heavy whipping cream
- ½ cup sharp Cheddar cheese, shredded
- ¼ cup ranch dressing
- Kosher salt and ground black pepper, to taste

Directions:
1. Combine all the ingredients in a large bowl. Toss to coat well broccoli well.
2. Pour the mixture into the baking pan.
3. Slide the baking pan into Rack Position 1, select Convection Bake, set temperature to 375ºF (190ºC) and set time to 30 minutes.
4. When cooking is complete, the broccoli should be tender.
5. Remove the baking pan from the oven and serve immediately.

511. Classic Worcestershire Poutine

Servings:2
Cooking Time: 33 Minutes
Ingredients:
- 2 russet potatoes, scrubbed and cut into ½-inch sticks
- 2 teaspoons vegetable oil

- 2 tablespoons butter
- ¼ onion, minced
- ¼ teaspoon dried thyme
- 1 clove garlic, smashed
- 3 tablespoons all-purpose flour
- 1 teaspoon tomato paste
- 1½ cups beef stock
- 2 teaspoons Worcestershire sauce
- Salt and freshly ground black pepper, to taste
- $^2/_3$ cup chopped string cheese

Directions:
1. Bring a pot of water to a boil, then put in the potato sticks and blanch for 4 minutes.
2. Drain the potato sticks and rinse under running cold water, then pat dry with paper towels.
3. Transfer the sticks in a large bowl and drizzle with vegetable oil. Toss to coat well. Place the potato sticks in the air fryer basket.
4. Put the air fryer basket on the baking pan and slide into Rack Position 2, select Air Fry, set temperature to 400ºF (205ºC) and set time to 25 minutes.
5. Stir the potato sticks at least three times during cooking.
6. Meanwhile, make the gravy: Heat the butter in a saucepan over medium heat until melted.
7. Add the onion, thyme, and garlic and sauté for 5 minutes or until the onion is translucent.
8. Add the flour and sauté for an additional 2 minutes. Pour in the tomato paste and beef stock and cook for 1 more minute or until lightly thickened.
9. Drizzle the gravy with Worcestershire sauce and sprinkle with salt and ground black pepper. Reduce the heat to low to keep the gravy warm until ready to serve.
10. When done, the sticks should be golden brown. Remove from the oven. Transfer the fried potato sticks onto a plate, then sprinkle with salt and ground black pepper. Scatter with string cheese and pour the gravy over. Serve warm.

512. Sumptuous Beef And Bean Chili Casserole

Servings:4
Cooking Time: 31 Minutes
Ingredients:
- 1 tablespoon olive oil
- ½ cup finely chopped bell pepper
- ½ cup chopped celery
- 1 onion, chopped
- 2 garlic cloves, minced
- 1 pound (454 g) ground beef

- 1 can diced tomatoes
- ½ teaspoon parsley
- ½ tablespoon chili powder
- 1 teaspoon chopped cilantro
- 1½ cups vegetable broth
- 1 (8-ounce / 227-g) can cannellini beans
- Salt and ground black pepper, to taste

Directions:
1. Heat the olive oil in a nonstick skillet over medium heat until shimmering.
2. Add the bell pepper, celery, onion, and garlic to the skillet and sauté for 5 minutes or until the onion is translucent.
3. Add the ground beef and sauté for an additional 6 minutes or until lightly browned.
4. Mix in the tomatoes, parsley, chili powder, cilantro and vegetable broth, then cook for 10 more minutes. Stir constantly.
5. Pour them in the baking pan, then mix in the beans and sprinkle with salt and ground black pepper.
6. Slide the baking pan into Rack Position 1, select Convection Bake, set temperature to 350ºF (180ºC) and set time to 10 minutes.
7. When cooking is complete, the vegetables should be tender and the beef should be well browned.
8. Remove from the oven and serve immediately.

513. Asian Dipping Sauce

Servings: About 1 Cup
Cooking Time: 0 Minutes
Ingredients:
- ¼ cup rice vinegar
- ¼ cup hoisin sauce
- ¼ cup low-sodium chicken or vegetable stock
- 3 tablespoons soy sauce
- 1 tablespoon minced or grated ginger
- 1 tablespoon minced or pressed garlic
- 1 teaspoon chili-garlic sauce or sriracha (or more to taste)

Directions:
1. Stir together all the ingredients in a small bowl, or place in a jar with a tight-fitting lid and shake until well mixed.
2. Use immediately.

514. Bartlett Pears With Lemony Ricotta

Servings:4
Cooking Time: 8 Minutes
Ingredients:
- 2 large Bartlett pears, peeled, cut in half, cored
- 3 tablespoons melted butter

- ½ teaspoon ground ginger
- ¼ teaspoon ground cardamom
- 3 tablespoons brown sugar
- ½ cup whole-milk ricotta cheese
- 1 teaspoon pure lemon extract
- 1 teaspoon pure almond extract
- 1 tablespoon honey, plus additional for drizzling

Directions:
1. Toss the pears with butter, ginger, cardamom, and sugar in a large bowl. Toss to coat well. Arrange the pears in the baking pan, cut side down.
2. Put the air fryer basket on the baking pan and slide into Rack Position 2, select Air Fry, set temperature to 375ºF (190ºC) and set time to 8 minutes.
3. After 5 minutes, remove the pan and flip the pears. Return to the oven and continue cooking.
4. When cooking is complete, the pears should be soft and browned. Remove from the oven.
5. In the meantime, combine the remaining ingredients in a separate bowl. Whip for 1 minute with a hand mixer until the mixture is puffed.
6. Divide the mixture into four bowls, then put the pears over the mixture and drizzle with more honey to serve.

515.   Crispy Cheese Wafer

Servings:2
Cooking Time: 5 Minutes
Ingredients:
- 1 cup shredded aged Manchego cheese
- 1 teaspoon all-purpose flour
- ½ teaspoon cumin seeds
- ¼ teaspoon cracked black pepper

Directions:
1. Line the air fryer basket with parchment paper.
2. Combine the cheese and flour in a bowl. Stir to mix well. Spread the mixture in the pan into a 4-inch round.
3. Combine the cumin and black pepper in a small bowl. Stir to mix well. Sprinkle the cumin mixture over the cheese round.
4. Put the air fryer basket on the baking pan and slide into Rack Position 2, select Air Fry, set temperature to 375ºF (190ºC) and set time to 5 minutes.
5. When cooked, the cheese will be lightly browned and frothy.
6. Use tongs to transfer the cheese wafer onto a plate and slice to serve.

516.   Sweet Cinnamon Chickpeas

Servings:2
Cooking Time: 10 Minutes

Ingredients:
- 1 tablespoon cinnamon
- 1 tablespoon sugar
- 1 cup chickpeas, soaked in water overnight, rinsed and drained

Directions:
1. Combine the cinnamon and sugar in a bowl. Stir to mix well.
2. Add the chickpeas to the bowl, then toss to coat well.
3. Pour the chickpeas in the air fryer basket.
4. Put the air fryer basket on the baking pan and slide into Rack Position 2, select Air Fry, set temperature to 390ºF (199ºC) and set time to 10 minutes.
5. Stir the chickpeas three times during cooking.
6. When cooked, the chickpeas should be golden brown and crispy. Remove from the oven and serve immediately.

517.   Air Fried Blistered Tomatoes

Servings:4 To 6
Cooking Time: 10 Minutes
Ingredients:
- 2 pounds (907 g) cherry tomatoes
- 2 tablespoons olive oil
- 2 teaspoons balsamic vinegar
- ½ teaspoon salt
- ½ teaspoon ground black pepper

Directions:
1. Toss the cherry tomatoes with olive oil in a large bowl to coat well. Pour the tomatoes in the baking pan.
2. Put the air fryer basket on the baking pan and slide into Rack Position 2, select Air Fry, set temperature to 400ºF (205ºC) and set time to 10 minutes.
3. Stir the tomatoes halfway through the cooking time.
4. When cooking is complete, the tomatoes will be blistered and lightly wilted.
5. Transfer the blistered tomatoes to a large bowl and toss with balsamic vinegar, salt, and black pepper before serving.

518.   Spanakopita

Servings:6
Cooking Time: 8 Minutes
Ingredients:
- ½ (10-ounce / 284-g) package frozen spinach, thawed and squeezed dry
- 1 egg, lightly beaten
- ¼ cup pine nuts, toasted
- ¼ cup grated Parmesan cheese
- ¾ cup crumbled feta cheese
- ⅛ teaspoon ground nutmeg
- ½ teaspoon salt
- Freshly ground black pepper, to taste

- 6 sheets phyllo dough
- ½ cup butter, melted

Directions:
1. Combine all the ingredients, except for the phyllo dough and butter, in a large bowl. Whisk to combine well. Set aside.
2. Place a sheet of phyllo dough on a clean work surface. Brush with butter then top with another layer sheet of phyllo. Brush with butter, then cut the layered sheets into six 3-inch-wide strips.
3. Top each strip with 1 tablespoon of the spinach mixture, then fold the bottom left corner over the mixture towards the right strip edge to make a triangle. Keep folding triangles until each strip is folded over.
4. Brush the triangles with butter and repeat with remaining strips and phyllo dough.
5. Place the triangles in the baking pan.
6. Put the air fryer basket on the baking pan and slide into Rack Position 2, select Air Fry, set temperature to 350ºF (180ºC) and set time to 8 minutes.
7. Flip the triangles halfway through the cooking time.
8. When cooking is complete, the triangles should be golden brown. Remove from the oven and serve immediately.

519. Air Fried Bacon Pinwheels

Servings: 8 Pinwheels
Cooking Time: 10 Minutes
Ingredients:
- 1 sheet puff pastry
- 2 tablespoons maple syrup
- ¼ cup brown sugar
- 8 slices bacon
- Ground black pepper, to taste
- Cooking spray

Directions:
1. Spritz the air fryer basket with cooking spray.
2. Roll the puff pastry into a 10-inch square with a rolling pin on a clean work surface, then cut the pastry into 8 strips.
3. Brush the strips with maple syrup and sprinkle with sugar, leaving a 1-inch far end uncovered.
4. Arrange each slice of bacon on each strip, leaving a ⅛-inch length of bacon hang over the end close to you. Sprinkle with black pepper.
5. From the end close to you, roll the strips into pinwheels, then dab the uncovered end with water and seal the rolls.
6. Arrange the pinwheels in the basket and spritz with cooking spray.
7. Put the air fryer basket on the baking pan and slide into Rack Position 2, select Air Fry,

set temperature to 360ºF (182ºC) and set time to 10 minutes.
8. Flip the pinwheels halfway through.
9. When cooking is complete, the pinwheels should be golden brown. Remove from the oven and serve immediately.

520. Kale Frittata

Servings:2
Cooking Time: 11 Minutes
Ingredients:
- 1 cup kale, chopped
- 1 teaspoon olive oil
- 4 large eggs, beaten
- Kosher salt, to taste
- 2 tablespoons water
- 3 tablespoons crumbled feta
- Cooking spray

Directions:
1. Spritz the baking pan with cooking spray.
2. Add the kale to the baking pan and drizzle with olive oil.
3. Slide the baking pan into Rack Position 2, select Convection Broil, set temperature to 360ºF (182ºC) and set time to 3 minutes.
4. Stir the kale halfway through.
5. When cooking is complete, the kale should be wilted.
6. Meanwhile, combine the eggs with salt and water in a large bowl. Stir to mix well.
7. Make the frittata: When broiling is complete, pour the eggs into the baking pan and spread with feta cheese.
8. Slide the baking pan into Rack Position 1, select Convection Bake, set temperature to 300ºF (150ºC) and set time to 8 minutes.
9. When cooking is complete, the eggs should be set and the cheese should be melted.
10. Remove from the oven and serve the frittata immediately.

521. Chicken Ham Casserole

Servings:4 To 6
Cooking Time: 15 Minutes
Ingredients:
- 2 cups diced cooked chicken
- 1 cup diced ham
- ¼ teaspoon ground nutmeg
- ½ cup half-and-half
- ½ teaspoon ground black pepper
- 6 slices Swiss cheese
- Cooking spray

Directions:
1. Spritz the baking pan with cooking spray.
2. Combine the chicken, ham, nutmeg, half-and-half, and ground black pepper in a large bowl. Stir to mix well.
3. Pour half of the mixture into the baking pan, then top the mixture with 3 slices of Swiss

cheese, then pour in the remaining mixture and top with remaining cheese slices.
4. Slide the baking pan into Rack Position 1, select Convection Bake, set temperature to 350ºF (180ºC) and set time to 15 minutes.
5. When cooking is complete, the egg should be set and the cheese should be melted.
6. Serve immediately.

522. Chorizo, Corn, And Potato Frittata

Servings:4
Cooking Time: 12 Minutes
Ingredients:
- 2 tablespoons olive oil
- 1 chorizo, sliced
- 4 eggs
- ½ cup corn
- 1 large potato, boiled and cubed
- 1 tablespoon chopped parsley
- ½ cup feta cheese, crumbled
- Salt and ground black pepper, to taste

Directions:
1. Heat the olive oil in a nonstick skillet over medium heat until shimmering.
2. Add the chorizo and cook for 4 minutes or until golden brown.
3. Whisk the eggs in a bowl, then sprinkle with salt and ground black pepper.
4. Mix the remaining ingredients in the egg mixture, then pour the chorizo and its fat into the baking pan. Pour in the egg mixture.
5. Slide the baking pan into Rack Position 1, select Convection Bake, set temperature to 330ºF (166ºC) and set time to 8 minutes.
6. Stir the mixture halfway through.
7. When cooking is complete, the eggs should be set.
8. Serve immediately.

523. Dehydrated Bananas With Coconut Sprnikles

Servings:x
Cooking Time:x
Ingredients:
- 5 very ripe bananas, peeled
- 1 cup shredded coconut

Directions:
1. Place coconut in a large shallow dish. Cut Press banana wedges in the coconut and organize in one layer on the dehydrating basket.
2. Hours Put basket in rack place 4 and then press START.
3. Dehydrate for 26 hours or until peanuts are Dry to the touch but still garnish with a sweet, intense banana taste.
4. Let bananas cool completely before storing in an Airtight container for up to 5 months.

524. Roasted Mushrooms

Servings: About 1½ Cups
Cooking Time: 30 Minutes
Ingredients:
- 1 pound (454 g) button or cremini mushrooms, washed, stems trimmed, and cut into quarters or thick slices
- ¼ cup water
- 1 teaspoon kosher salt or ½ teaspoon fine salt
- 3 tablespoons unsalted butter, cut into pieces, or extra-virgin olive oil

Directions:
1. Place a large piece of aluminum foil on the sheet pan. Place the mushroom pieces in the middle of the foil. Spread them out into an even layer. Pour the water over them, season with the salt, and add the butter. Wrap the mushrooms in the foil.
2. Select Roast, set the temperature to 325ºF (163ºC), and set the time for 15 minutes. Select Start to begin preheating.
3. Once the unit has preheated, place the pan in the oven.
4. After 15 minutes, remove the pan from the oven. Transfer the foil packet to a cutting board and carefully unwrap it. Pour the mushrooms and cooking liquid from the foil onto the sheet pan.
5. Select Roast, set the temperature to 350ºF (180ºC), and set the time for 15 minutes. Return the pan to the oven. Select Start to begin.
6. After about 10 minutes, remove the pan from the oven and stir the mushrooms. Return the pan to the oven and continue cooking for anywhere from 5 to 15 more minutes, or until the liquid is mostly gone and the mushrooms start to brown.
7. Serve immediately.

525. Parsnip Fries With Garlic-yogurt Dip

Servings:4
Cooking Time: 10 Minutes
Ingredients:
- 3 medium parsnips, peeled, cut into sticks
- ¼ teaspoon kosher salt
- 1 teaspoon olive oil
- 1 garlic clove, unpeeled
- Cooking spray
- Dip:
- ¼ cup plain Greek yogurt
- ⅛ teaspoon garlic powder
- 1 tablespoon sour cream
- ¼ teaspoon kosher salt
- Freshly ground black pepper, to taste

Directions:

1. Spritz the air fryer basket with cooking spray.
2. Put the parsnip sticks in a large bowl, then sprinkle with salt and drizzle with olive oil.
3. Transfer the parsnip into the basket and add the garlic.
4. Put the air fryer basket on the baking pan and slide into Rack Position 2, select Air Fry, set temperature to 360ºF (182ºC) and set time to 10 minutes.
5. Stir the parsnip halfway through the cooking time.
6. Meanwhile, peel the garlic and crush it. Combine the crushed garlic with the ingredients for the dip. Stir to mix well.
7. When cooked, the parsnip sticks should be crisp. Remove the parsnip fries from the oven and serve with the dipping sauce.

526. Ritzy Pimento And Almond Turkey Casserole

Servings:4
Cooking Time: 32 Minutes
Ingredients:
- 1 pound (454 g) turkey breasts
- 1 tablespoon olive oil
- 2 boiled eggs, chopped
- 2 tablespoons chopped pimentos
- ¼ cup slivered almonds, chopped
- ¼ cup mayonnaise
- ½ cup diced celery
- 2 tablespoons chopped green onion
- ¼ cup cream of chicken soup
- ¼ cup bread crumbs
- Salt and ground black pepper, to taste

Directions:
1. Put the turkey breasts in a large bowl. Sprinkle with salt and ground black pepper and drizzle with olive oil. Toss to coat well.
2. Transfer the turkey to the air fryer basket.
3. Put the air fryer basket on the baking pan and slide into Rack Position 2, select Air Fry, set temperature to 390ºF (199ºC) and set time to 12 minutes.
4. Flip the turkey halfway through.
5. When cooking is complete, the turkey should be well browned.
6. Remove the turkey breasts from the oven and cut into cubes, then combine the chicken cubes with eggs, pimentos, almonds, mayo, celery, green onions, and chicken soup in a large bowl. Stir to mix.
7. Pour the mixture into the baking pan, then spread with bread crumbs.
8. Slide the baking pan into Rack Position 1, select Convection Bake, set time to 20 minutes.
9. When cooking is complete, the eggs should be set.

10. Remove from the oven and serve immediately.

527. Dehydrated Honey-rosemary Roasted Almonds

Servings:x
Cooking Time:x
Ingredients:
- 1 heaping tablespoon demerara sugar
- 1 teaspoon finely chopped fresh rosemary
- 1 teaspoon kosher salt
- 8 ounces (225g) raw almonds
- 2 tablespoons kosher salt
- Honey-Rosemary glaze
- ¼ cup (80g) honey

Directions:
1. Place almonds and salt in a bowl. Add cold tap water to cover the almonds by 1-inch
2. (2cm). Let soak at room temperature for 12 hours to activate.
3. Rinse almonds under cold running water, then drain. Spread in a single layer on the dehydrate basket.
4. Dehydrate almonds for 24 hours or till tender and somewhat crispy but additionally spongy in the middle. Almonds may be eaten plain or roasted each the next recipe.
5. Put honey in a small saucepan and heat over Low heat. Put triggered nuts
6. At a medium bowl and then pour over warm honey. Stir To coat nuts equally. Add rosemary, sugar
7. And salt and stir to blend.
8. Spread Almonds in one layer on the skillet.
9. Insert cable rack into rack place 6. Select BAKE/350°F (175°C)/CONVECTION/10 moments and empower Rotate Remind.
10. Stirring almonds when Rotate Remind signs.
11. Let cool completely before storing in an airtight container.

528. Chinese Pork And Mushroom Egg Rolls

Servings: 25 Egg Rolls
Cooking Time: 33 Minutes
Ingredients:
- Egg Rolls:
- 1 tablespoon mirin
- 3 tablespoons soy sauce, divided
- 1 pound (454 g) ground pork
- 3 tablespoons vegetable oil, plus more for brushing
- 5 ounces (142 g) shiitake mushrooms, minced
- 4 cups shredded Napa cabbage
- ¼ cup sliced scallions
- 1 teaspoon grated fresh ginger

- 1 clove garlic, minced
- ¼ teaspoon cornstarch
- 1 (1-pound / 454-g) package frozen egg roll wrappers, thawed
- Dipping Sauce:
- 1 scallion, white and light green parts only, sliced
- ¼ cup rice vinegar
- ¼ cup soy sauce
- Pinch sesame seeds
- Pinch red pepper flakes
- 1 teaspoon granulated sugar

Directions:
1. Line the air fryer basket with parchment paper. Set aside.
2. Combine the mirin and 1 tablespoon of soy sauce in a large bowl. Stir to mix well.
3. Dunk the ground pork in the mixture and stir to mix well. Wrap the bowl in plastic and marinate in the refrigerator for at least 10 minutes.
4. Heat the vegetable oil in a nonstick skillet over medium-high heat until shimmering. Add the mushrooms, cabbage, and scallions and sauté for 5 minutes or until tender.
5. Add the marinated meat, ginger, garlic, and remaining 2 tablespoons of soy sauce. Sauté for 3 minutes or until the pork is lightly browned. Turn off the heat and allow to cool until ready to use.
6. Put the cornstarch in a small bowl and pour in enough water to dissolve the cornstarch. Put the bowl alongside a clean work surface.
7. Put the egg roll wrappers in the basket.
8. Put the air fryer basket on the baking pan and slide into Rack Position 2, select Air Fry, set temperature to 400ºF (205ºC) and set time to 15 minutes.
9. Flip the wrappers halfway through the cooking time.
10. When cooked, the wrappers will be golden brown. Remove the egg roll wrappers from the oven and allow to cool for 10 minutes or until you can handle them with your hands.
11. Lay out one egg roll wrapper on the work surface with a corner pointed toward you. Place 2 tablespoons of the pork mixture on the egg roll wrapper and fold corner up over the mixture. Fold left and right corners toward the center and continue to roll. Brush a bit of the dissolved cornstarch on the last corner to help seal the egg wrapper. Repeat with remaining wrappers to make 25 egg rolls in total.
12. Arrange the rolls in the basket and brush the rolls with more vegetable oil.
13. Select Air Fry and set time to 10 minutes. Return to the oven. When done, the rolls should be well browned and crispy.
14. Meanwhile, combine the ingredients for the dipping sauce in a small bowl. Stir to mix well.
15. Serve the rolls with the dipping sauce immediately.

529. Sumptuous Vegetable Frittata

Servings:2
Cooking Time: 20 Minutes
Ingredients:
- 4 eggs
- $^1/_3$ cup milk
- 2 teaspoons olive oil
- 1 large zucchini, sliced
- 2 asparagus, sliced thinly
- $^1/_3$ cup sliced mushrooms
- 1 cup baby spinach
- 1 small red onion, sliced
- $^1/_3$ cup crumbled feta cheese
- $^1/_3$ cup grated Cheddar cheese
- ¼ cup chopped chives
- Salt and ground black pepper, to taste

Directions:
1. Line the baking pan with parchment paper.
2. Whisk together the eggs, milk, salt, and ground black pepper in a large bowl. Set aside.
3. Heat the olive oil in a nonstick skillet over medium heat until shimmering.
4. Add the zucchini, asparagus, mushrooms, spinach, and onion to the skillet and sauté for 5 minutes or until tender.
5. Pour the sautéed vegetables into the prepared baking pan, then spread the egg mixture over and scatter with cheeses.
6. Slide the baking pan into Rack Position 1, select Convection Bake, set temperature to 380ºF (193ºC) and set time to 15 minutes.
7. Stir the mixture halfway through.
8. When cooking is complete, the egg should be set and the edges should be lightly browned.
9. Remove the frittata from the oven and sprinkle with chives before serving.

530. Creamy Pork Gratin

Servings:4
Cooking Time: 21 Minutes
Ingredients:
- 2 tablespoons olive oil
- 2 pounds (907 g) pork tenderloin, cut into serving-size pieces
- 1 teaspoon dried marjoram
- ¼ teaspoon chili powder
- 1 teaspoon coarse sea salt
- ½ teaspoon freshly ground black pepper
- 1 cup Ricotta cheese
- 1½ cups chicken broth
- 1 tablespoon mustard

- Cooking spray

Directions:
1. Spritz the baking pan with cooking spray.
2. Heat the olive oil in a nonstick skillet over medium-high heat until shimmering.
3. Add the pork and sauté for 6 minutes or until lightly browned.
4. Transfer the pork to the prepared baking pan and sprinkle with marjoram, chili powder, salt, and ground black pepper.
5. Combine the remaining ingredients in a large bowl. Stir to mix well. Pour the mixture over the pork in the pan.
6. Slide the baking pan into Rack Position 1, select Convection Bake, set temperature to 350ºF (180ºC) and set time to 15 minutes.
7. Stir the mixture halfway through.
8. When cooking is complete, the mixture should be frothy and the cheese should be melted.
9. Serve immediately.

531. Shawarma Spice Mix

Servings: About 1 Tablespoon
Cooking Time: 0 Minutes
Ingredients:
- 1 teaspoon smoked paprika
- 1 teaspoon cumin
- ¼ teaspoon turmeric
- ¼ teaspoon kosher salt or ⅛ teaspoon fine salt
- ¼ teaspoon cinnamon
- ¼ teaspoon allspice
- ¼ teaspoon red pepper flakes
- ¼ teaspoon freshly ground black pepper

Directions:
1. Stir together all the ingredients in a small bowl.
2. Use immediately or place in an airtight container in the pantry.

532. Greek Frittata

Servings:2
Cooking Time: 8 Minutes
Ingredients:
- 1 cup chopped mushrooms
- 2 cups spinach, chopped
- 4 eggs, lightly beaten
- 3 ounces (85 g) feta cheese, crumbled
- 2 tablespoons heavy cream
- A handful of fresh parsley, chopped
- Salt and ground black pepper, to taste
- Cooking spray

Directions:
1. Spritz the baking pan with cooking spray.
2. Whisk together all the ingredients in a large bowl. Stir to mix well.
3. Pour the mixture in the prepared baking pan.

4. Slide the baking pan into Rack Position 1, select Convection Bake, set temperature to 350ºF (180ºC) and set time to 8 minutes.
5. Stir the mixture halfway through.
6. When cooking is complete, the eggs should be set.
7. Serve immediately.

533. Oven Grits

Servings: About 4 Cups
Cooking Time: 1 Hour 5 Minutes
Ingredients:
- 1 cup grits or polenta (not instant or quick cook)
- 2 cups chicken or vegetable stock
- 2 cups milk
- 2 tablespoons unsalted butter, cut into 4 pieces
- 1 teaspoon kosher salt or ½ teaspoon fine salt

Directions:
1. Add the grits to the baking pan. Stir in the stock, milk, butter, and salt.
2. Select Bake, set the temperature to 325ºF (163ºC), and set the time for 1 hour and 5 minutes. Select Start to begin preheating.
3. Once the unit has preheated, place the pan in the oven.
4. After 15 minutes, remove the pan from the oven and stir the polenta. Return the pan to the oven and continue cooking.
5. After 30 minutes, remove the pan again and stir the polenta again. Return the pan to the oven and continue cooking for 15 to 20 minutes, or until the polenta is soft and creamy and the liquid is absorbed.
6. When done, remove the pan from the oven.
7. Serve immediately.

534. Butternut Squash With Hazelnuts

Servings: 3 Cups
Cooking Time: 23 Minutes
Ingredients:
- 2 tablespoons whole hazelnuts
- 3 cups butternut squash, peeled, deseeded and cubed
- ¼ teaspoon kosher salt
- ¼ teaspoon freshly ground black pepper
- 2 teaspoons olive oil
- Cooking spray

Directions:
1. Spritz the air fryer basket with cooking spray. Spread the hazelnuts in the pan.
2. Put the air fryer basket on the baking pan and slide into Rack Position 2, select Air Fry, set temperature to 300ºF (150ºC) and set time to 3 minutes.

3. When done, the hazelnuts should be soft. Remove from the oven. Chopped the hazelnuts roughly and transfer to a small bowl. Set aside.
4. Put the butternut squash in a large bowl, then sprinkle with salt and pepper and drizzle with olive oil. Toss to coat well. Transfer the squash to the lightly greased basket.
5. Put the air fryer basket on the baking pan and slide into Rack Position 2, select Air Fry, set temperature to 360ºF (182ºC) and set time to 20 minutes.
6. Flip the squash halfway through the cooking time.
7. When cooking is complete, the squash will be soft. Transfer the squash to a plate and sprinkle with the chopped hazelnuts before serving.

535. Arancini

Servings: 10 Arancini
Cooking Time: 30 Minutes
Ingredients:
- $^2/_3$ cup raw white Arborio rice
- 2 teaspoons butter
- ½ teaspoon salt
- $1^1/_3$ cups water
- 2 large eggs, well beaten
- 1¼ cups seasoned Italian-style dried bread crumbs
- 10 ¾-inch semi-firm Mozzarella cubes
- Cooking spray

Directions:
1. Pour the rice, butter, salt, and water in a pot. Stir to mix well and bring a boil over medium-high heat. Keep stirring.
2. Reduce the heat to low and cover the pot. Simmer for 20 minutes or until the rice is tender.
3. Turn off the heat and let sit, covered, for 10 minutes, then open the lid and fluffy the rice with a fork. Allow to cool for 10 more minutes.
4. Pour the beaten eggs in a bowl, then pour the bread crumbs in a separate bowl.
5. Scoop 2 tablespoons of the cooked rice up and form it into a ball, then press the Mozzarella into the ball and wrap.
6. Dredge the ball in the eggs first, then shake the excess off the dunk the ball in the bread crumbs. Roll to coat evenly. Repeat to make 10 balls in total with remaining rice.
7. Transfer the balls in the air fryer basket and spritz with cooking spray.
8. Put the air fryer basket on the baking pan and slide into Rack Position 2, select Air Fry, set temperature to 375ºF (190ºC) and set time to 10 minutes.
9. When cooking is complete, the balls should be lightly browned and crispy.
10. Remove the balls from the oven and allow to cool before serving.

536. Garlicky Spiralized Zucchini And Squash

Servings:4
Cooking Time: 10 Minutes
Ingredients:
- 2 large zucchini, peeled and spiralized
- 2 large yellow summer squash, peeled and spiralized
- 1 tablespoon olive oil, divided
- ½ teaspoon kosher salt
- 1 garlic clove, whole
- 2 tablespoons fresh basil, chopped
- Cooking spray

Directions:
1. Spritz the air fryer basket with cooking spray.
2. Combine the zucchini and summer squash with 1 teaspoon of the olive oil and salt in a large bowl. Toss to coat well.
3. Transfer the zucchini and summer squash to the basket and add the garlic.
4. Put the air fryer basket on the baking pan and slide into Rack Position 2, select Air Fry, set temperature to 360ºF (182ºC) and set time to 10 minutes.
5. Stir the zucchini and summer squash halfway through the cooking time.
6. When cooked, the zucchini and summer squash will be tender and fragrant. Transfer the cooked zucchini and summer squash onto a plate and set aside.
7. Remove the garlic from the oven and allow to cool for 5 minutes. Mince the garlic and combine with remaining olive oil in a small bowl. Stir to mix well.
8. Drizzle the spiralized zucchini and summer squash with garlic oil and sprinkle with basil. Toss to serve.

537. Simple Teriyaki Sauce

Servings: ¾ Cup
Cooking Time: 0 Minutes
Ingredients:
- ½ cup soy sauce
- 3 tablespoons honey
- 1 tablespoon rice wine or dry sherry
- 1 tablespoon rice vinegar
- 2 teaspoons minced fresh ginger
- 2 garlic cloves, smashed

Directions:
1. Beat together all the ingredients in a small bowl.
2. Use immediately.

538. Lemony Shishito Peppers

Servings:4
Cooking Time: 5 Minutes
Ingredients:
- ½ pound (227 g) shishito peppers (about 24)
- 1 tablespoon olive oil
- Coarse sea salt, to taste
- Lemon wedges, for serving
- Cooking spray

Directions:
1. Spritz the air fryer basket with cooking spray.
2. Toss the peppers with olive oil in a large bowl to coat well.
3. Arrange the peppers in the basket.
4. Put the air fryer basket on the baking pan and slide into Rack Position 2, select Air Fry, set temperature to 400ºF (205ºC) and set time to 5 minutes.
5. Flip the peppers and sprinkle the peppers with salt halfway through the cooking time.
6. When cooked, the peppers should be blistered and lightly charred. Transfer the peppers onto a plate and squeeze the lemon wedges on top before serving.

539. Cinnamon Rolls With Cream Glaze

Servings:8
Cooking Time: 5 Minutes
Ingredients:
- 1 pound (454 g) frozen bread dough, thawed
- 2 tablespoons melted butter
- 1½ tablespoons cinnamon
- ¾ cup brown sugar
- Cooking spray
- Cream Glaze:
- 4 ounces (113 g) softened cream cheese
- ½ teaspoon vanilla extract
- 2 tablespoons melted butter
- 1¼ cups powdered erythritol

Directions:
1. Place the bread dough on a clean work surface, then roll the dough out into a rectangle with a rolling pin.
2. Brush the top of the dough with melted butter and leave 1-inch edges uncovered.
3. Combine the cinnamon and sugar in a small bowl, then sprinkle the dough with the cinnamon mixture.
4. Roll the dough over tightly, then cut the dough log into 8 portions. Wrap the portions in plastic, better separately, and let sit to rise for 1 or 2 hours.

5. Meanwhile, combine the ingredients for the glaze in a separate small bowl. Stir to mix well.
6. Spritz the air fryer basket with cooking spray. Transfer the risen rolls to the basket.
7. Put the air fryer basket on the baking pan and slide into Rack Position 2, select Air Fry, set temperature to 350ºF (180ºC) and set time to 5 minutes.
8. Flip the rolls halfway through the cooking time.
9. When cooking is complete, the rolls will be golden brown.
10. Serve the rolls with the glaze.

540. Sweet And Sour Peanuts

Servings:9
Cooking Time: 5 Minutes
Ingredients:
- 3 cups shelled raw peanuts
- 1 tablespoon hot red pepper sauce
- 3 tablespoons granulated white sugar

Directions:
1. Put the peanuts in a large bowl, then drizzle with hot red pepper sauce and sprinkle with sugar. Toss to coat well.
2. Pour the peanuts in the air fryer basket.
3. Put the air fryer basket on the baking pan and slide into Rack Position 2, select Air Fry, set temperature to 400ºF (205ºC) and set time to 5 minutes.
4. Stir the peanuts halfway through the cooking time.
5. When cooking is complete, the peanuts will be crispy and browned. Remove from the oven and serve immediately.

541. Fast Cinnamon Toast

Servings:6
Cooking Time: 5 Minutes
Ingredients:
- 1½ teaspoons cinnamon
- 1½ teaspoons vanilla extract
- ½ cup sugar
- 2 teaspoons ground black pepper
- 2 tablespoons melted coconut oil
- 12 slices whole wheat bread

Directions:
1. Combine all the ingredients, except for the bread, in a large bowl. Stir to mix well.
2. Dunk the bread in the bowl of mixture gently to coat and infuse well. Shake the excess off. Arrange the bread slices in the air fryer basket.
3. Put the air fryer basket on the baking pan and slide into Rack Position 2, select Air Fry, set temperature to 400ºF (205ºC) and set time to 5 minutes.
4. Flip the bread halfway through.

5. When cooking is complete, the bread should be golden brown.
6. Remove the bread slices from the oven and slice to serve.

542. Golden Nuggets

Servings: 20 Nuggets
Cooking Time: 4 Minutes
Ingredients:
- 1 cup all-purpose flour, plus more for dusting
- 1 teaspoon baking powder
- ½ teaspoon butter, at room temperature, plus more for brushing
- ¼ teaspoon salt
- ¼ cup water
- ⅛ teaspoon onion powder
- ¼ teaspoon garlic powder
- ⅛ teaspoon seasoning salt
- Cooking spray

Directions:
1. Line the air fryer basket with parchment paper.
2. Mix the flour, baking powder, butter, and salt in a large bowl. Stir to mix well. Gradually whisk in the water until a sanity dough forms.
3. Put the dough on a lightly floured work surface, then roll it out into a ½-inch thick rectangle with a rolling pin.
4. Cut the dough into about twenty 1- or 2-inch squares, then arrange the squares in a single layer in the basket. Spritz with cooking spray.
5. Combine onion powder, garlic powder, and seasoning salt in a small bowl. Stir to mix well, then sprinkle the squares with the powder mixture.
6. Put the air fryer basket on the baking pan and slide into Rack Position 2, select Air Fry, set temperature to 370ºF (188ºC) and set time to 4 minutes.
7. Flip the squares halfway through the cooking time.
8. When cooked, the dough squares should be golden brown.
9. Remove the golden nuggets from the oven and brush with more butter immediately. Serve warm.

543. Chocolate And Coconut Macaroons

Servings: 24 Macaroons
Cooking Time: 8 Minutes
Ingredients:
- 3 large egg whites, at room temperature
- ¼ teaspoon salt
- ¾ cup granulated white sugar
- 4½ tablespoons unsweetened cocoa powder
- 2¼ cups unsweetened shredded coconut

Directions:
1. Line the air fryer basket with parchment paper.
2. Whisk the egg whites with salt in a large bowl with a hand mixer on high speed until stiff peaks form.
3. Whisk in the sugar with the hand mixer on high speed until the mixture is thick. Mix in the cocoa powder and coconut.
4. Scoop 2 tablespoons of the mixture and shape the mixture in a ball. Repeat with remaining mixture to make 24 balls in total.
5. Arrange the balls in a single layer in the basket and leave a little space between each two balls.
6. Put the air fryer basket on the baking pan and slide into Rack Position 2, select Air Fry, set temperature to 375ºF (190ºC) and set time to 8 minutes.
7. When cooking is complete, the balls should be golden brown.
8. Serve immediately.

544. Banana Cake

Servings:8
Cooking Time: 20 Minutes
Ingredients:
- 1 cup plus 1 tablespoon all-purpose flour
- ¼ teaspoon baking soda
- ¾ teaspoon baking powder
- ¼ teaspoon salt
- 9½ tablespoons granulated white sugar
- 5 tablespoons butter, at room temperature
- 2½ small ripe bananas, peeled
- 2 large eggs
- 5 tablespoons buttermilk
- 1 teaspoon vanilla extract
- Cooking spray

Directions:
1. Spritz the baking pan with cooking spray.
2. Combine the flour, baking soda, baking powder, and salt in a large bowl. Stir to mix well.
3. Beat the sugar and butter in a separate bowl with a hand mixer on medium speed for 3 minutes.
4. Beat in the bananas, eggs, buttermilk, and vanilla extract into the sugar and butter mix with a hand mixer.
5. Pour in the flour mixture and whip with hand mixer until sanity and smooth.
6. Scrape the batter into the pan and level the batter with a spatula.
7. Slide the baking pan into Rack Position 1, select Convection Bake, set temperature to 325ºF (163ºC) and set time to 20 minutes.

8. After 15 minutes, remove the pan from the oven. Check the doneness. Return the pan to the oven and continue cooking.
9. When done, a toothpick inserted in the center should come out clean.
10. Invert the cake on a cooling rack and allow to cool for 15 minutes before slicing to serve.

545. Mediterranean Quiche

Servings:4
Cooking Time: 30 Minutes
Ingredients:
- 4 eggs
- ¼ cup chopped Kalamata olives
- ½ cup chopped tomatoes
- ¼ cup chopped onion
- ½ cup milk
- 1 cup crumbled feta cheese
- ½ tablespoon chopped oregano
- ½ tablespoon chopped basil
- Salt and ground black pepper, to taste
- Cooking spray

Directions:
1. Spritz the baking pan with cooking spray.
2. Whisk the eggs with remaining ingredients in a large bowl. Stir to mix well.
3. Pour the mixture into the prepared baking pan.
4. Slide the baking pan into Rack Position 1, select Convection Bake, set temperature to 340ºF (171ºC) and set time to 30 minutes.
5. When cooking is complete, the eggs should be set and a toothpick inserted in the center should come out clean.
6. Serve immediately.

546. Burgundy Beef And Mushroom Casserole

Servings:4
Cooking Time: 25 Minutes
Ingredients:
- 1½ pounds (680 g) beef steak
- 1 ounce (28 g) dry onion soup mix
- 2 cups sliced mushrooms
- 1 (14.5-ounce / 411-g) can cream of mushroom soup
- ½ cup beef broth
- ¼ cup red wine
- 3 garlic cloves, minced
- 1 whole onion, chopped

Directions:
1. Put the beef steak in a large bowl, then sprinkle with dry onion soup mix. Toss to coat well.
2. Combine the mushrooms with mushroom soup, beef broth, red wine, garlic, and onion in a large bowl. Stir to mix well.
3. Transfer the beef steak in the baking pan, then pour in the mushroom mixture.

4. Slide the baking pan into Rack Position 1, select Convection Bake, set temperature to 360ºF (182ºC) and set time to 25 minutes.
5. When cooking is complete, the mushrooms should be soft and the beef should be well browned.
6. Remove from the oven and serve immediately.

547. Teriyaki Shrimp Skewers

Servings: 12 Skewered Shrimp
Cooking Time: 6 Minutes
Ingredients:
- 1½ tablespoons mirin
- 1½ teaspoons ginger juice
- 1½ tablespoons soy sauce
- 12 large shrimp (about 20 shrimps per pound), peeled and deveined
- 1 large egg
- ¾ cup panko bread crumbs
- Cooking spray

Directions:
1. Combine the mirin, ginger juice, and soy sauce in a large bowl. Stir to mix well.
2. Dunk the shrimp in the bowl of mirin mixture, then wrap the bowl in plastic and refrigerate for 1 hour to marinate.
3. Spritz the air fryer basket with cooking spray.
4. Run twelve 4-inch skewers through each shrimp.
5. Whisk the egg in the bowl of marinade to combine well. Pour the bread crumbs on a plate.
6. Dredge the shrimp skewers in the egg mixture, then shake the excess off and roll over the bread crumbs to coat well.
7. Arrange the shrimp skewers in the basket and spritz with cooking spray.
8. Put the air fryer basket on the baking pan and slide into Rack Position 2, select Air Fry, set temperature to 400ºF (205ºC) and set time to 6 minutes.
9. Flip the shrimp skewers halfway through the cooking time.
10. When done, the shrimp will be opaque and firm.
11. Serve immediately.

548. Milky Pecan Tart

Servings:8
Cooking Time: 26 Minutes
Ingredients:
- Tart Crust:
- ¼ cup firmly packed brown sugar
- $^1/_3$ cup butter, softened
- 1 cup all-purpose flour
- ¼ teaspoon kosher salt
- Filling:
- ¼ cup whole milk

- 4 tablespoons butter, diced
- ½ cup packed brown sugar
- ¼ cup pure maple syrup
- 1½ cups finely chopped pecans
- ¼ teaspoon pure vanilla extract
- ¼ teaspoon sea salt

Directions:
1. Line the baking pan with aluminum foil, then spritz the pan with cooking spray.
2. Stir the brown sugar and butter in a bowl with a hand mixer until puffed, then add the flour and salt and stir until crumbled.
3. Pour the mixture in the prepared baking pan and tilt the pan to coat the bottom evenly.
4. Slide the baking pan into Rack Position 1, select Convection Bake, set temperature to 350ºF (180ºC) and set time to 13 minutes.
5. When done, the crust will be golden brown.
6. Meanwhile, pour the milk, butter, sugar, and maple syrup in a saucepan. Stir to mix well. Bring to a simmer, then cook for 1 more minute. Stir constantly.
7. Turn off the heat and mix the pecans and vanilla into the filling mixture.
8. Pour the filling mixture over the golden crust and spread with a spatula to coat the crust evenly.
9. Select Bake and set time to 12 minutes. When cooked, the filling mixture should be set and frothy.
10. Remove the baking pan from the oven and sprinkle with salt. Allow to sit for 10 minutes or until cooled.
11. Transfer the pan to the refrigerator to chill for at least 2 hours, then remove the aluminum foil and slice to serve.

549. Sweet Air Fried Pecans

Servings: 4 Cups
Cooking Time: 10 Minutes
Ingredients:
- 2 egg whites
- 1 tablespoon cumin
- 2 teaspoons smoked paprika
- ½ cup brown sugar
- 2 teaspoons kosher salt
- 1 pound (454 g) pecan halves
- Cooking spray

Directions:
1. Spritz the air fryer basket with cooking spray.

2. Combine the egg whites, cumin, paprika, sugar, and salt in a large bowl. Stir to mix well. Add the pecans to the bowl and toss to coat well.
3. Transfer the pecans to the basket.
4. Put the air fryer basket on the baking pan and slide into Rack Position 2, select Air Fry, set temperature to 300ºF (150ºC) and set time to 10 minutes.
5. Stir the pecans at least two times during the cooking.
6. When cooking is complete, the pecans should be lightly caramelized. Remove from the oven and serve immediately.

550. Pão De Queijo

Servings: 12 Balls
Cooking Time: 12 Minutes
Ingredients:
- 2 tablespoons butter, plus more for greasing
- ½ cup milk
- 1½ cups tapioca flour
- ½ teaspoon salt
- 1 large egg
- $^2/_3$ cup finely grated aged Asiago cheese

Directions:
1. Put the butter in a saucepan and pour in the milk, heat over medium heat until the liquid boils. Keep stirring.
2. Turn off the heat and mix in the tapioca flour and salt to form a soft dough. Transfer the dough in a large bowl, then wrap the bowl in plastic and let sit for 15 minutes.
3. Break the egg in the bowl of dough and whisk with a hand mixer for 2 minutes or until a sanity dough forms. Fold the cheese in the dough. Cover the bowl in plastic again and let sit for 10 more minutes.
4. Grease the baking pan with butter.
5. Scoop 2 tablespoons of the dough into the baking pan. Repeat with the remaining dough to make dough 12 balls. Keep a little distance between each two balls.
6. Slide the baking pan into Rack Position 1, select Convection Bake, set temperature to 375ºF (190ºC) and set time to 12 minutes.
7. Flip the balls halfway through the cooking time.
8. When cooking is complete, the balls should be golden brown and fluffy.
9. Remove the balls from the oven and allow to cool for 5 minutes before serving.

CPSIA information can be obtained
at www.ICGtesting.com
Printed in the USA
LVHW060302040121
675643LV00004B/36